As an instructor who has taught undergraduate theology inside a prison-based seminary program, I can say without hesitation that this commentary on Hebrews reflects serious scholarship and real pastoral depth. Nobles read the text with care, handles the major interpretive challenges responsibly, and writes with a clarity that serves both students and ministers. What makes this work uniquely compelling is the way it draws thoughtfully on the lived realities of incarceration - endurance, suffering, temptation to despair, and the long work of hope - without ever turning Hebrews into mere autobiography. Instead, his experience sharpens his attention to the epistle's central themes and gives the reader a grounded, hard-won perspective on what it means to "hold fast" and persevere in faith.

Brandon L Warren, EdD., MDiv., Lee College

Perseverance Through the Eyes of the Condemned: Commentary of Hebrews is a powerful and authentic commentary, written from behind prison walls by Michael Nobles. With uncommon depth and hard-earned insight, Nobles reveals how the message of Christ speaks most clearly to those who know guilt, loss, and longing for freedom. This work is a compelling reminder that redemption is not theoretical-it is lived, tested, and proven even in the darkest places.

Terry Solley,
President, Global Prison Outreach
Co-author of *Exiles: A Prisoner's Daily Devotion*

Forged in prison cells and refined in the classroom, Michael Nobles' *Perseverance Through the Eyes of the Condemned* approaches Hebrews from a perspective few possess. By bridging life within the modern justice system and serious theological study, Nobles exposes how the realities of incarceration illuminate the ancient call to endurance, revealing how perseverance under judgment connects the world of Hebrews to our own. As the author of a prisoner's perspective on the book of Romans, and knowing Nobles personally, I am proud and honored to commend and recommend this book to anyone who wants an easy to understand, yet, with strong interaction by other giants who've written on the book of Hebrews. Make sure to get a copy of this book.

John Montana,
Graduate of Southwestern Baptist Theological Seminary, and author of *Redemption Through the Eyes of the Condemned*: Commentary on Romans

It is the privlege of every Christian to read the Scripture with God's help. Michael Nobles has taken up his responsibility and knows its blessing. His commentary on Hebrews shows the humility of reading with prayerful dependence on God and God's work through respected Christian scholars. By reading with eyes opened and eyesight shaped by a culture more like the 1st century Christians faced, the culture of a maximum-security prison, Nobles helps us read with new more grateful eyes. Take up and read!

Ben Phillips, PhD.
Dean, College of Christian Studies,
Professor of Christian Studies,
Charleston Southern University

PERSEVERANCE

through the Eyes of the Condemned

COMMENTARY ON HEBREWS

Michael S. Nobles

PERSEVERANCE THROUGH THE EYES OF THE CONDEMNED

Copyright© 2026 Michael S. Nobles

ISBN: 979-8-9945886-0-4

CONTENTS

Author's Preface

Prison is like a twisted version of the movie Groundhog Day, and after two decades of incarceration you look for ways to disrupt the repetitiousness of prison life. I choose to write. I write to gather my thoughts, reflect on my past, and share my experiences. I imagine the biblical authors wrote for similar reasons. Their writings were the products of their reflections and experiences (divinely inspired of course). They had been through some things that dramatically transformed the way they saw the world. They were not perfect men, they had done things which they were not proud of, but they had been transformed through an encounter with God. They were moved by an unquenchable desire to share their stories of transformation with all those they came into contact with. I can relate to them.

In 2014, I was given the opportunity of a lifetime. I was invited to attend Southwestern Baptist Theological Seminary while in prison! I was transferred to the Darrington unit (now Memorial) to attend college and earn a bachelor's degree in biblical studies. During my time there, a few of the other incarcerated students pitched the idea of a commentary series written by inmates for inmates. Men chose books and began to research and write. However, like most projects in prison, the idea was left unfinished. I graduated from seminary in 2018 and began my ministry as a Field Minister sharing the Gospel and my story of transformation with all those I met. In 2022, I was transferred to the Coffield unit and reunited with a former classmate, John Montana. I was shocked to learn that he had not only finished his commentary, but also had it published. He inspired me to write and publish mine.

I have always been a little intimidated by the book of Hebrews. It seemed so different from the rest of the New Testament; the Greek was way beyond my rudimentary understanding of the language, and so much was unknown about the introductory material. But I love a challenge. I began reading, writing on, preaching and teaching the book of Hebrews. I have preached and taught verse by verse through this book in order to gather my thoughts. I thank the church at the Coffield unit for their long suffering. I almost left this book unfinished. When A.I. was unleashed on the world and I learned that people were using it to write books, I was crushed. I knew I couldn't compete with A.I. Yet the message of perseverance called to me from the pages of this sermon. I could not preach and teach perseverance while failing to persevere in my personal life. I also realized that A.I. could not walk in my shoes, A.I. lacks lived experience. So this commentary is personal. It is the scholarship of others, but the experiences are mine alone. I write for the prisoner.

There are numerous people who were instrumental in making sure this book was finished. John Montana inspired me to write and provided me with a guide to follow. Without him, this book would still be the unfinished idea of a college student. To my brothers on the Coffield unit, thank you for allowing me to share all the wonderful things I learned about Hebrews. The men of the G-3 Bible study and Sheepfold service encouraged me to persevere when I wanted to quit. They shared many helpful insights as I preached and taught through Hebrews. Shout out to Anthony Scott (H.O.T.) your desire to learn is a constant reminder of why ministry and discipleship are so important. To my Aunt Lois, my cousin Karen, and my sister Amy, these three women have provided me with a living example of Hebrews 13:3. They have never failed to shower me with encouragement, love, and affection for over two decades of incarceration. This journey is almost complete. I can't wait for what is next.

I want to thank Grove and Brenna Norwood with the Heart of Texas Foundation for providing me with an opportunity of a lifetime. Without their leadership of the Field Ministry program, I would not have been capable of writing this book. I want to give a special shoutout to all the Field Ministers throughout the state. Your work is often overlooked and underappreciated; continue to persevere. I want to thank all the staff and volunteers at Nations University for an opportunity to continue my education; thank you Randi for your patience. To Lance and Kathi Rogers, you encouraged me to believe in myself and my ability to lead and help others. To chaplain Uzzel, you were there to help me at the end. Thank you. Thanks to Brandon Warren, Terry Solley, and Ben Phillips your blurbs added value to my book.

Finally, a special thanks to Fyrst Ayd (Aaron Brown) my fellow Field Minister and brother in Christ. You shouldered the majority of the ministry while I chased my goals of writing this book and earning my degree. I couldn't have completed this without your faithfulness. Now it's your turn to write your devotional. Get to work!

Introduction to Hebrews

Much like the inmate, the epistle to the Hebrews has a sketchy past. Its structure defies description. Is it a sermon or a letter? The authorship is debated and very little is known about its provenance, destination, or audience. Some in the church valued it, others ignored it; nevertheless, it has withstood the test of time. For this reason alone, it is worthy of consideration.

The book of Hebrews is the biblical theologian's playground. It begins at creation and ends at the heavenly Jerusalem addressing the entirety of the biblical story in between. It is hands down the most beautifully crafted letter in all the New Testament, and contains theological concepts left untouched by other authors. Its use of the Old Testament has puzzled some and opened the whole of Scriptures to others. It contains both some of the most dividing and unifying Scriptures in all the Bible. Any person who takes the time to understand this letter will never see the Bible the same again. This book, more than any other, aims to elevate the person and work of Jesus while arguing the need for perseverance. All believers are on a journey to the Heavenly Jerusalem where their pioneer welcomes them into the presence of God, and their final rest. Until that day arrives, they are called to endure the struggle of this world from faith to faith. Semper Reformanda!

A Note on Scholarship

I am not a New Testament scholar. All the research and scholarship found in this book belongs to men and women more capable than I. I have simply done my best to compile the thoughts and ideas of numerous experts on the book of Hebrews. With that said, if you see your thoughts or ideas and I failed to acknowledge the source, I apologize. I have benefited greatly from the knowledge of the many scholars cited in this book even when I disagreed with their conclusions. I did my best to withhold my opinion. After all I am not a scholar! I do take responsibility for all things prison contained in this book. My experience as an incarcerated Christian influenced both my interpretation and application of this letter. I cannot help but see the relationship between the author's listeners and the incarcerated believer. Both are trying to persevere in a hostile, unbelieving environment. Both are in need of constant understanding, warning, and encouragement. Both must look to Jesus in order to persevere.

The Authorship of Hebrews

The authorship issues surrounding Hebrews are as old as the book itself and throughout the centuries many have put forth their prospected candidate. Some of the ancient candidates were Luke, Paul, Barnabas, and Clement of Rome. More recent scholarship has offered Apollos, Priscilla, Philip, and even Mary the mother of Jesus.[1] While the probability of the theories varies, four appear to stand above the others: Paul, Barnabas, Luke, and Apollos.

Paul

By the end of the second century Pauline authorship was reported in the East by Patristics such as Clement of Alexandria (150-215 AD) and Origen (185-254 AD); although the latter also mentions others holding to Luke and Clement of Rome as prospective authors. In the West, Pauline authorship did not gain support until the time of Jerome (347-420 AD) and Augustine (354-430 AD) where support for the epistle was probably related

[1] For an excellent overview of authorship see: Donald Guthrie, *New Testament Introduction* (Downers Grove: IVP, 1990), 673.

to its need of canonicity. The early church struggled to authorize biblical letters which were not directly or indirectly associated with an apostle. Cockerill has noted that one can see the rise of Pauline authorship from East to West in relation to support for "Hebrews' canonical status."[2] As a result, Pauline authorship remained largely unquestioned until the time of the Reformation when Luther and Calvin, both opposed it. Very few scholars support Paul as a potential author today.

The weightiest support for Pauline authorship lies in its antiquity. Paul was regarded as the author by the church for over a thousand years. While this cannot stand as sole support for Pauline authorship, it also must not be easily disregarded. Scholars through the centuries have attempted to shore up the historical argument for Pauline authorship by addressing some of the strongest points against Paul. For example, the style which differs from Paul's other works was addressed by Clement of Alexandria who believed that Hebrews was originally written by Paul in Hebrew and translated into Greek by Luke. However, as Witherington has noted, the eloquence of the author's Greek makes it "almost impossible" to be an "awkward translation Greek," and furthermore, the author's use of the Greek LXX for citing the Old Testament would not be something someone writing in Hebrew would do.[3] Others have attempted to answer the stylistic issues by arguing that someone in the Pauline circle recorded what they had heard Paul preach. However, there is no extant evidence of a Hebrew original and no textual evidence for

---

[2] D. A. Carson and Douglas Moo, *An Introduction to the New Testament* (Grand Rapids: Zondervan, 1992), 601.

[3] Ben Witherington III, *Letters and Homilies for Jewish Christians: A Socio-Rhetorical Commentary on Hebrews, James, and Jude* (Downers Grove: IVP Academic, 2007), 19.

Hebrews being translated. As far as the oral transmission argument is concerned, other issues such as difference in theological emphasis makes it unlikely. Donald Guthrie notes that the author of Hebrews' theology emphasizes exaltation over Pauline resurrection, and purification over Pauline justification. The author also focuses on Christ as high priest, a theme absent in Paul's letters.[4]

Many scholars have noted the internal issues that oppose Pauline authorship. For example, Hebrews 2:3 states that the author received the Gospel from those who had heard the Lord, thus making him a second-generation believer. It is unlikely that Paul who had a direct encounter with the resurrected Lord Jesus would have spoken this way about himself. David Allen notes that Paul in his other epistles considered himself an eyewitness to the resurrected Lord (Acts 9), a requirement for apostleship.[5] As a result, it is unlikely that Paul penned Hebrews firsthand. While there are several similarities to the Pauline corpus, they are easily addressed by the close relationship the author had with the Pauline circle.

Barnabas

The argument for Barnabas, like Paul, has the benefit of antiquity, although it does not hold the prolonged witness by the church. One of the earliest references to Barnabas' authorship was provided by Tertullian (196-212 AD) in the West who stated his authorship as if it was common knowledge. It has also been noted that Barnabas was a Levite who would have been capable of producing work so dependent on the Old Testament. Furthermore,

---

[4] Donald Guthrie, *New Testament Introduction,* 673.

[5] David Allen, *Hebrews*, New American Commentary (Nashville: B&H, 2010), 40.

Barnabas is referred to as the Son of Exhortation (Acts 4:36) and the author of Hebrews refers to his epistle as a word of exhortation (Heb. 13:22). This could possibly be a play on Barnabas' name. However, one major weakness lies in the fact that there is no known existing text that can be legitimately attributed to Barnabas. The so-called epistle of Barnabas was most likely not penned by him. However, if it was, it would exclude him because of the vast differences between the two epistles. Guthrie notes that Barnabas being a Jew with close ties to Jerusalem would not likely hold such a Hellenistic outlook as found in Hebrews.[6] Many scholars have noted that the author displayed a high level of Greek education similar to Philo and generally associated with Alexandria, Egypt.

Luke

Luke's candidacy also has the support of antiquity and has become one of the more popular views within the church. Origen testified that some during his time believed Luke wrote Hebrews. Luke was a traveling companion of the apostle Paul so the correlation between Hebrews and the Pauline epistles would be natural. He also wrote in a polished Greek similar to the author of Hebrews. Finally, one can find similar vocabulary between Luke/Acts and Hebrews which is not found elsewhere in the New Testament.

One of the most recent treatments of Lukan authorship is provided by David Allen where he spends fifteen of his thirty-one pages on authorship addressing Lukan strengths and weaknesses. Allen believes that Luke wrote Hebrews after the death of Paul

---

[6] Donald Guthrie, *New Testament Introduction*, 675-76.

and before the destruction of the temple in AD 70.[7] Allen begins his argument by establishing Luke's presence in Rome. In 2 Timothy 4:11 Paul states; "Only Luke is with me" which places Luke in Rome around AD 67-68. He argues that Paul penned 2 Timothy from prison in Rome, possibly around 66-67 AD. In his letter, Paul tells Timothy to come quickly (2 Timothy 4:9) and likely dies around Timothy's arrival. Timothy is imprisoned and later released which fits with Hebrews 13:23. Finally, Hebrews refers to Timothy as "our brother" placing him in the Pauline circle and making him an associate of the author. Allen also argues that Luke/Hebrews are the only New Testament works that come near to the classical Greek style. There is a similarity in vocabulary and style, and Hebrews shares 53 words with Luke and Acts that are not found elsewhere in the New Testament.

Apollos

Apollos' authorship is a view that has gained a lot of recent support. Witherington provides the following evidence in support of Apollos using Acts 18-19 and First Corinthians to strengthen his argument. First, these texts place Apollos in the Pauline circle making him a possible associate of Timothy and accounting for the Pauline influence in Hebrews. Second, Apollos was from Alexandria and learned in the Scriptures (Old Testament) indicating a familiarity with the LXX from which he taught Christ as does the author of Hebrews. Third, he is referred to as an eloquent man which means he was trained in rhetoric as most assuredly was the author of Hebrews. Finally, Witherington ties the confusion surrounding the plural form of "baptisms" found in Hebrews 6:2 to the Acts 18:25 account surrounding Apollos. He argues that the plural form of baptism can be explained by the

---

[7] David Allen, *Hebrews,* 48.

distinction between John's baptism and Christian baptism. As a result, Witherington states; "No one fits the bill so well as Apollos to be author of this document."[8]

Witherington takes the Apollos' position a step further by arguing his likelihood of authorship. Witherington offers eleven parallels between Apollos and the author of Hebrews: (1) both were of Jewish ancestry, (2) Apollos was from Alexandria which is also likely for the author of Hebrews, (3) both were eloquent men trained in rhetoric, (4) both were powerful in the use of Scriptures in a Christological way, (5) both taught accurately the things concerning Jesus, (6) both spoke boldly, (7) both were missionary minded, (8) both had a fervency of spirit, (9) both had knowledge of Roman Christians, (10) both were of the Pauline circle, (11) both had a relation possibly to Corinth.[9]

While these are most definitely powerful similarities, the description of the author likely would have fitted numerous people from that time. Commentators who argue for a specific biblical character for authorship appear to assume that the author of Hebrews is known to the biblical witness. It is likely that the author of Hebrews was never mentioned in any other biblical book.

Many scholars today address the authorship issues from a historical perspective and generally do not take a position, but instead, devote their time to describing the "type" of person the author was. Cockerill has noted that the description of Apollos in Acts 18-19 definitely describes the type of person who would have written Hebrews and points one to the rhetorical skill used

---

[8] Ben Witherington, *Letters and Homilies for Jewish Christians,* 24.
[9] Ibid., 23-24.

throughout Hebrews.[10] Cockerill, while stating that authorship is inconclusive, describes the writer as a man who "was a master of elegant Greek" and understood the art of rhetoric and oral persuasion. "He had a thorough knowledge of the Old Testament" and was deeply concerned about the social issues which influenced his audience.[11] Lane describes the author similarly when he states that he was a Hellenistic Jewish Christian, trained in rhetoric, very religious and concerned for the community to which he wrote.[12] Both these authors state that the biblical description of Apollos fits the type of person who was capable of writing Hebrews. Apollos was someone in the Pauline circle who is described as an elegant man (Acts 18:24; 19:1).[13] However, it appears that no one from antiquity held this view and as Guthrie has stated it would seem, "The Alexandrian church would have preserved such a fact."[14] Allen further adds that there are no extant works written by Apollos to compare with Hebrews.[15] As a result, the author of Hebrews remains unknown.

The Audience of Hebrews

While the authorship issues surrounding Hebrews are interesting and have produced many spirited debates, their relevance for interpretation pale in comparison to the need for the understanding of the biblical audience.[16] Craig Koester provides a helpful overview of the church's circumstances.

---

[10]Gareth Cockerill, *Hebrews*, The New International Commentary on the New Testament (Grand Rapids: Eerdmans, 2012), 10.
[11] Ibid., 2-3.
[12] William Lane, *Hebrews*, 2 vols. WBC, 47a-47b (Dallas: Word Books, 1991), xlix-li.
[13] Cockerill, *Hebrews,* 9.
[14] Donald Guthrie, *New Testament Introduction,* 679.
[15] David Allen, *Hebrews,* 47.
[16] Gareth Cockerill, *Hebrews*, 19.

Hebrews addressed a Christian community that had existed for some time. At several points the author refers to the group's history, allowing us to discern three phases. First, the community was formed when Christian evangelists proclaimed a message of salvation, performing miracles to validate their preaching. Some persons came to faith, experiencing the power of the Holy Spirit and a sense of enlightenment; they received baptism and the laying on of hands. Second, non-Christians instigated hostilities against the community by physically accosting Christians and denouncing them before local authorities, who imprisoned them and allowed Christian property to be plundered. During the conflict, Christians maintained their faith commitments and supported each other, attending to the needs of those in prison. Third, overt persecution gave way to a lower level of conflict in which non-Christians continued to verbally harass Christians. Some from the community were in prison, and others felt the effects of being marginalized in society. Although some continued to show faith and compassion, others experienced malaise that was evident in tendencies to neglect the faith and community gatherings. Hebrews was written during this third phase.[17]

Hebrews is most likely addressed to a group of Jewish Christians who lived outside of Palestine.[18] They were well versed in the Old Testament and capable of understanding elegant Greek. They probably moved into the Pauline circle and constituted a relatively large house church. They had come to faith as a result

---

[17] Craig Koester, *Hebrews: A New Testament Translation with Introduction and Commentary*, AB 36 (New York: Doubleday, 2001), 64-65.

[18] The term Jewish Christian used in this commentary includes both ethnic Jews and Gentiles who had adopted Jewish religious practices. In Koester, *Hebrews,* 20.

of the evangelism of first-generation believers but did not witness Jesus' ministry firsthand.[19]

The audience at one point suffered imprisonment and the loss of property for the sake of the Gospel (Heb. 10:32-33). Now once again, they were being marginalized (Heb. 12:4). This new pressure was causing the believers to grow lax.[20] The author is worried that the Hebrews may be "in danger of compromising their commitment to Christ."[21] They likely could be suffering temptation to identify with the unbelieving world of which they once belonged.[22] By turning away from their former associations, they had made themselves targets. This turning away resulted in persecution from the groups to which they once belonged. As Koester states, "By turning away from certain patterns of belief, the convert makes a negative judgment—either explicitly or implicitly—on beliefs and values that continue to be held by those who do not share the same faith."[23]

---

[19] Lane, *Hebrews,* lv.
[20] Ibid., lvi.
[21] Cockerill, Hebrews, 16.
[22] Ibid., 17.
[23] Koester, *Hebrews,* 67.

The Date of Hebrews

The exact dating of Hebrews faces as many obstacles as determining authorship and audience. Nevertheless, there are several pieces of evidence that will enable one to confidently narrow a time frame. Most biblical scholars are comfortable with dating Hebrews between 60-90 AD. Their starting reference point is generally derived from two pieces of evidence. First, the author appears to be a second-generation believer (Heb. 2:3). This means a date prior to 60 AD would be unlikely. The author also refers to an earlier persecution which his listeners had faced. If the community addressed was in Rome, then this persecution was likely Claudius' expulsion mentioned concerning Aquila and Priscilla in Acts 18:1-2. Scholars who advocate for a range between 60-90 AD use 1 Clement's reference of Hebrews as their stopping points. Most scholars hold that 1 Clement was written around 95 AD. Therefore, for Clement to use Hebrews it would have had to be written and in circulation before 95 AD.

Other scholars would narrow the range to somewhere between 60-70 AD. These scholars use the same arguments for their starting point; however, they believe that several other factors warrant a pre-70 date. Douglas Moo argues that in light of the author's view of Old Testament worship practices that if the Temple was already destroyed he would have mentioned this.[24] Allen believes that Luke wrote Hebrews which influences his date between 67-68 AD.[25] Other scholars are not persuaded by the silence of the Temple's destruction and instead point to the silence surrounding Nero's persecution beginning in 64 AD. The recipients of Hebrews had not yet experienced a persecution

[24] Douglas Moo, *Hebrews, Exegetical Commentary on the New Testament* (Grand Rapids: Zondervan, 2024), 6-7.
[25] Allen, *Hebrews*, 75, 78.

resulting in death which most definitely described the times of Nero.[26] The overall evidence likely favors the 60-70 AD date.[27]

A Note on Interpretation Methods

Understanding how the author viewed the Old Testament is vital for today's readers. The author did not believe that the Old Testament provided a satisfactory means for fellowship with God; it was always meant to be partial and progressive. The preacher viewed all of God's acts and people as part of one continuous story. For him, there were nott Jews and Christians but one people of God who had placed faith in his final revelation—Jesus Christ.

For example, the author's understanding of entering God's rest is colored by the background story of the wilderness wandering and Promised Land. However, the author appears to see the same rest being offered to the children of Israel as the rest being offered to the First Century Christian (Heb. 4:1-2). For the author, the land was never the point. Access to God through faith in Christ was always the plan. To some this may sound like a form of replacement theology; however, to the author of Hebrews, it is simply the fulfillment of God's one plan of salvation for all people. For today's readers, this offers a level of comfort and security. The believer is not part of God's backup plan of salvation. God is speaking his authoritative word into the noisy, chaotic world, bringing order and rest to all those that will heed his voice.

---

[26] Lane, *Hebrews*, lxii-lxvi; Guthrie, *Hebrews*, 22.

[27] For thorough explanations of authorship see: Koester, *Hebrews,* 50-54; Cockerill; *Hebrews*, 34-41.

Outline of Hebrews

I God's Ultimate Message for the Weary Traveler (1:1-4:13)

- A) Jesus: A Superior Guide (1:1-2:18)
    - 1) The Supremacy of the Message (1:1-4)
    - 2) The Supremacy of the Messenger (1:5-14)
    - 3) The Importance of the Message (2:1-4)
    - 4) The Need of the Message (2:5-9)
    - 5) The Benefits of the Message (2:10-18)
- B) Jesus: Faithfulness through Obedience (3:1-4:13)
    - 1) Consider the Faithfulness of a Son (3:1-6)
    - 2) Remember the Disobedience of a People (3:7-19)
    - 3) Strive for the Blessing of Obedience (4:1-11)
    - 4) Live by the Standard of the Word (4:12-13)

II God's Companion for the Weary Traveler (4:14-10:18)

- A) Jesus: The People's Great High Priest (4:14-6:20)
    - 1) The High Priest Who Sympathizes (4:14-5:10)
    - 2) The Necessity of Spiritual Maturity (5:11-6:12)
    - 3) The Reliability of God's Character and Promise (6:13-20)
- B) Jesus: A Superior Priesthood (7:1-28)
    - 1) Melchizedek: A Unique High Priest (7:1-10)
    - 2) Jesus: A Superior High Priest (7:11-28)
- C) Jesus: The High Priest of the New Covenant (8:1-10:18)
    - 1) The Supremacy of the New Covenant (8:1-13)
    - 2) The Failure of the Old Covenant (9:1-14)
    - 3) The Mediator of the New Covenant (9:15-28)
    - 4) The Superior Sacrifice of the New Covenant (10:1-18)

III God's Examples of Faithfulness for the Weary Traveler (10:19-12:29)

- A) Jesus: The Foundation of Perseverance (10:19-39)
  - 1) Perseverance: Draw Near. Hold Fast, and Consider (10:19-25)
  - 2) Perseverance: No Turning Back Now (10:26-39)
- B) Jesus: The Goal of Faith (11:1-40)
  - 1) Faith Defined (11:1-3)
  - 2) Faith from Creation to Flood (11:4-7)
  - 3) Abraham's Faithful Journey (11:8-22)
  - 4) Moses' Faithful Leadership (11:23-31)
  - 5) The Triumph and Trials of the Faithful (11:32-40)
- C) Jesus: The Example of Endurance (12:1-29)
  - 1) Staying Focused on Jesus (12:1-3)
  - 2) The Discipline of the Father (12:4-13)
  - 3) Esau's Failure to Endure (12:14-17)
  - 4) The Goal of Endurance (12:18-24)
  - 5) A Final Warning to Persevere (12:25-29)

IV God's Final Instructions for the Weary Traveler (13:1-25)

- A) Showing Love to One Another (13:1-6)
- B) Imitate and Obey Leaders (13:7-17)
- C) A Final Word of Exhortation (13:18-25)

A Note on How to Use This Commentary

Any serious study of Scripture should begin with prayer. Just as God used many Old Testament texts to minister to the recipients of this letter in their time of need, he will use the same texts to minister to your needs. However, you must prepare your heart and mind to hear the voice of God. In prayer, ask God to open the Scriptures to you in a special way. The Bible allows us to hear God's voice, but we must attempt to remove all distractions.

Next familiarize yourself with the section of Hebrews you will be studying. This may require you to read all the epistle first to get the overall flow of the letter, then really focus on the section you will be studying. This book assumes that you are familiar with the letter and should be read with Bible close by. This commentary is simply a guide to help you tackle some of the more difficult parts of Hebrews.

As you read Hebrews, jot down your initial thoughts and questions. I hope that many of them will be answered as you read this commentary. If not, there are numerous resources available in the bibliography. I chose Gareth Cockerill's commentary to serve as an overall guide to my research. You will recognize many of his ideas in this book, I hope I did not misrepresent them too badly!

Finally, my understanding of how the two testaments relate to one another is derived from my understanding of men like G.K. Beale, and Graeme Goldsworthy. Their books on biblical interpretation have been invaluable to my research. Check some of their works out, you will never read the Bible the same again.[28]

[28] All Scriptures are taken from the ESV translation of the Bible.

I. God's Ultimate Message for the Weary Traveler (1:1-4:13)

Section Summary

Since the beginning of time, God has spoken to his people. He walked and talked with Adam in the cool of the Garden and called Abraham from a foreign land into covenant fellowship. He spoke with Moses about the oppression of his people and called him to guide Israel to the Promised Land. He cried out for repentance and obedience and sent prophets to deliver the message of covenant faithfulness. God has always spoken but his people rarely listened. Yet into the "last days" he sent Jesus, a superior spokesman with a superior message. The eternal heir of all creation took on flesh to deliver a final message and guide his people to a heavenly kingdom. Those who follow his example and persevere will enter into God's rest, but for those who fail to endure and harden their hearts, judgment awaits. God's living and active word cries out to have faith in the person and work of Jesus. Hear his voice!

Introduction to the Section

Life in Christ is not always easy. Believers are on a journey that takes them from faith to faith. Along the way, there are hills of triumphs and valleys of trials. Believers will often find themselves standing atop of one or stuck at the bottom of another. The author's audience is in a valley. They are experiencing opposition that is causing them to question whether they should continue forward or possibly turn back. The author encourages his listeners not to grow weary in their travels. They have a superior guide who has delivered a superior message with superior benefits (Heb. 1:1-2:18).

The audience's responsibility is to "consider Jesus" and follow his example of faithfulness and obedience. They are to resist the urge to turn back like the disobedient wilderness generation and instead strive for the promised rest of God. Along the journey, the living, active word of God is always examining the thoughts and intentions of their hearts (Heb. 3:1-4:13).

A. Jesus: A Superior Guide (1:1-2:18)

1. The Supremacy of the Message (1:1-4)

Prisoner's Insight for the Journey

Prison is never quiet. For those visiting or new to the system, one of the first things noticed is the constant roar produced by dozens of conversations happening at once. TVs blare mindless programing at all hours, and fans circulate the stale prison air with a never ceasing hum. Over time, one adjusts, and the endless roar of many noises becomes the background clamor of everyday life. Hearers become indifferent to the roar, no longer able to distinguish any particular voice or sound. The noise becomes deafening.

Attempting to get the attention of someone across a crowded dayroom at times can seem impossible. The louder one yells, the louder the roar becomes, overpowering everything in its path. In order to overcome the roar, the speaker must drag his listeners into his presence by breaking through the background noise. In prison, there are numerous ways to grab the attention of a noisy dayroom, some more dangerous than others, but all equally effective. Beating on a stainless-steel table with a cup is sure to get the attention of your listeners, but you had better have something to say. Less advised, but probably most effective, would be to unplug the TV, killing the mindless programing, and likely yourself. Yet drastic times call for drastic measures. If you are to grab the attention of a crowded dayroom it requires a new voice, *a voice of authority* to break through to the hearers.

In many ways, the children of Israel had become accustomed to how God spoke. In the past, God's word was given through prophets, signs, and wonders. He delivered his Law through the means of angels and called men to proclaim his covenant faithfulness. For thousands of years, God spoke at various times and various ways into the roar of the background noise. Yet the children of Israel failed to heed his voice and soon the voice of God was drowned out by the roar of countless other voices. The Lord's voice became rare (1 Sam. 3:1).

At the close of the Old Testament, the prophet Malachi proclaims the future coming of the Day of the Lord (Mal. 3:1), and Israel longed to see this day arrive. Yet when John the Baptist came fulfilling the role of Elijah preparing the way of the Lord (Mal. 4:5, Matt. 3:1-3), the people rejected both him and the Messiah. In their hardness of heart, God's people crucified the Lord of Glory, but in love, God raised him from the dead, exalting him to his right hand (Acts 2:22-36). From his exalted position of authority, the Son is speaking into the background noise of the believer's life and: "Today if you hear his voice, don't harden your hearts" (Heb. 4:7).

The Jewish Christians in Hebrews are struggling with the background noise of their day, so much so, many appear to be second guessing the faith and desiring to revert to the more established form of Judaism. The author reminds them that God has spoken through his Son, and his Son is still speaking to their struggles. The author calls his flock to heed the authoritative voice of Christ who is God's final revelation.

Commentary

1:1-2a

Messages come in all shapes and forms. Some are spoken and others written, but the greatest messages are embodied. When God was ready to deliver his most important word to humanity, he did not write it on stone nor entrust it to a prophet. He sent his only begotten Son into the world to not only proclaim the Gospel with words but to show it through his actions. The author of Hebrews shares the greatest revelation of all time by revealing the person and work that personifies the message: Jesus. The author understands that his audience is struggling to persevere in faith. Yet he also understands that if they will listen closely to what is said and follow the example of the message then they will endure to the end.

The author captures his listeners' attention by crafting possibly the most beautiful sentence in all the New Testament. In one breath, he carries his listeners from "long ago" to these "last days" to show the continuation of God's work. The same God who walked with Adam in the Garden is the same God who reveals himself in Jesus. The author highlights this continuation with a four part comparison: (1) Long ago/in these last days, (2) God spoke many times and in many ways/God spoke in a Son, (3) God spoke to the fathers/God spoke to us, (4) God spoke by the prophets/God spoke by a Son.[29]

The author's comparison is essential for understanding his point. He knows that God's word is effectual over the lives of his listeners. The Holy Spirit can apply the word spoken long ago to the church's current struggle. The Spirit that hovered over creation in the beginning is the same Spirit that both convicts the heart of sin and comforts the soul after correction. God has not forgotten his people. Like a loving father, God's word guides the believer all throughout life. God spoke long ago, he has spoken with finality in his Son, and he continues to speak by upholding and guiding his redemptive plan. The book of Hebrews is about the fulfillment of God's plan of salvation. The author cites numerous Old Testament Scriptures, often placing them on the lips of God, and reveals how they are fulfilled in Jesus. The author presents the Old Testament as if God was presently speaking the words to his church.

(1) *Long ago/ in these last days* highlights God's continual work in the lives of his people. For a group of Christians with a Jewish background, emphasizing that God's work in the New Testament is a continuation of his work in the Old would be vital. The author is not attempting to portray two different gods or even two different plans, but one God bringing to fulfillment one faith in his Son Jesus. God's work is progressive. It is the same God who has always spoken into the noise. The God who said, "Let

---

[29] For similar examples of contrast see Allen, *Hebrews*, 96-115; Cockerill, *Hebrews* 88; Lane, *Hebrews*, 9-11.

there be light" is the same God who calls today's believers into the church.

The phrase "in the last days" was commonly used by biblical authors to signify the end times. The arrival of Jesus inaugurated the last days. The author of Hebrews understood the "last days" to encompass the life of Jesus through his second coming when his enemies will be made his footstool (Heb. 1:13). Therefore, the author's audience was currently living during the last days and was being encouraged to remain faithful and "avail themselves of the benefits of God's redemption in the son."[30] The Old Testament saints looked forward to this day, and the New Testament saints were aware that the day had arrived. The prophet Joel writing 800 years before the event looks forward to a day when God would pour out his Spirit on all people (Joel 2:28). The apostle Peter, in his sermon on the day of Pentecost, proclaims that this day has arrived (Acts 2). Jesus while preaching in a synagogue in Nazareth read from Isaiah 61:1-2. After closing the scroll, he proclaims to his listeners: "Today this scripture has been fulfilled in your hearing" (Luke 4:17-21). Jesus understood his presence as the fulfillment of the promises concerning the last days. By linking the old way of God's communication with the new, the author shows his understanding of God's continual work.

(2) *God spoke many times and, in many ways, /God spoke in a Son.* The author also points to the various modes of past revelation. By simply reading the Old Testament accounts one sees that God did not limit himself to any one form. God spoke through signs and wonders that were mediated by bushes, angels, and even donkeys (Exod. 3:4; Gen. 22:15; Num. 22:28). God spoke to Moses on Sinai and delivered the Commandments to a

---

[30] Cockerill, *Hebrews*, 90; Allen, *Hebrews*, 102.

fearful people (Exod. 20:18-19). God's most common means of communication in the Old Testament was tied primarily to his presence in the Tabernacle/Temple. When the glory of the Lord would descend on the tent of meeting, the people would go to worship and hear the message of God delivered through Moses (Exod. 33:7-11).

God also chose the time at which he would reveal himself. The Old Testament saints did not have unrestricted access to God's revelation. Before calling young Samuel, the Bible says, "The word of the Lord was rare in those days, there was no frequent vision" (1 Sam. 3:1). Thus, when God finally spoke it was almost always because he was preparing to do something new. When God revealed himself to Moses in a burning bush it was because he was preparing to deliver the children of Israel. As a result, God's ultimate message in his Son reveals that he is providing a new way of access and fellowship; the many times and many ways have now found its fulfillment in the one and only Son. All of God's past revelations are summed up in Christ (2 Cor. 1:20). This means the author's listeners should not be looking for God to reveal himself in some new way because Jesus has fully made known the Father (John 1:18). The author shows that God's revelation has become more focused and stable by revealing himself in a Son.

(3) *God spoke to the fathers/God spoke to us.* God's revelation has also become more personal. Long ago God spoke to the "fathers" but in these last days he spoke to "us." This statement brings the voice of God into the listener's current situation. Just as God spoke to Abraham, Isaac, and Jacob in the past, he is presently speaking to his people in the person of Christ. The audience needed to understand that God had not abandoned them in their trials, but just as he guided the Old Testament saints in their wilderness wanderings, he would also guide them in their time of need. The apostle Paul reminds his readers, "What was written in former days was written for our instruction, that through endurance and through the encouragement of the scriptures we might have hope" (Rom. 15:4). No longer is God's revelation part of an ancient religious history but it is the "powerful word" that is currently at work in the world.

(4) *God spoke by the prophets/God spoke by a Son.* Finally, God's medium has changed. God spoke by the prophets but now has spoken by a Son. The prophets spoke with authority of God as messengers, but the Son speaks as God in the flesh. The finality of Jesus' message is easily seen in his interpretation and application of the Old Testament Law and Prophets. It was Jesus' authoritative renderings that brought the displeasure of the religious leaders of his day. At the conclusion of the Sermon on the Mount, the people were amazed because he taught "as one who had the authority, and not as their scribes" (Matt. 7:29). Moreover, Jesus also saw himself as the fulfillment of the Old Testament (Luke 4:16-21). On the road to Emmaus, Jesus reminded his followers, "Everything written about me in the Law of Moses and the prophets, and the Psalms must be fulfilled" (Luke 24:44).

The distinction between how God spoke long ago and how he spoke in the last days is similar to the difference between reading someone's book and having the author explain it. I remember when I was training to become a Field Minister in Seminary at the Darrington Unit. A friend introduced me to a small book that transformed how I read the Bible. G. K. Beale's *Handbook on the New Testament Use of the Old Testament* introduced me to a new understanding of the Scriptures.[31] For the very first time, the Old Testament made sense. I was able to see the relation between the Old and the New Testaments. I devoured this small book even though as a young student I didn't have the necessary framework to understand many of its concepts. So, needless to say, I was excited to hear that Dr. Beale would be a visitor at my school. I wanted to meet the man and ask him questions about his book. I was not disappointed on either front. Dr. Beale was warm and engaging, displaying comfort inside a maximum-security prison rare to first-time visitors. His explanation concerning his work also answered many of my questions. While Dr. Beale's book is great, his character and explanation brought it to life. Dr. Beale was passionate about his work. In the same way, Jesus made real all of what God had spoken through the prophets long ago. Jesus' person embodied the content of the Old Testament.

A Note on the New Testament's Use of the Old

To fully understand the relation between Testaments, the content of the prophetic Old Testament message must be examined in light of its New Testament fulfillment. The New Testament authors never degrade the message of the prophets. The author is not attempting to downplay the message that the prophets proclaimed but desired to emphasize the superiority of the way the message was delivered. Thus, the author is not stressing the inferiority of the messengers or the discontinuity of the message, but he desires to emphasize the superiority of the Son and the finality of the message. Jesus the superior voice has fulfilled the message of the past. Jesus in the Sermon on the Mount makes it

[31] G.K. Beale, *Handbook on the New Testament use of the Old Testament* (Grand Rapids: Baker Academic, 2012).

clear that he had not come to abolish the Law and the Prophets (Matt. 5:17). Paul in the epistle to the Romans while discussing Abraham's faith stated, "But the words 'it was counted to him' were not written for his sake alone, but for ours also" (Rom. 4:23-24). Both these statements show that the New Testament authors had a high view of the Old Testament. They believed that the Old Testament Scriptures were being fulfilled during their day.

The Old Testament prophets' primary role was to call the people of God to covenant faithfulness by reminding them of the promises of God. The promises given to Israel by God functioned as an important aspect of their daily lives. The people of God knew that even in the face of trials and tribulations, God's promises would be realized. While the promises mediated temporal blessings, they also pointed to a day of complete fulfillment. The Old Testament saints often saw the partial fulfillment of God's blessing but never the complete attainment (Heb. 11:40). The future consummation of God's blessing was revealed in types and shadows pointing toward a future fulfillment. When the Old Testament is interpreted through the lens of the New, one can easily see that God's ultimate promise and blessing is most clearly revealed in the person and work of his Son. Jesus when rebuking the religious leaders of his day stated, "You search the scriptures [Old Testament] because you think that in them you have eternal life; and it is they that bear witness about me" (John 5:39). The author uses the same biblical interpretation methods as Jesus. The New Testament is a continuation of God's redemptive story that began at creation. By examining the method of the earliest New Testament writers, one sees that they held a very high view of the unity of the biblical story. What God spoke in the past through the prophets in types and shadows, he has made plain in the person of his Son, God's final and most complete revelation.

1:2b-4

After the author establishes the unity of God's message, he focuses his attention on the superiority of the messenger. Much of the author's message could be summed up as: "Jesus is better." First, Jesus is better because God has appointed him "heir of all things." Jesus is not just another messenger like the prophets, but as the Son of God, he is the heir of all creation. He has inherited a kingdom, a people, and a name above all names. The fullness of his inheritance will be realized at his second coming when his enemies will become his footstool and believers will inherit the fullness of salvation (Heb. 1:14).

The concept of heir and inheritance is one of the many prominent themes of the Bible. In the Old Testament the inheritance of Israel was signified by the Promised Land. Each generation of Israelites inherited the promise given to Abraham and the land tied to that blessing. Thus, as Moses is preparing to deliver Israel from Egyptian captivity, God commands him to say, "I will bring you into the land that I swore to give to Abraham, to Isaac, and to Jacob. I will give it to you as a possession. I am the Lord" (Exod. 6:6-8). However, the concept of heir and inheritance in the New Testament shifts. Jesus, the true Israel becomes the heir of all creation (Gal. 6:16). All the promises of God find their "yes" in him (2 Cor. 1:20). Paul expands Abraham's inheritance to the entire world (Rom. 4:13), and the author of Hebrews follows Paul's thought by expanding the inheritance of the land to the heavenly city (Heb. 11:8-10). Therefore, the New Testament authors understood Jesus as the heir of all the promises given to Israel. Believers inherit their blessings and access to God's promises through their relationship with Jesus. In Galatians, Paul tells the church, "If you are Christ's then you are Abraham's offspring, heirs according to promise" (Gal. 3:29).[32] The appointment of Jesus as heir of all things is significant for the author's audience. They are being persecuted and alienated from all sides. By separating themselves from mainline Judaism they suddenly feel cut off from the promises given to Israel.[33] They feel like a people without a home. The persecution they face has previously resulted in a loss of property (Heb. 10:34). Therefore, the author's unifying theme of the one people of God in Christ provides comfort for those who "have no lasting city" in this world, while they "seek the city that is to come" in the next (Heb. 13:14).

Lest his listeners assume that the Son became something he once was not, the author clarifies his statement by emphasizing the Son's eternal nature: "through whom also he created the ages." The author emphasizes, much like the apostles John and Paul, that Jesus was present and instrumental in the creation of the universe (John 1:3; Col. 1:16). The Son may be appointed heir, but he is the eternally present Son of creation. Just as Jesus took on flesh for the purpose of his death, burial, and resurrection, he also took on the role of heir. The Son is the eternal heir through whom and for whom God created an inheritance.[34] The author provides his listeners with a glimpse of the unity of the biblical story by reflecting back on the Genesis account of creation and looking forward to Revelation's account of a new creation. In between these bookends, stands Jesus, the beginning and end of all creation (Gen. 1; Rev. 21).

---

[32] G. K. Beale, *A New Testament Biblical Theology: The Unfolding of the Old Testament in the New* (Grand Rapids: Baker Academic, 2011), 671; 766.
[33] Cockerill, *Hebrews*, 702-703.
[34] Allen, *Hebrews*, 113-114.

Understanding the relationship between Jesus' appointment as heir and his being the eternal Son of creation is difficult. If Jesus is the eternal Son, then why did he need to be appointed heir? Jesus' appointment is directly related to his obedience. In verse 3, the author states, "After making purification for sins, he sat down at the right hand of majesty on high." This statement reflects both Christ's obedience to the cross, (making purification for sins), and his appointment as heir, (he sat down at the right hand of majesty on high). Jesus' obedience in the flesh was a necessary aspect of his appointment as heir. While all analogies ultimately break down in their description of God, an illustration might be helpful.

When I was growing up my dad restored classic Mustangs. He would take these cars and give them as gifts to his children when they became old enough to drive. Each of my older brothers received fully restored 60's model Mustangs. I remember working with my dad building the Mustang that would eventually become mine. I was at the same time both creator and heir to this beautiful car. However, my inheritance of this Mustang required that I act as a son worthy of this gift. Unfortunately, my disobedience during my teen years resulted in forfeiting my right to inherit the car. Jesus as the eternal Son was also responsible for creation of his future inheritance and as an obedient Son he also showed himself worthy of this beautiful gift.

Building on this previous argument of the Son's superiority, the author introduces a third clause describing the Son which contains some of the highest Christology found in all the New Testament. The above Greek clause is replete with words which need explanation. The Son is not simply an heir, but in his person and work, is the very revelation of God. The Son shines forth the "radiance" of God's glory. The word "radiance" is found only here in the New Testament. It can have both an active sense, which means to shine forth, and a passive use, which means to reflect. The author most likely means to convey that the Son shines forth (in an active way) the very nature of God. In light of the Old Testament Tabernacle imagery found throughout the book of Hebrews, "radiance" could also be seen as an allusion to the Shekinah glory of God's presence on the Tabernacle (Exod. 13:21).[35] This understanding correlates well with the author's contrast between old and new revelation. God's speaking was somewhat fleeting as seen in his presence with the Tabernacle; however, in the Son it has found permanence. This statement helps relate the Son to the Father. The Son reveals the glory of God to mankind.

The Son is also the exact imprint of God's nature. The Greek word "exact imprint" generally denotes the stamping of a coin or wax seal with an image.[36] The Son's image is the nature and attributes of God. The Son manifests not only the word of God but also his essence. The Son is not simply one sent to deliver the word of God but reveals God in both word and deed. The author's use of the phrase "exact imprint" stresses the relationship between the Father and Son. When humanity comes to know the Son, they also know the Father. In the Gospel of John, Philip asks Jesus to show him the Father. Jesus responds by stating, "Whoever has seen me has seen the father" (John 14:8-11). Paul also stresses Jesus' role as the manifestation of the Father when he states, "[Jesus] is the image of the invisible God" (Col. 1:15). Thus, the author of Hebrews reveals to his listeners in the strongest of terms

---

[35] Albert Mohler, *Christ-Centered Exposition: Exalting Jesus in Hebrews* (Nashville, TN: Holman Reference, 2017), 10.
[36] Cockerill, *Hebrews*, 94

the divine nature of the Son. Koester rightly notes that it required "boldness … for early Christians to confess Jesus' divine sonship in contexts where there were competing claims."[37] Such statements were likely the cause behind much of the listeners' persecution.

It is amazing how children display the characteristics and mannerisms of their parents, even when the parent has been absent from the child's life. I have a son who was 8 years old when I came to prison 20 years ago. However, my sister tells me how much my son resembles me, not only in looks, but also temperament and mannerism. She tells me when she sees and talks to him, it is like seeing and talking to me. He is the "exact imprint" of his father.

The idea of upholding the universe points to the Son's providence. Jesus is able to sustain the people of God in periods marked by stress.[38] The Son is continually present by the power of his word in the lives of his listeners. This theme of God's sustaining word is found continuously throughout this epistle. The author aims to comfort his listeners by reminding them that God is always present in his powerful word. Throughout this letter, the author emphasizes the speech of God and calls his listeners to hear and obey God's voice "today." As often the case with translations, the full meaning of the word "upholds" is missed. While the word most definitely has the sense of upholding and sustaining, it also denotes guiding. This means the same word that holds all things together is also the same word that guides all reality to its final conclusion.[39] The guiding aspect of the word is important for the

---

[37] Koester, *Hebrews*, 187.
[38] Lane, *Hebrews*, 18.
[39] Cockerill, *Hebrews*, 95.

author who sees the people of God as pilgrims on a journey, pilgrims that through the power of the word must persevere to the end. It is the word of God that brought all things into existence, and it is the word of God that will bring all things to its consummation.

After making purification for sins. The author pulls from the Old Testament's wording and imagery in order to introduce the priestly role of the Son. This is evident as the author is able to draw from the rich Old Testament heritage and interpret the actions of God through a Christological lens. The concept of purification draws heavily from the Day of Atonement (Exod. 30:10) and would have easily been recognized by the listeners.

A Note on Purification

In the Old Testament purification from sin was necessary in order to approach God.[40] *Sin places a barrier between one's relationship with God which must be removed.*[41] *The anticipation that Christ's sacrifice will be compared and found superior to the Old Testament sacrificial system by complete removal (Heb. 9-10) is hinted at in the phrase "after making." The middle voice can carry a reflexive aspect of "after making in himself," and in the original Greek, the word signifies a definite action performed once and for all.*[42] *This simple phrase anticipates the further discussion that Christ is both the sacrifice (he made purification in himself) and the one performing the offering as priest (he sat down).*

The rules for purification in the Old Testament were clearly defined. It was Israel's purification laws that set them

---

[40] Allen, *Hebrews*, 125-26.
[41] Lane, *Hebrews*, 15.
[42] Ibid.

apart from other nations and afforded them access to God.[43] *Early in Judaism, purification was tied closely to temple worship and the priesthood. As the children of Israel were led into captivity and developed communities of worship in foreign lands, synagogues became the focus of worship. This also required a rethinking of purification practices. During Jesus' day there was a shift from concern of outward purity to a focus of inward purity. Jesus' statement that it is not what goes into the body, but what comes out that defiles a person was programmatic of the shift in thinking (Mark 7:15).*

This shift found favor in the eyes of many Jewish Christians that were grappling with concepts of worship amongst Gentiles. The struggle for clarity is seen at the so-called Jerusalem counsel in Acts 15. Early believers were attempting to understand their new freedom in Christ. However, clear distinction between the worship practices of Jews and Christians took time to develop. In the Hellenistic environment, the loosing of outward purity restrictions and the focus on moral purity enabled early Christianity to thrive. Jesus' willingness to eat and fellowship with those perceived as unclean enabled Christianity to flourish in the Hellenistic world.[44] *This is especially true as Jesus' death came to be understood by his followers as a perfect sacrifice able to perform what the Mosaic Law could not. The death of Christ was interpreted in light of O.T. prophecies and Jesus is seen as fulfillment of the sacrificial system. As a result, faith in Christ came to replace the need for sacrifice. This theme is emphasized throughout Hebrews. Jesus' death as a sacrifice*

---

[43] Bruce Chilton, "Purity and Impurity." In *Dictionary of the Later New Testament and Its Developments*. Edited by Ralph P. Martin and Peter Davids. (Downers Grove: Intervarsity Press, 1997), 988.

[44] Chilton, "Purity and Impurity," 995.

made the Old Covenant and its sacrificial institutions obsolete (Heb. 8:13). This was especially appealing to Jewish Christians because Jesus came to be seen as part of God's redemptive plan and not as a replacement. This enabled Hellenistic Jews to keep ties to their rich Jewish heritage while also freeing them of the more restrictive worship practices of Judaism.

Returning to the distinction of inward versus outward purification the author states that the Old Covenant was unable to forgive sins and clear the conscience (Heb. 10:4, 11). The sacrificial death of Christ was prefigured by the priest, the tabernacle, and the sacrificial system which culminated in worship on the Day of Atonement. The former were mere shadows and types (Heb. 8:5) of the reality in Christ. While the old system was replaced, its imagery is retained for the purpose of explanation of Christ's atoning work. Christ's death is also seen as destroying the power of the devil, delivering captives, and providing access to God (Heb. 2:14-16). As a result, Christ's entrance into heaven enables him to function continually before God as our mediator and as a "pioneer" who establishes the pattern that future believers will follow. He is the first fruit of resurrection who carries the believer's humanity into heaven (Heb. 6:20).

Christ's death also provides propitiation of divine wrath that is established by the removal of sin (expiation). The removal of God's wrath is seen in Christ's becoming a merciful high priest (Heb. 2:17). The substitutionary aspect of Christ's death is also seen in Hebrews 9:23 which draws from Is. 53:4-12. Christ has borne the sins of many. The sanctifying aspect of Christ's death is not seen as "moral improvement" but as forgiveness. Christ's death provides salvation not from the material to the immaterial but from this age to the age to come. Thus, perfection is eschatological and realized at the completion of God's salvific plan. Salvation in Hebrews also implies community because as the one people of God, past and present, Christ's death has provided for all access to the sanctuary of God. As a body, they experience the rest of God together. Notable is Jesus' actions in the temple in Matt. 21. Jesus cleanses the temple and then receives the unclean to make them clean. Jesus does the same for the believer today; he sits in God's temple and receives sinners making them clean before God. Jesus tells his disciples to say to this mountain, "Move from here to there, and it will move" (Matt. 17:20). The mountain is the Temple Mount. It is in the way of true worship. Jesus echoes this understanding concerning the physical Temple Mount with the Samaritan woman. The day had arrived when people would worship God through Jesus in the Spirit instead of in a physical location.[45]

He sat down at the right hand of the majesty on high is a clear allusion to Ps. 110:1 which the author uses as a key verse of his sermon.[46] Lane states that the priestly language "he sat down" anticipates a full treatment of Jesus as High Priest later in the letter.[47] All that the author has stated concerning the Son finds its completion in the phrase "he sat down." This phrase denotes both the completion of his atoning work and his continual reign from the position of authority. Lane argues the statement, "the son has been exalted to God's right hand means that he lives and rules with the authority and power of God himself."[48] For the author's

---

[45] Michael Horton, *The Christian Faith: A Systematic Theology for Pilgrims on the Way* (Grand Rapids: Zondervan, 449), 2011.
[46] Cockerill, *Hebrews*, 97.
[47] Lane, *Hebrews*, 18.
[48] Ibid., 16.

audience, the continual rule of Jesus from heaven is significant. His presence at the right hand of God implies that he is in control of their current struggles. All that the author will reveal to his listeners concerning the benefits of faith in Jesus are dependent on his sacrificial work and his continual intercession from heaven. Jesus has prepared the way into the presence of God. Now listeners must continue their journey of faith until they arrive at the heavenly city.

In prison everything is locked, and inmates are not allowed to touch the keys. This means we depend on others to access just about any area. I worked for a chaplain who would arrive at work first thing in the morning and unlock all the necessary closets and cabinets before sitting down behind his desk. We knew that once he sat down that unlocking anything else was not going to happen. Once he got behind the desk in his office, his work of unlocking was complete. In the same way, Jesus' purification of sins is complete, and he is not getting up to purify sins again. When the Lord descends from his office in heaven once again, it will not be to purify sins but to judge all those who have not been purified.

Having become as superior to the angels. Finally, the author closes this section with a comment concerning Jesus' superiority to the angels. Many scholars have attempted to see a form of angel worship being addressed by this statement. However, this is unlikely in light of the author's main idea: God's final revelation in the Son. This section has been about the various times and ways that God has communicated with his people. Therefore, just as God spoke through prophets, he has also spoken through angels. Jewish tradition held that the angels were responsible for delivering the Law to Moses on Mt. Sinai. This same idea is also found in the New Testament (Acts 7:30-38; Gal.

3:19). Therefore, the author aims to show that Jesus is a superior messenger than the angels. The author's use of comparison is a prominent literary device which he will continually employ throughout his sermon. Moo highlights this point well; "The author, for the first time, uses a literary device that will undergird most of his major arguments: synkrisis, or 'comparison.' And here the author introduces for the first time the word that he will use twelve other times to mark this comparison: 'greater,' or as it is usually translated, 'better.'"[49] The author uses terms such as "better" and "more excellent" to stress the superiority of the Son. The Greek fathers stated that the word "superior" denoted a difference in kind not just degree.[50] While the Son stands in comparison to prophets and angels it is not his person that is being examined but his function as one superior to the angels because he has revealed God's redemptive plan.

He has inherited a name more excellent than theirs. Not only is Jesus superior to angels as a messenger but he has also inherited a more excellent name than theirs. The "name" which he inherited is most likely a reference to his title of exalted Son. The angels were considered sons of God, but Jesus is "the Son" of God signified by his unique role in creation, redemption, and rule of the universe. Jesus as Son sits in the place of authority at the right hand of God. The angels which will be addressed further in the following section are created to serve both the Son and his people.

A Note on the Deity of Jesus

Critics of the deity of Christ have historically focused on passages such as Hebrews 1:4 to claim that Jesus became

[49] Moo, *Hebrews*, 36.
[50] Witherington, *Letters and Homilies for Jewish Christians*, 108.

something in his person that he once was not. This error in thinking has fueled just about every Christological heresy throughout the history of the church. The Kenosis heresy was supported by Philippians 2:7 when they argued that Jesus emptied himself of his divinity.[51] *The Jehovah Witnesses have attempted to support their modern view of Arianism with John 1:1 by arguing that the word could not be "with God" and "be God" at the same time. Thus, they translated the passage to say, "the word was with God and the word was a god."*[52]

This trend had the tendency to use the Scriptures for the opposite of what they were written: the elevation of Jesus. Richard Bauckham in his essay: "The Divinity of Jesus Christ in the Epistle to the Hebrews" states, "The earliest Christology was already... the highest Christology."[53] *The early church had no issue with identifying Jesus as God in the flesh. Modern interpreters must keep this in mind. Moo notes two extremes when interpreting these statements which must be avoided. "On the one hand, we must be careful not to read later developed Christological reflection into these verses ... However, on the other hand ... neither should we minimize the import of these lines for that later Christological development."*[54] *Thus the author of Hebrews beautifully navigates between the divinity and humanity of Jesus with no theological issue. Much of the issues surrounding*

---

[51] The Kenosis theory is derived from the Greek word κενόω which means to empty.

[52] Arianism is an ancient heresy that argues that Jesus was a created being of similar but not equal substance as the Father.

[53] Richard Bauckham, "The Divinity of Jesus Christ in the Epistle to the Hebrews," In the *Epistle to the Hebrews and Christian Theology*, Edited by Richard Bauckham, Daniel R. Driver, Trevor A. Hart, and Nathan MacDonald (Grand Rapids: Eerdmans, 2009), 17.

[54] Moo, *Hebrews*, 38-39.

the deity of Jesus stem from a disregard of the overall context of the Bible. This is especially the case in the book of Hebrews.[55] *Those who fail to acknowledge the divine characteristics of Jesus have not honestly considered how the author of Hebrews presents him to his listeners. Bauckham notes that Hebrews presents Jesus in three primary categories: Son, Lord, and High Priest. He argues that each of these categories requires Jesus to be "both truly God and truly human."*[56]

The author of Hebrews uses a chain of biblical texts in the first chapter to reveal the divine nature of Jesus. In the first four verses, Jesus is presented as the eternal Son responsible for the creation and providence of the universe. This eternal Son also sits in the place of authority at the right hand of the Father. Those who deny the deity of Jesus must consider the implications of these statements. First, a Jewish listener would consider the statements blasphemous. Jesus in the Gospel of John offends the Jewish leaders of his day for making less direct statements concerning his person and work (John 5:17; 8:58). Any Jewish reader would immediately recognize the author's emphasis on the deity of Christ. Moreover, the author provides numerous Old Testament citations that clearly place Jesus in the realm of divinity (Ps. 45:6-7/Heb. 1:8-9; Ps. 102:25-27/Heb. 1:10-12). Bauckham states that the citations make "entirely clear that the exalted Lord Jesus is the one who shares the divine identity in two crucial respects of creation of all things and sovereignty over all things."[57] *As Son, therefore, Jesus is also Lord. Finally, Hebrews' picture of Jesus as High Priest speaks to his divine character. Jesus' priesthood derives from the order of Melchizedek an obscure biblical*

---

[55] Moo, *Hebrews*, 25.
[56] Ibid., 18.
[57] Ibid., 25.

character briefly mentioned in Genesis 14:17-20 and Psalm 110:4. While Psalm 110:1 relates to the Lordship of the Messiah, Psalm 110:4 relates to his priestly role. The Genesis account provides the historical backdrop of Melchizedek but does not offer much other information surrounding his role. It is the author's interpretation of Genesis that drives home the point of Jesus' deity. The author describes Melchizedek as without mother, father, genealogy, and beginning or end of days. Bauckham states this language signifies true deity.[58] *However, it is not the person of Melchizedek that Hebrews seeks to emphasize but his office as priest. The Melchizedekian High Priesthood is of a divine origin. The author of Hebrews clarifies his point by stating that the Melchizedekian Priest which resembles the Son of God continues as priest forever (Heb. 7:3). Jesus' priesthood does not resemble Melchizedek's, but Melchizedek's resembles Jesus'. Thus, the author of Hebrews begins his sermon with the divinity of Christ. This theological point is vital to what he will argue later concerning what Jesus has accomplished. In chapter 2, the author will address the humanity of Jesus and its role in salvation. For the author, it was necessary that Jesus be fully divine and fully human in one person.*

Application

THE WORD OF GOD SPEAKS

Much like the church of the first century, today's church faces many obstacles. This is especially true for the incarcerated church. Believers on the inside have a unique set of challenges that they must face on a daily basis. Many of the everyday freedoms that churches enjoy on the outside are non-existent in prison. For

[58] Moo, *Hebrews*, 28-29.

example, a rhythm of worship can be at times almost impossible. In prison, where security trumps all, church services and religious programing are regularly cancelled (as I write this, we are on a security lockdown 9/10/2023).

For many believers, it is during these times of separations that they find it hardest to hear from God. Some, who depend solely on worship services and programs for spiritual nourishment, find themselves struggling to maintain a relationship with God. The background noise of lockdown begins to drown out the voice of God and the longer the separation lasts the quieter his voice becomes. It is during these times of prolonged absence that the believer must realize that God is still speaking. The believer's relationship with God is not tied to a certain service or program. They are not Old Testament saints required to approach God through a priest's sacrifices. God is present right where the believer is. He is present in the cell; he is present in the cubicle. The believer must simply open the word of God to hear him speak. The believer's access is made possible because the Son sits at the right hand of the Father continually making intercessions on our behalf. Read 2 Timothy 2:15; 3:16; Hebrews 4:12-13; 2 Peter 1:20-21; Joshua 1:9; Psalms 119:9-11. How important is it for the believer to spend time listening to the voice of God from the Scriptures?

DOCTRINE DEFINES RELATIONSHIP

Many people struggle with the idea of doctrine. They argue that doctrine is what divides the church and it really doesn't matter "what" you know but only matters "who" you know: "Isn't Christianity really about a relationship with Jesus?" The problem is that you cannot truly have a relationship with someone you know nothing about. Relationships imply knowledge. So, understanding who Jesus is and what he has accomplished is vital for a healthy relationship. The doctrines of Christianity are what our union with Christ is built upon. The author of Hebrews knows this very well. He desires that his audience have a strong relationship with Jesus, so he begins by describing who Jesus is followed by what he has accomplished. This knowledge is what will enable the church to persevere through trials and tribulations. The same is true for the church today. The believer should search the Scriptures for biblical truths about the character and work of God. The more they come to know about God, the more they will be able to experience his awesome presence. Take time today to read and meditate on Hebrews 1:1-4; John 1:1-14; Col. 1:15; and Phil. 2:5-11. What do these Scriptures tell you about the nature of Jesus? How does this knowledge help you deal with the chaotic world of prison life?

2. *The Supremacy of the Messenger (1:5-14)*

Prisoner's Insight for the Journey

Almost every person in prison will testify that the most important day of their entire incarceration is the day they finally become eligible for parole. Some have worked hard to change in anticipation of their chance for release. On this day, their crime will be considered in light of the time they have served and the level of rehabilitation they have achieved. Unlike the movies, inmates do not get to plead their case before a panel. Decisions are made based on their file. Everything they have achieved or failed to achieve is contained within a few meager pieces of paper. Inmates are allowed to submit their best evidence in support of rehabilitation. They examine and reexamine years of achievements trying to decide which will speak rehabilitation and change in their absence. In brief, they lay out their claim: "I am remorseful for my past crimes, I have served X amount of years, and I have achieved the following to help me become a productive member of society, I am ready for release." On that day, only the best evidence of rehabilitation will do because it may be years before you get another opportunity to sway the opinions of the voters: "What evidence will you put forth?"

In Hebrews the author has presented his claim: Jesus is superior to the angels because he is the eternal Son, the complete revelation of God who sits in the position of authority. To prove this, the author provides his listeners with seven pieces of evidence, the best evidence available; the very word of God. For the Jewish believer, the Old Testament Scriptures functioned as the voice of God; what the Scriptures proclaimed God proclaimed.

In this section, the author introduces seven Old Testament passages which he breaks into pairs in order to make a point with each about the supremacy of Jesus as the messenger of God. The seven Old Testament claims are meant to provide support to seven claims made about the Son in the first four verses. [59] Psalm 2:7 and 2 Samuel 7:14 show the unique and intimate relationship between the Father and Son, something the angels do not possess. Deut. 32:43/ Psalm 97:7 and Psalm 104:4 speak about Jesus' enthronement at the right hand of God and the angels' role to worship the Son. Furthermore, the larger context of the first four Old Testament citations has to do with defeating enemies. In light of the current struggle of the author's audience these texts also serve to provide comfort to a body under persecution.[60] With Ps. 45:6-7 and Ps. 102:25-27, the author shows the deity of the Son. Jesus is addressed as both God in verse 8 and creator in verse 10. The author closes this section with Ps. 110:1 which focuses the listener's attention once again on the supremacy of the Son by emphasizing his position of authority.[61]

Commentary

1:5-14

Verse five introduces the first scriptural support for the superiority of the Son. These verses also serve to introduce a contrast between the Son and the angels. The Son holds a special place in relation to the Father; he is the enthroned king. The angels on the other hand are represented as worshipers and servants of

---

[59] Lane, *Hebrews*, 22.

[60] George Guthrie, "Hebrews" In *Commentary on the New Testament use of the Old Testament*, ed. By G. K. Beale and D.A. Carson (Grand Rapids: Baker Academic, 2007), 931.

[61] George Guthrie, *Hebrews,* The NIV Application Commentary (Grand Rapids: Zondervan, 1998), 75-77.

the Son. Psalm 2 and Psalm 110 are both Royal enthronement Psalms and serve as bookends to the author's argument. The author shows his rhetorical skills by connecting the preceding section (1:1-4) with the current (1:5-14) by the use of the word "angels" at v.4 and v.5.[62] This further makes a connection between v.5 and v.13.[63] The author makes these connections in order to focus his listener's attention on the subject of Jesus' superiority over the angels. The author begins with two Old Testament texts that were commonly interpreted as messianic scriptures in the first century (Ps. 2:7; 2 Sam. 7:14).[64] In Psalm 2, the context refers to the appointment of the Davidic king and ends with a reminder of the blessing found in the Son. Thus, the idea of begetting the Son is not about bringing him into existence or some form of adoptionism but references the Son's induction as ruler of all God's created order. The Son is not brought into existence; creation was made through him. The Son has not been adopted because he is the eternal Son.[65]

Now the author aims to support his claims concerning the Son from the first four verses. With Psalm 2:7 and 2 Samuel 7:14, the author defends the claim that the Son is the heir of all things (v.2). He uses these two texts to emphasize "the son's unique relationship to the father and his enthronement."[66] These two verses are related with the Rabbinic interpretive principle called

---

[62] Witherington, *Letters and Homilies for Jewish Christians*, 125
[63] Lane, *Hebrews*, 24.
[64] Lane, *Hebrews*, 25.
[65] Moo, *Hebrews*, 45.
[66] Guthrie, "Hebrews" In *Commentary on the New Testament use of the Old Testament*, 925.

"Gezerah Shavah," which allowed interpreters to hone in on key words (i.e. son) to link texts.[67]

Angels were often referred to as sons of God in the Old Testament (Job 1:6) and were believed to dwell in the presence of God in order to do his bidding, such as the delivery of the Law at Mt. Sinai (Acts 7:53, Gal. 3:19).[68] As a result, the author opens with a rhetorical question, "To which of the angels" in order to emphasize the preeminence of the Son in light of the angelic host.[69] God has spoken something special to "the Son" which he has not said to the many sons (angels). The author argues that Jesus is revealed as the Son of God through his exaltation and enthronement which shows his special relationship with God the Father, a relationship not possessed by the angels.[70] The author also introduces this text as if God is the one speaking.[71] This shows the author's understanding of Scripture as divine speech and its present impact on the lives of the hearers.[72] The word of God delivered long ago is relevant for the author's audience.

There are three primary ways that we communicate with loved ones from prison: letters, phone calls, and visits. Each one is special and serves its purpose, but a phone call is a little more special than a letter. It is real-time, and you can hear the emotion in your family's voice. While a phone call is nice, the greatest privilege by far is a personal visit. At visits you can both hear and see the emotion in your loved ones. You also have the benefit of

---

[67] Ibid., 927.
[68] Cockerill, *Hebrews*, 101.
[69] Guthrie, "Hebrews" In *Commentary on the New Testament use of the Old Testament*, 925.
[70] Ibid., 927
[71] Witherington, *Letters and Homilies for Jewish Christians,* 127.
[72] Allen, *Hebrews*, 170

physical contact, making communication more intimate, something which is impossible through letters or phone calls. So, while all communication in prison is valuable, contact visits are the most special form. God's message through angels was like letters and phone calls. They performed a special task on behalf of God. They delivered the message the people needed. Jesus, however, was like that contact visit. The message he delivered was both real-time and personal. The author is not degrading the angels as messengers; he just wants his listeners to know that a visit from Jesus was the best message of all.

2 Samuel 7:14 is located within the context of a series of promises given to King David by God. God promised David an heir who would build a house for God and establish the Davidic kingdom forever. This prophecy originally focused on Solomon; however, when the perpetual rule of the Davidic line was not realized, Jewish interpreters anticipated a future fulfillment.[73] This fulfillment was eventually transferred to a messianic figure that would establish the Davidic kingdom forever. This idea brings about the peoples' question concerning Jesus in John 7:40-44: "has not the Scripture said that the Christ comes from the offspring of David" (John 7:42).[74]

The larger context of 2 Samuel 7:1-17 contains numerous themes that relate to the book of Hebrews as a whole. As already mentioned, Jesus is the offspring anticipated in 2 Samuel 7:12 and thus earns the title Son of God (Heb. 1:5/Ps. 2:7). Also 2 Samuel 7:10-11 mentions the appointment of a place for the people of God which will provide rest from their enemies. The author's audience

---

[73] Guthrie, "Hebrews" In *Commentary on the New Testament use of the Old Testament*, 928- 929.
[74] Lane, *Hebrews*, 25.

is encouraged to strive for that ultimate rest (Heb. 4:11) which is found in the heavenly Jerusalem, the place God has appointed for his people (Heb. 12:22). 2 Sam. 7:11 also mentions that God will establish a house for David. As the Davidic heir, Jesus reigns over God's house to which believers now have access (Heb. 3:6). Finally, 2 Sam. 7:14-15 mentions the discipline of the Davidic heir followed by God's steadfast and never-ending love. This corresponds well with the author of Hebrews' explanation of God's discipline concerning his children. The discipline of the Lord is proof of one's sonship (Heb. 12:3-11). The author uses this text to both elevate Jesus over the angels by emphasizing his unique relationship to God[75] and to provide comfort and assurance to his audience during their time of persecution. God has prepared a place of rest for the weary traveler. Jesus, the offspring of David has endured the discipline of the Lord and inherited a people and eternal kingdom.

1:6-7

The author now shifts focus to the angels. He introduces two new Old Testament citations (Deu. 32:43, Ps 104:4) and again connects them by verbal analogy linking the word angel in both. Deuteronomy 32:43/Psalm 97:7 and Psalm 104:4 speak about Jesus' enthronement at the right hand of God and the angels' role to worship the Son. The author cites Deuteronomy 32:43 taken from the Psalm of Moses that was sung prior to Israel's entrance into the Promised Land.[76] The author has already established that the eternal Son is also the Messianic king (Ps. 2:7; 1 Sam. 7:14).

---

[75] Guthrie, "Hebrews" In *Commentary on the New Testament use of the Old Testament*, 930.

[76] Guthrie, "Hebrews" In *Commentary on the New Testament use of the Old Testament*, 931.

Now by referring to Jesus as the firstborn, the author alludes to the fact that the eternal Son is also the true Israel of God. By quoting Deuteronomy 32:43, the author alludes to the exaltation/enthronement of the Son as fulfillment of Israel's entrance into the Promised Land. Thus, by Jesus entering into the presence of God, he has also inherited the rest signified by the Promised Land. This idea of Christ being our forerunner into God's rest and thereby providing the one people of God access to the ultimate rest is prevalent throughout the letter.

In verse 7, the author uses Psalm 104:4 to show that the angels who are created beings are also servants sent out to minister. The uncreated Son is appointed to rule and reign from heaven. The angels are created to serve the Son. To emphasize this point, the angels are described by changeable elements such as wind and fire which contrast with the Son's uncreated, unchangeable, sovereign nature. This contrast is revisited in Hebrews 1:13-14 where Christ is depicted as sovereign and the angels are depicted as serving believers.[77] As will be further emphasized with the next two verses, the author's use of Deuteronomy implies the deity of Jesus. In Deuteronomy 32:43 the "him" who receives the worship of the angels is YHWH. However, in Hebrews the "him" who receives worship is the Son, a clear allusion to the deity of Christ.[78]

1:8-12

The author now describes the Son in relation to the temporal, created nature of the angels.[79] He introduces Psalm 45:6-7 as his fifth piece of evidence with a contrasting phrase that

---

[77] Moo, *Hebrews*, 48.
[78] Cockerill, *Hebrews*, 108.
[79] Ibid., 109.

is rarely brought out in English translation. The contrasts between introductory statements in v.7 and v.8 can be rendered as following: "on the one hand he says to the angels … but on the other he says to the Son." The author's contrast introduces his use of Psalm 45:6-7 which is a clear reference to the deity of the Son. The author places the Psalm in the mouth of God which results in the Father calling the Son God. While the systematic formulation of the Trinity would not be complete until the 4th century, the seeds of the doctrine are clearly evident in the author's use of the seven Old Testament texts found in this section.[80]

The author's use of the word "throne" and the phrase "forever and ever" denote the Son's eternal reign as God. The author also describes the Son's reign as one of uprightness, a characteristic of a king and a trait that many of the former kings of Israel did not possess. The statement he has "loved righteousness and hated lawlessness" describes the character of the Son as a whole.[81] This statement anticipates the discussion of the Son's incarnation in Hebrews 2:5-18 and references his active obedience to the will of the Father.[82] The Son was obedient to the Father in the flesh and his active obedience is generally a reference to his crucifixion. Jesus was obedient to the point of the cross (Phil. 2:8). As a result, God the Father has anointed the Son. The anointing of one by another usually took place at special events. In this case, as the Son assumes his role as sovereign king of the universe, he is anointed by his Father. The phrase "oil of gladness" represents the festive nature of the anointing. This also corresponds well with the worship of the Son by the angels in

---

[80] Guthrie, *Hebrews*, NIV, 75.

[81] Daniel Wallace, *Greek Grammar Beyond the Basics: An Exegetical Syntax of the New Testament* (Grand Rapids: Zondervan, 1996), 557.

[82] Cockerill, *Hebrews*, 111.

v.6.[83] Hebrews depicts the entrance into the presence of God as a joyous event. This same imagery is found in Hebrews 12:1 which depicts the believer as running before a stadium of cheering fans. The believer's approach to the heavenly Jerusalem is depicted as a festal gathering (Heb. 12:22). This picture of God's rest as a joyous occasion is beneficial for an audience which is struggling with trials and tribulations. The final phrase "beyond your companions" is debated among scholars. Some see the companions as the angels and therefore continue the comparison of the preceding context. Others believe that the word "companions" refers to believers which points to the phrase many sons in Hebrews 2:10. Most likely, considering the author's other depictions of heavenly joy, he has both angels and believers in mind.

The author again places Psalm 102:25-27, the sixth piece of evidence, on the lips of God. This Psalm reaffirms the Son's participation in creation that was first announced in v.2 of the prologue. This Psalm's use of the word "beginning" is a reference to the Genesis account of creation.[84] The eternal Son laid the foundation of the heavens and the earth. Thus, the author is clear that the Son is the maker of all reality. This theme is prevalent with many N.T. authors as seen in John 1:1-14 and Colossians 1:16. This contrast continues to emphasize the author's distinction between angels and the Son. Included in the Son's creative ability is the creation of the angels. Thus, the Son is superior to them in every way because he is their maker.

The author also wants to highlight the Son's eternal and sovereign authority over creation. The heavens that he created will

---

[83] Cockerill, *Hebrews*, 111.
[84] Ibid., 112.

perish but the Son will remain. The creation will grow old like a worn-out garment and like a robe the Son will roll them up. The author uses the Psalm to highlight the temporal nature of creation. This world will not last forever, but like a garment, it will be changed. The two uses of garment imagery "growing old" and "changing" point to the day when God will ultimately renew all things.[85] However, as the world grows old and perishes, the Creator stays the same. This verse anticipates the author's claim in Hebrews 13:8 that Jesus Christ is the same yesterday, today, and forever. His years will not end.

Psalm 102 also begins with a lament, a cry to God for help. In light of the struggles of the audience, the author employs this Psalm to achieve two purposes: (1) highlight the Son's superiority to the angels as their Creator, (2) provide comfort to a group of believers during times of uncertainty. For the author, Jesus' superiority and the believer's comfort are two sides of the same coin. Because the eternal Son is sovereign over creation, believers can rest assured that he is also sovereign over their lives. The author wants his listeners to know that trials are temporary and under control of the sovereign Lord.

All the previous quotations culminate in the author's final Psalm. Psalm 110:1 also completes the connection which began in v.5. It is the most quoted Old Testament verse in the New Testament. It is quoted or alluded to 22 times, five times of which are found here in the epistle to the Hebrews.[86] The concept of enthronement which was alluded to in previous verses is now fully stated in verse 13. The Psalm again is placed on the lips of the

---

[85] Moo, *Hebrews*, 50-51.

[86] Guthrie, "Hebrews" In *Commentary on the New Testament use of the Old Testament*, 943.

Father and directed to the Son. The Son is commanded to sit at the right hand of the Father which is designated as the position of authority. Thus, the author concludes the grand comparison between the angels and the Son. The angels minister in the presence of God. The Son reigns from the throne as God. The eternal reign of the Son looks toward a day when all his enemies will ultimately be subjected to him. All things are currently under the control of the Son. However, creation awaits its full subjugation. The world may seem out of control, but the believer can be assured that Jesus will one day conquer all the enemies of the kingdom, making them a footstool for his feet.

Ministering in a fallen world is a difficult job. This is especially true inside a maximum-security prison. Drugs and violence are everywhere, and the people generally gravitate toward darkness. It often seems the more one preaches "be like Jesus" the less like Jesus the people become. The Christian is at war with sin and the fallen culture it produces, a war they appear to be losing. But they must not grow weary in doing good. The war is already won. Jesus reigns victorious from the right hand of the Father awaiting the day he will return to once and for all stomp out sin and this fallen world. There are just a few battles left to fight.

The chapter closes with a rhetorical question which expects a positive answer: "Yes, the angels are ministering spirits…" The angels' purpose is to serve those "about to inherit salvation." In a final comparison with verse 13, the author has the Son sitting and reigning while the angels serve the saints. Again, the idea "about to inherit" looks forward to the day that believers' salvation will be fully realized.[87] The author's idea of salvation is

---

[87] Moo, *Hebrews*, 53.

tied closely to his understanding of perseverance. In light of his audiences' struggle they are on the verge of obtaining what they have hoped for. They must simply persevere.

The author has laid out his best evidence to support his claim of Jesus' superiority over the angels: (1) the Father and Son have a unique relationship that the angels do not have; (2) The Son is God's firstborn who is worthy of the angels' worship; (3) The angels are created servants but the Son is God who rules from heaven; (4) the Son is the creator of even the angels, all the created order will pass away but the Son remains forever; (5) The Son reigns victoriously from the right hand of the Father anticipating a day that his people will be triumphant over their enemies.

Application

COMPETING MESSAGES

In prison there are a lot of messengers and messages competing for the attention of the believer. The TV cries "watch me, wrestling is on." The Rec. yard screams, "It is a beautiful day outside, and you're getting a little fat." Friends draw you to the domino table for just "one game." While the activities are not sinful, they have a way of taking control of our lives. These seemingly innocent activities take up hours of our day and reign over our attention. Before long, we have less and less time to listen to the voice of God. Take time this week to compare the hours you spend engaging in leisure activities with the hours you spend developing your relationship with God. Do you see a potential problem? If so, set aside some dedicated time for the Lord and study Psalm 1. Write down what you learn about spending time with God.

3. The Importance of the Message (2:1-4)

Prisoner's Insight for the Journey

Prison is meant to serve two purposes in our lives: punishment and rehabilitation. Despite popular belief, it is not the prison system's responsibility to punish. Prison is simply the place we serve out our forced separation from society. It is the loss of some of the most basic freedoms and separation from our loved ones that serves as our punishment. On the other hand, the prison system does have a responsibility to provide opportunities for rehabilitation. On the most basic level, this is the purpose of many of those nonsensical rules we love so much: no clothes lines up during the day!

On a larger scale, the system provides daily programming that is geared toward helping us to identify the thinking errors that led to our incarceration. Educational, religious, and rehabilitative programs exist on every facility and provide the knowledge and skills to help us achieve rehabilitation. However, the classes alone cannot accomplish this; we have a responsibility to live in accordance with what we have learned. Now that we know, we are that much more accountable for how we live: "For this reason, we must pay closer attention to what we have heard lest we drift away from it" (Heb. 2:1).

In the introduction, the preacher made his claim: Jesus is superior. In the second section, he lays out his best evidence, the word of God. He has provided his audience with all they need to know: "God has said." Now he warns them to pay close attention to the voice of God. If God held people accountable for what was said through the angels, how much more accountable will they be held for what he has spoken in his Son. God has spoken with final authority and all who have heard his voice are much more responsible for what they know.

In this section the author introduces his first warning passage. He warns his listeners to pay close attention to what he has previously said about the superiority of Jesus as messenger of God. Jesus is God's final word on redemption. The author uses one of his favorite methods for presenting an argument: the lesser to the greater. If God's message by the angels was reliable and people were punished for not heeding it (lesser) then how much more will they be accountable for failure to heed a message by his Son (greater). Furthermore, God's final message was witnessed by the full Godhead: Father, Son, and Holy Spirit. As a result, the one who fails to pay attention will not escape judgment.

A Note on the Warning Passages in Hebrews

Some of the most hotly debated and difficult to interpret Scriptures in the Bible are the warning passages in Hebrews (2:1-4; 3:7-19; 6:4-8; 10:26-31; 12:25-29). This debate is generally divided between two theological camps. The first position commonly referred to as the Arminian view holds that those addressed in Hebrews were converted believers in danger of losing their salvation. The second position referred to as the Calvinist view holds that the people described in the passages were never true believers. Thus, these texts fall square in the middle of the loss of salvation vs eternal security debate.

It must be noted that these are extremely difficult passages to interpret. Both positions offer strong arguments and have an abundance of scholarly support. While it would be nice to simply remain neutral in the debate, it would be impossible to write a commentary while doing so. Therefore, just to be clear, I hold the Calvinist position on the debate. I do not believe it is possible for a person who God has saved to fall away from salvation. I affirm that those who are saved will persevere to the end. I also hold to my understanding of the hypothetical view of the warning passages. This position "suggests that the author crafts his harsh warning for rhetorical impact, to blast the hearers out of their spiritual slumber, but that the state described cannot really happen."[88] *Thus I believe the author employs these warnings as a means of perseverance. This view will be further explained at Hebrews 5:11-6:12.*

Commentary

2:1-4

In the previous section, the author painstakingly laid out his argument for the superiority of the Son over the angels. His comparison anticipates what would be said in this section. A greater message requires greater attention because there are greater consequences. The author introduces this new section with a conjunction "therefore" that closely ties what he has said about the Son in the previous section with his warning here about failure to listen. For the author, the word of God requires obedience. He is concerned that the trials that his listeners are facing will result in their failure to heed the word of God. Therefore, it is necessary that they pay close attention to what they are hearing.

The switch from exposition to exhortation is easily seen by the subtle rebuke that is implied in his warning. This is a reminder of what they already have been told, what they already know to be true. His warning employs the imagery of a ship drifting off course

[88] Guthrie, *Hebrews*, NIV, 226.

or possibly slipping its anchor: “lest we drift away.”[89] The believers are in danger of missing out on the salvation which God has to offer. If they continue to focus their attention on their circumstances, they will miss out on the blessings of God. Thus, his audience is to stay anchored to the word of God in order to stay on course.

Imagine you are taking a trip to a city you have never visited. You have no idea how to get there, but you do have a reliable GPS in your car. You begin your journey and the GPS has you on a proper course. But what would happen if you stopped paying attention to the GPS? Suppose suddenly your phone rings and it is your boss giving you a hard time about taking off work. Then an accident happens up ahead, and you have to change lanes several times. By the time your attention is focused once again on the GPS’ directions, you learn that you have missed your exit. You have failed to pay attention and allowed your turn to “drift away.” The word of God serves as the believer’s GPS. But the phone calls and accidents of life will try to distract one from arriving at their destination. Nevertheless, if believers pay close attention to the directions it gives, then they will not have to worry about drifting away amid the chaos.

Verse 2 begins one long extended sentence in Greek, which ends in verse 4. English translations break this long sentence for convenience. Thus, in the original, this is one long, closely related comparison of the message delivered by the angels versus the message delivered by the Son. Jewish tradition held that the angels delivered the Commandments to Moses at Mt. Sinai. The author’s argument is that if the people of God were

[89] Moo warns against this interpretation, *Hebrews*, 66-67.

accountable to the Law delivered by angels how much more accountable will they be held for a message delivered by the Son.[90]

However, verse 2 also makes a point not to degrade the message of the Law delivered to Moses. God's law did not fail. The message was reliable. The word for "reliable" in the original language was a legal term that emphasized the binding nature of the Law. The author stresses his point by reminding his audience that people did not go unpunished for their "every transgression and disobedience." The Old Testament is replete with examples of Israel's failure to heed the word of God and the subsequent penalties that resulted from their disobedience. As a result, this section likely anticipates the author's discourse on Israel's wandering in the wilderness where he states that they failed to enter God's rest because of "disobedience" (Heb. 3:18).

God's demand for obedience to his word is applicable for all generations. If it was important to the former generation, how much more vital is it for the current people who are living in the "last days." In the Greek, the word for "disobedience" is similar to the word for "hearing" used in Hebrews 2:1 but here in verse 2, this word likely entails a "failure" to hear. Thus, the author reminds his audience to hear/listen (v.1) because a failure to hear (disobedience) comes with a just punishment (v.2).

Verse 2 is also introduced with a conditional sentence in the original that is often missed in English translations. The author's argument is the following: "If the message declared by angels was reliable (and it was) then the message declared by the Son who is superior to the angels is that much more reliable." If people were held accountable for failure to heed the first message,

---

[90] Moo, *Hebrews*, 63.

how much more accountable would they be held for failure to heed the second? The author is not attempting to elevate the Gospel over the Law; they are different sides of the same coin. His point is to stress the authority of the messenger. The Gospel carries more weight because it is the fulfillment of the Law delivered by God himself.

Verse 3 picks up the second half of the author's conditional clause. In verse 3, the author contrasts the two different aspects of the two messages: Law and Gospel. Failure to heed the first brought punishment, failure to heed the second entails missing out on a "great salvation." The author uses the contrast between the former message and the current one in order to stress the importance of the believer's obedience. The Law required an outward obedience; the Gospel requires an inward faith that results in obedience. God continues to speak to his people, and his message continues to carry absolute authority, both Law and Gospel.

Now the author highlights the confirmation of the message. All messages were to be confirmed by two or more witnesses. The Good News was declared "first by the Lord." This looks back to the author's introduction and references God's speaking by the Son (Heb. 1:2). Yet the message was also confirmed by "those who heard the Lord." In this verse, the author separates himself from those who originally heard the Lord preach. Thus, the author is most likely a second-generation believer who received the Gospel from the apostles. The word "attested" (ESV) is a similar form of the legal term used in verse 2 for "reliable," continuing the author's theme of the message's binding nature.[91] The themes of speaking, declaring, and hearing

---

[91] Moo, *Hebrews*, 65.

show that the message is not a dead word but living and active; it requires accountability (Heb. 4:12-13).

Texas has an enhancement law. If a person is convicted of a second-degree felony and commits another, the new felony can be enhanced to a first-degree offense. The difference is significant. A second-degree felony holds a maximum of 20 years, a first-degree felony holds a maximum of 99 years. The second conviction is harsher than the first. In the same way, disobedience to the Law was like a second-degree felony, but disobedience to Jesus carries an eternal life sentence.

Finally, the author invokes his third witness. The message was first given by the Son, confirmed by those who were witnesses to the Son, and finally witnessed together by signs and wonders from God. The New Testament idea of the Gospel's confirmation by signs and wonders is found in many New Testament letters. The phrase "bore witness or witnessed together" looks back to the confirmation of the message by the apostles. The apostles preached the Good News and God confirmed their message by performing miraculous works through them.

There is a sense of completion found in this verse. The fact that the author appeals to past signs and wonders instead of any current manifestation of miracles or gifts is revealing. He does not appeal to his ability to perform signs and wonders. It appears that the author's point is that God confirmed the Gospel in the past through the apostles with signs and wonders, there is no need for further confirmation. This section adds support to the argument that as the Gospel message became more unified in the post-apostolic age, the manifestation of signs and gifts also began to wane. However, one views the use of gifts today, verse 4 makes it clear that their use is in accordance to the will of God.

Application

FOLLOWING GOD'S COMMANDS

As believers, we tend to plead ignorance as a defense, or more often, only follow Christ when his will is in line with our own. The voice of God often sounds a lot like our own voice. Somehow, we believe this method will make us less accountable, somehow a little less guilty. However, this is far from the truth. Believers will be held accountable for both what they know and what they do not know. Therefore, we must "pay close attention" because we don't want to miss a word. Missing out on the word of God can have eternal implications. God has spoken to his people and we are accountable to what he has said.

However, we should not see following God's will as burdensome; especially, if we consider that God's will is meant to make us more Christ-like. God's word should not be seen as punishment or his commands as words to avoid. God's will is much like a cure for an illness, it may sometimes taste bad and make us feel uncomfortable, but it is what we need. God desires that we be conformed to the image of his Son, this is for our betterment.

Therefore, we should take every opportunity to learn and understand the will of God for our lives. We should never plead ignorance or only keep the easy commands. All of God's words are binding and authoritative. So, the next time you hear or read the word of God pay close attention and ask yourself: "Is this an opportunity for me to do the will of God and become more like my Lord and Savior?"

PAY ATTENTION SO YOU DON'T MISS OUT

In society today people rarely pay attention to anything. Everyone is in such a hurry they never slow down long enough to focus on details. As a result, so much of life is missed. This is especially true concerning the things of God. The Bible says that the heavens declare the glory of God (Ps. 19:1) but many never pay attention to the beauty of his handiwork.

In prison one learns to appreciate the small things. The ability to watch a sunrise or sunset is rare. The freedom to choose how one spends their day is nonexistent. So, on the rare occasion when one is allowed to see a starry sky, the time is suddenly more meaningful. Take a moment today and read Psalm 19. Consider what it says about God's creation and his word. How do these two things work together to bring about a relationship with our Creator?

WE ARE ALL ACCOUNTABLE TO SOMEONE

Accountability is an essential part of our Christian walk. Whether we like it or not we are accountable to both the word of God and our fellow believer. As the word of God convicts us of sin, we should share our struggles with a fellow Christian. By doing this, we admit our struggle and submit to the accountability of another. This enables us to move forward in our walks with Christ without carrying all our sinful burdens. Read James 1:22-25 and meditate on these verses. Then read James 5:16. How does James 5:16 help us live out James 1:22-25?

4. The Need of the Message (2:5-9)

Prisoner's Insight for the Journey

Prison breeds pessimism. As in Dante's *Divine Comedy,* we are reminded daily that hope is not welcome. Separated from loved ones, freedom and often our dignity, we are forced to live in filthy cages like animals. Violence and drug addiction are perpetuated by a system meant to rehabilitate. Hopelessness and despair become our existence. Yet somehow, some way, thousands upon thousands of men and women find a way to exist, sometimes even thrive in the worst of conditions. We find a way to be human in our inhumane circumstances, pushed forward by a subconscious knowledge that we are created for more. In defiance of our often-hopeless existence, we stand hopeful, dreaming and looking forward to what we could be, what we should be. The image of God bestowed on all of humanity fights against the animalistic tendencies that our cages create. We were not meant to dwell in cages. God created us to reign.

Adam's sin opened the door for hopelessness and despair; our sin kept the door open. Adam introduced the need for prison; we ensure that the need remains. Yet God, in his infinite grace and mercy, sent the eternal Son in to the world. For a little while Jesus was "made lower than the angels" that he had created so that "he might taste death for everyone." In Christ, our hope and freedom cannot be caged in despair. In Christ our humanity is restored despite the inhumane. In Christ we struggle from a place of victory. The second Adam, Jesus Christ, took on flesh to accomplish what the first Adam did not; provide for us an example of what we could be, what we should be!

In Hebrews the church is struggling with the hopelessness and despair created by their current persecution. The reality of being social outcasts, loss of property, and even death threatens to rob them of the hope they have in the Lord. Their brother in Christ reminds them that things are not as they seem. In the midst of their struggles, Christ still reigns. The Creator of the universe who suffered and died on their behalf is now reigning, crowned with glory and honor. Therefore, they are to have hope, because he has overcome death and delivered them from the authority of the devil, the author of hopelessness and despair.

In this section, the author moves from the exalted Son seated at the right hand of glory to the incarnate Jesus made lower than the angels. He shows how man was created to reign and rule but failed to subjugate all creation. Yet Jesus, who is crowned with glory and honor, accomplished what man did not through his obedience to the point of death.

Commentary

2:5-9

After warning the believers to pay close attention to what was discussed in Hebrews 1:5-14, the author resumes his comparison of the Son with the angels. In chapter one, the author's focus was on highlighting the exalted reign and rule of the eternal Son. Jesus, as God, rules from the right hand of the Father over all of creation. In verse 5, the author narrows his focus on Jesus' role as man. He introduces Psalm 8:4-6 in order to discuss what Jesus has accomplished in his humanity. The author's point so far is that the Son as God is exalted superior to the angels. Now the author turns his attention to the Son's superiority over the angels as man. Thus, the author understands that Jesus is both 100% God and

100% man in one person. Some of the finest minds in history have stood in awe of Jesus' two natures. Many others have called the two natures a contradiction. But for the author of Hebrews, no contradiction exists. He seamlessly moves from one nature to the next without second thought.

The author introduces the theme of subjection by asserting that God has not placed angels in a position of authority. He likely does this for two reasons. First, there was an idea in Jewish thought that God had divided the nations among the angels to rule.[92] The author wants to eliminate this possibility from the discussion. Second, the author wants to emphasize that it was man whom God chose to rule and reign over his creation. Man may have been created lower than the angels, but he was created for a higher purpose. The author also references "the world to come" which alludes to Christ's present reign in heaven. However, the idea of subjection that is prominent in this section also has in mind a new heaven and earth where total subjection will be finally realized. For his audience, the chaotic world in which they lived did not appear to be in subjection to anyone. So, the author moves to reassure his listeners that things are not as they appear.

In verses 6-8, the author once again omits the name and location of his Old Testament text (Psalm 8:4-6) in order to highlight that God is the ultimate author of all Scripture.[93] The use of the Psalm begins by considering man's original relationship to his Creator. Why would the sovereign Creator of the universe think about or care for man? The obvious answer is that God created man for a purpose.

---

[92] Guthrie, *Hebrews*, NIV, 97.
[93] Moo, *Hebrews*, 72.

Psalm 8:4-6 in its original context addresses man's relationship to God, especially his responsibility to reign and rule over creation. This Psalm looks back to Adam's role in the Garden to have dominion over the earth (Gen. 1:26). The author uses this text to place a question in the minds of his listeners: "If the world was not subjected to angels, and man who was meant to be in control obviously is not, then who is?" The author draws his listeners in so that he may share with them the story of redemption. God created man a little lower than the angels but crowned him with honor and glory, a reference to man's responsibility to reign. However, Adam failed and forfeited his right to rule. The author also points out that all things were put under the control of man but obviously it does not appear that way. The author's audience did not see control. They saw persecution and fear. The author reminds them that while they do not see control, they do see Jesus. The eye of faith enables the believer to see what is not currently present.[94] Their faith in the resurrection and exaltation of Jesus helps the audience see the ultimate rest of God.

The author spent a whole chapter proving that the Son is the sovereign God of the universe. Now he uses this text to help his listeners understand how God can be in control of a chaotic world. Jesus, the eternal Son, sovereign Creator of the universe took on flesh becoming "for a little while" lower than the angles. As man, Jesus is the last Adam, fulfilling the role that the first Adam forfeited.[95] The first Adam was disobedient to the Father, the Last Adam was obedient to the point of death. The first Adam brought sin and death into the world, the Last Adam conquered them both by tasting death for everyone.[96] The first Adam was

---

[94] Moo, Hebrews, 74.
[95] Allen, *Hebrews*, 228.
[96] Moo, *Hebrews*, 76.

meant to reflect true humanity; in the last Adam, people become truly human. The trials the listeners are experiencing will not last forever. Jesus' exaltation to the right hand of the Father proves that everything will ultimately be subjected to him. He has overcome the world. The author assures his audience that since Jesus has been "crowned with glory and honor," they too will also one day be crowned. The believers' future reward is a result of Jesus suffering death on their behalf. Adam's sin brought about the penalty of death on all mankind, but Jesus' death brought about forgiveness for many (1 Cor. 15:22). This is God's act of grace. God does not give humanity what they deserve (death). He gives them what they do not deserve (life). Jesus cleaned up Adam's mess on the believer's behalf.

Prison is an extremely filthy place. Most people do not clean up after themselves. Furthermore, the inmates assigned to clean up rarely do a good job. This uncleanliness affects everyone. It provides an opportunity for sickness and disease to spread. However, there are some people who cannot stand the filthy conditions. They take it upon themselves to clean up the mess of others for the benefit of the whole population. This is what Jesus did on behalf of all humanity. He cleaned up Adam's mess once and for all.

Application

CLEANING UP A MESS SOMEONE ELSE MADE

The believer has a responsibility to be a good steward with the blessing God has given him. This could be as simple as relationships with other believers or as important as the responsibility of an entire congregation. All believers are called to perform some tasks for the kingdom of God. Take the time today to identify what that task may be. Then ask yourself: "Am I performing my duty effectively, or is someone having to constantly clean up my mess?" Read 1 Corinthians 4:1-2 and meditate on your faithfulness to God's ministry

5. The Benefits of the Message (2:10-18)

Prisoner's Insight for the Journey

The old saying goes, "You cannot understand peoples' struggles until you walk a mile in their shoes." Unfortunately, this is why so many people are misunderstood. We all have our own unique set of circumstances that are made up by our own unique issues, needs, and desires. Nevertheless, we all want to be understood. This is especially true for the prisoner.

Prison is its own little world and, much like its larger counterpart, it is full of misunderstood individuals. In this world, we have our own way of doing and saying things that are difficult for the uninitiated to understand. Sometimes we wash our clothes in the toilet. We carry our cups and spoons everywhere we go. Yes everywhere! We have our own dialect. We do not eat together, we "spread." We drink shots of coffee and not cups (although a shot is actually a full cup). Probably most difficult to understand are the weird rules that prisons enforce on prisoners. We can only call people who are on our approved phone list. You wonder why you have not heard from us in over a decade, it's probably because you haven't registered your phone, so register it! Yes it is 115 degrees in our living area, but the state provides us with ice water, sometimes.

Communicating the chaos of prison to someone who has never been here is difficult, sometimes even frustrating. Fortunately for us, there are a growing number of advocacy groups whose sole purpose is to communicate on our behalf. And the most beautiful part is they have walked in our shoes. More men and women everyday are re-entering society and becoming our voice.

They understand our needs and struggles because they have experienced them firsthand. They wore our white uniforms and overcame the struggles of this world; therefore, they are able to help those of us who are currently struggling.

For the author's audience, much of their persecution resulted from a lack of understanding. The Greeks believed a God in the flesh was foolishness, the Romans believed the Christians were atheists, and the Jews simply thought they were blasphemous; but for the first-century Christian who has experienced the transforming influence of Christ, Christianity was wondrous. The author of Hebrews beautifully communicates Christ's two natures to a struggling congregation. He wants them to know that the God they serve understands their struggles. By taking on flesh he walked in their shoes, and by overcoming temptation, he is able to help them with their temptation.

Commentary

2:10-18

The author begins this verse with a phrase that links his new section with the previous one. The author highlights that Christ's suffering and death was part of the plan to bring many believers to glory. "It was fitting" for the Creator and Sustainer of the universe to perfect Jesus through suffering and death. God's plan and Jesus' sacrificial death achieved two things that need further explanation: (1) brings many people to glory, (2) perfects Jesus, the founder of salvation. In order to better understand God's plan and Christ's work, the two issues above will be discussed in reverse order.

Many people struggle with the idea of Christ being "perfected" through suffering. They naturally ask: "In what way was Christ as God not already perfect?" First, as God, Jesus was, is, and will always be perfect. Second, as man, Jesus was, is, and will always be perfect. The author's statement is not intended to imply that Jesus was lacking in any way. So, in what way was Jesus perfected? Here, an illustration may be helpful.

Have you ever had a perfect plan where you executed every step perfectly? Probably not, but God did. God planned to come into the world, take on flesh, suffer, die, and be victoriously resurrected. Jesus perfectly executed every aspect of a perfect plan. Thus, by Jesus accomplishing God's plan of salvation, he adds perfection to perfection. Furthermore, this plan perfectly provides access to God through the Son. This continues the theme of Christ's representation of humanity discussed above. What Adam failed to do, Christ fulfilled perfectly. Through Jesus' obedience, he "brings many sons" into the presence of God. This is why the author refers to him as the founder or pioneer of salvation. As a pioneer, Jesus has charted the course for all believers to follow.[97] He goes before believers both providing and showing the way to God. The suffering of Jesus was important for the author's audience to understand. If their founder suffered while overcoming the world, they too should expect trials and tribulations. However, as their pioneer, Jesus has also shown them the way to become victorious in suffering.[98] He is able to help those who are being tempted (v.18).

The author now highlights the saving relationship between the Son and believers.[99] First, the Son is the one "who sanctifies." Because of the predominance of Old Testament imagery in

---

[97] Moo, *Hebrews*, 82.
[98] Cockerill, *Hebrews*, 136.
[99] Moo, *Hebrews*, 82-83.

Hebrews the concept of sanctification most likely alludes to defilement. Whereas in the Old Testament defilement was directly related to outward impurity, in the New Testament, it is purity of the heart that is the focus. It is the inward defilement of sin that keeps one from the presence of God. The author here shows that it is through Christ that believers are sanctified. He also shows that believers are in need of sanctification. Thus, the author here highlights both the problem (sin) and the solution (sanctification through Jesus). Both the one who provides access and the one who needs access have their origin in "one source." This statement clarifies that salvation is of God. God sent his Son into the world to save his people from their sins (Matt 1:21). The believers' right to be called sons of God unifies them with the only begotten Son in brotherhood, thus, God has many sons and daughters who have become brothers and sisters to Christ through faith.

As a result, the Son will proclaim the name of God to his people. In verse 12, the author introduces Psalm 22:22 by placing it on the lips of Jesus. This continues his theme of divine speech. It is the authoritative word of God that speaks to their issues. The main point of the author's use of Psalm 22 is to highlight Christ's suffering in his humanity and the unity with his people. However, the current suffering of the listeners cannot be far from his thought. The context of Psalm 22 helps the listener understand the author's use. In this Psalm, David cries to God during a time of distress. He feels abandoned by God: "My God my God why have you forsaken me?" David is surrounded by his enemies, his hands and feet have been pierced, they have divided and cast lots for his clothing. The correlation between David's suffering and Jesus is evident. Jesus as the Messianic King fulfills Psalm 22 through his suffering on the cross. The first 21 verses of Psalm 22 are a cry for help. The author cites Psalm 22:22 in order to emphasize Christ's victory over suffering. The exalted Christ proclaims victory from heaven to those in the midst of their struggles. The author reminds his listeners that while they may feel separated from God in their current circumstances, God is nearby. The Son who provides access speaks from the throne of heaven into their struggles.

In verse 13, the author continues the theme of Christ's unity with his people. Here he introduces a quote from the prophet Isaiah. Isaiah's circumstances are very similar to the circumstances of King David above. He finds himself in the midst of a rebellious people. The Lord warns in Isaiah 8:11 not to walk in the way of the rebellious. Yet in the face of danger, how will the people of God respond? Will they succumb to fear of the rebellious and walk in their ways, or will they fear the Lord and find sanctuary in him? For the rebellious, the Lord will become a "stone of offense and a rock of stumbling." But Isaiah and the children of God will trust in the Lord. The author shows how Christ fulfills the Old Testament by overcoming their enemies in their time of need. For the author's audience, the context of the Old Testament passages is vital. How will they respond in the face of their trials? Will they "pay much closer attention" to what they have heard or will they "drift away" from it? Christ faced and overcame the same struggles they are facing by trusting in God.[100]

The author now drives home the purpose of the incarnation. The unifying aspect of humanity is humanness (flesh and blood). Christ became unified with humanity when he took on flesh. The necessity of the incarnation is evident when one considers who became flesh and for what purpose. The eternal Son found it necessary to assume the weakness of flesh and blood so that he may use our nature to pay our penalty. The author here also

---

[100] Moo, *Hebrews*, 84-85.

highlights two results of the incarnation. First, through death and resurrection, Jesus overcame the "one who has the power of death." Again, the author alludes to the Genesis account of Satan's deception of Adam and Eve which resulted in the death of all people. The apostle Paul stated that sin entered the world through one man resulting in death for all (Rom. 5:1). Christ, through his obedience to the point of death, overcame the devil who wielded the fear of death over humanity. The author describes the fear of death as slavery. Christ has set us free from the fear of death. This does not mean that believers do not die, but simply they have nothing to fear in death. The pioneer of their salvation has assured the believer through his resurrection that death cannot hold them.[101] The listeners have nothing to fear from their trials and suffering.

Prison is a stressful place and much of the stress stems from the unknown. We worry about our loved ones or the results of an upcoming parole answer. We think that if we just knew the answer, we would be less stressed. But the reality is we would find something else to worry about. There will always be something we do not know which stresses us out. This is why many people fear death. They fear the unknown. But the believer has no need to worry. Jesus provided us with a picture of what to expect. By overcoming death, he removes the fear of the unknown. The believer can rest assured that his last breath in this life will be followed by his first breath in the next.

In verse 16, the author displays his ability to say a lot with few words. He accomplishes this by alluding to two Old

[101] Cockerill, *Hebrews*, 148.

Testament texts: Isaiah 41:8-10, Jeremiah 31:31.[102] In order to understand the author's use of the Scriptures it is important to understand their original context. In Isaiah 41, the children of Israel are facing persecution and the eventual captivity by the nation of Assyria. In the face of this persecution, Isaiah reminds them that Israel, "Abraham's offspring" who God took from captivity in Egypt will not be cast away. Therefore, they should not "fear" because God will strengthen and help them in their day of need.

Furthermore, the author alludes to Jeremiah 31:32 which references God's New Covenant, a text the author quotes at length in Hebrews 8. Much like Isaiah, the prophet Jeremiah was warning a rebellious Israel of the persecution and eventual captivity by the Babylonians. Here the prophet also reminds Israel of their past deliverance when God "took them by the hand to bring them out of Egypt" and also looks forward to a day of restoration (Jer. 31:31-40). These two Old Testament texts have several common themes that help apply them to the audiences' current situation.

First, both Old Testament citations contain imminent persecution. Second, both aim to encourage the listeners by appealing to God's past work of deliverance. Third, God is portrayed as the deliverer/pioneer who takes or leads his people out of captivity. Finally, the texts have numerous words and themes in common with the overall message of Hebrews. With the above similarities in mind, the author's intent becomes clear. The author of Hebrews reminds his listeners of the promise of God's deliverance in the face of their persecution. The same God who long ago spoke to the fathers by the prophets is the same God who

---

[102] Guthrie, "Hebrews" In *Commentary on the New Testament use of the Old Testament*, 951-52.

speaks today in his Son (Heb. 1:1-2). The eternal Son, who is superior to the angels in every way, became lower than the angels by taking on flesh (Heb. 2:9). In his humanity, Jesus suffered and died in order to perfect the plan of God thus becoming the pioneer of salvation (Heb. 2:10). By overcoming death in the flesh, Jesus broke the power of the devil, and by delivering them from the slavery of "fear," he is able to lead the "offspring of Abraham" (believers) through their current trials. Their deliverer is not some lofty deity out of touch with their struggles, a point the author drives home in Hebrews 2:17-18.[103]

In verse 17, the author draws his conclusion. In order for the eternal Son to help humanity, it was necessary that he be made like his brothers in every way. This is one of the strongest statements of Jesus' complete unity with humanity found in all the New Testament. This also introduces a discussion of Jesus' humanity in relation to mankind's sinful nature, (a discussion that this commentary will address at Hebrews 4:15 where the author of Hebrews adds clarity to the issue).

Not only was it necessary for Jesus to take on flesh to overcome death, the devil, and temptation, but the author also states that the incarnation was necessary for Jesus to intercede on the believer's behalf. As a result, he became the believer's high priest. The function of the priestly office in the Old Testament was to represent the worshiper before God. In order for him to do this, the priest had to be selected from amongst the people (Exod. 28:1) to offer sacrifices on their behalf. By taking on flesh, Jesus fulfilled this requirement. However, the author also points out that he became a merciful and faithful high priest. At many times

[103] Guthrie, "Hebrews" In *Commentary on the New Testament use of the Old Testament*, 951-52.

throughout Israel's history, the priesthood was everything but merciful and faithful. Here the author again alludes to the Old Testament and the story of the priest Eli and his evil sons. In this story, a man of God proclaims to Eli that God will raise up a faithful priest to serve him (1 Sam. 2:27-36). This prophecy is ultimately fulfilled in Jesus.

Furthermore, the priest's duty was to offer sacrifices on behalf of the people. The sacrifices served as a means of providing access to God. Biblical scholars have explained the function of the sacrifice in two ways: propitiation or expiation. It is not the place here to discuss the theological nuances of the above words; however, a simple comparison of meanings will be helpful. Propitiation entails the idea of satisfying God's justice by turning away divine wrath. Thus, the idea of paying a penalty for sin. Expiation conveys the idea of washing away or covering of sin and derives from the Old Testament.[104] The most important thing to take away from the author's use is that Jesus has provided access to God through his sacrifice by dealing with sin.

The author now focuses on the cost of providing access. He states that Jesus suffered when tempted. This statement accomplishes two things for the author. First, it emphasizes the humanity of Jesus. He was "made like his brothers in every respect" (2:17). Second, this helps the author bring to reality their current suffering. Jesus suffered in the service to God and was victorious. They should expect nothing different. Finally, the author concludes with a note of comfort. They are not alone in their struggles. The one who was tempted and victorious can also help all those who are in the midst of their temptation.

---

[104] Moo, *Hebrews*, 89.

Application

I KNOW YOUR STRUGGLES

Not many years ago, the Texas Department of Criminal Justice started utilizing inmates to minister, counsel, and educate other inmates. They found that many of the various peer programs were extremely effective. As a result, they began to multiply overnight. The effectiveness of these programs resulted from one inmate's ability to understand the struggles of another, something the prison staff could not do. Inmates are more open to sharing their trials with other inmates. Take a moment and read the Great Commission (Matt. 28:18-20). This is a call for peer-to-peer ministry. Look for a way that you can answer this call today.

A Note on Jesus as the True Israel

The book of Hebrews is about the fulfillment of God's plan of redemption. The author continually drives home the point that the Old Testament institutions are fulfilled in the person and work of Jesus. The author implies this in his introduction when he states that God's final revelation was revealed in his Son (Heb. 1:2). Every subsequent chapter will support his claim of the Old Testament's fulfillment in Jesus. Jesus is the superior message and messenger who fulfills the role of the prophets and angels (1:1-2:4). Jesus is the superior humanity who accomplished what Adam did not (Heb. 2:5-18). As a result, Jesus is what humanity should be.[105] *Jesus is also presented as superior to Moses (Heb. 3:1-6), the Levitical priesthood (Heb. 7-9), the sacrificial system (Heb. 10) and is the institutor of a better covenant (Heb. 8). However, there is also a strong argument that the author of Hebrews and*

---

[105] See article in Moo, *Hebrews*, 75-76.

other New Testament authors saw Jesus as the True Israel of God who fulfilled what the nation of Israel did not. G.K. Beale states:

> *Matthew portrays Jesus to be recapitulating the history of Israel because he sums up Israel in himself. Since Israel disobeyed, Jesus has come to do what it should have, so he must retrace Israel's step up to the point where it failed and then continue to obey and succeed in the mission that Israel should have carried out.*[106]

This concept of Jesus as the True Israel is important for understanding the author of Hebrews' exposition on how his first-century audience is God's house (Heb. 3:6) and is called to enter God's rest. In Genesis, humanity is created to bear the image of God, spread this image through procreation, and subdue the earth (Gen. 1:27-28). However, as a result of the fall, humanity is unable to accomplish its mandate perfectly. Nevertheless, the call to bear, procreate, and subdue is passed on to subsequent generations. Noah receives the mandate (Gen. 9:1-7) followed by Abraham (Gen. 12:2-3; 17:2, 6, 8) and the rest of the patriarchs (Gen. 26:3; 28:3-4, 14). The descendants of Jacob who became the nation of Israel also received the commission (Gen. 47:27; Exod. 1:7; Deut. 7:13). However, the biblical narrative reveals that Israel was rebellious against God's mandate and never fully realized his commission. Therefore, the Psalmist and prophets looked to a day when God would see his mandate fulfilled through an obedient representative (Ps. 8:5-8; 107:37-38; Is. 51:2-3; Jer. 3:16-18; Ez. 36:9-12; Hos. 1:10). A careful reading of the New Testament will reveal that its authors viewed Jesus as the obedient

---

[106] G.K. Beale, *A New Testament Theology: The Unfolding of the Old Testament in the New* (Grand Rapids: Baker, 2011), 406.

Adamic/Israel figure which the Old Testament anticipated (Acts 7:38). Jesus viewed himself as the fulfillment of the Old Testament mandate (Luke 4:17-21; 24:44) and the biblical authors followed his understanding (Matt. 2:15/Hos. 11:1). This led the apostle Paul to remark, "All the promises of God find their yes in him [Jesus]" (2 Cor. 1:20). This means what the Old Testament anticipated found its complete fulfillment in Jesus. This fulfillment aims to benefit the believer. Paul in Romans wrote that what was written in the former days (Old Testament) was written for the New Testament believer's benefit (Rom 15:4). The Old Testament served as a tutor bringing the saints to the knowledge of Jesus (Gal. 3:24-25). The Gospel has served to remove the division between Jew and Gentile and make one people of God in Christ. This means that if you are in Christ then you are Abraham's offspring and heirs of the promise (Gal. 3:29). Therefore, believers become the household of God (Heb. 3:6) and are able to enter God's eternal rest (Heb. 4:6-7) as a result of their relationship with Jesus who is the true Israel of God (Gal 6:16).

B. Jesus: Faithfulness through Obedience (3:1-4:13)

1. Consider the Faithfulness of a Son (3:1-6)

Prisoner's Insight for the Journey

Prison is full of people who did not count the cost. For most of us, we lived from moment to moment never giving much thought to the "big picture." We failed to truly consider the outcome of our actions. We did not think about the time and opportunities that would be lost. We did not consider the loved ones that would pass. We did not think about the pain and hardship our actions would cause. We just lived.

In prison time has slowed. The fast-paced life that kept us from considering the big picture is gone. Now we spend countless hours, years, and even decades meditating on our actions. We relive in our minds the moment of our demise thousands of times over, thinking, "If only I had truly counted the cost." We have learned to consider the big picture and realize the great cost of not thinking before we act.

In Hebrews 3:1-6, the author appeals to his listeners during a time of persecution to "consider Jesus" the apostle and high priest of their confession. The author calls his audience to count the cost of turning away from their "heavenly calling." He reminds them that God is building a household of the faithful and that they must "hold fast" to their confidence in the work of God. He appeals to them to "consider" the big picture of God's plan for his people.

In this section, the author transitions from his comparison of Jesus and the angels to Jesus and Moses. Moses, one of the greatest leaders in the history of Israel, was a faithful servant in God's house (Heb. 3:5). He led the children of Israel from captivity in Egypt and received the Law at Sinai. As a representative of the Old Covenant, he testified "to the things that were to be spoken [fulfilled] later" in the New Covenant. For the Jewish people, Moses played a significant role in their story of redemption. However, the author calls his brothers and sisters to consider Jesus (v.1). Jesus is superior to Moses as a leader because he is faithful over God's house as a Son. Moses served in God's house, but Jesus is its architect. As apostle and high priest, Jesus leads God's people on their journey to a heavenly calling. Therefore, the people must "hold fast" to their confidence and persevere through their struggles. This comparison of Jesus and Moses anticipates what will be said concerning the children of Israel's disobedience in the following section (Heb. 3:16-19). Israel fell in the wilderness because of unbelief. The True Israel of God (Jesus) triumphantly entered God's ultimate rest at the head of his people through obedience.

Commentary

3:1-6.

In verse 1, the author links this section to the previous one with "therefore." This "therefore" stands as a bridge between all that has been said concerning Jesus' person and work (Heb. 1:1-2:18) with the author's exhortation to "consider Jesus."[107] The word "consider" conveys the idea to "fix the eyes of the spirit upon … someone."[108] This is a call for listeners to exercise their faith

[107] Moo, *Hebrews*, 95.
[108] See "κατανοέω" in BDAG.

by focusing and meditating on the past work and present position of Jesus. This anticipates what the author will discuss in chapter 11. The assurance of things hoped for and the evidence of things not seen (Heb. 11:1) is what Jesus has accomplished for the believer. It also entails what they have to look forward to in the future. They must not only pay very close attention to what they have heard (Heb. 2:1) but they must also continually look to Jesus with their eyes of faith. This enables believers to press forward on their journey. By focusing on Jesus, believers are forced to consider the cost of turning away from the faith to their old lifestyles. Nothing beneficial lies behind them; the journey to God's kingdom, their heavenly calling, is the ultimate goal.

The author also reveals his skill as a writer by using key phrases such as holy brothers, share, heavenly calling, apostle, and high priest to neatly tie important themes of his sermon together. In verse 1, he refers to his audience as "holy brothers" which points back to his statement in Hebrews 2:11: "those who are sanctified." These phrases are two ways of saying the same thing. The author's point is to remind his listeners of their standing in Christ and relation to God. His audience has been sanctified, set apart, and made holy.[109] This is an encouraging phrase for a group of struggling believers who feel alienated. They have been set apart for a purpose. They have been singled out for a heavenly calling. A further connection with the previous section is seen in the author's use of "share." Just as Jesus "shared" in humanity's flesh and blood, believers are to share in the work accomplished by Christ which is the believer's heavenly calling.[110] God calls to believers from out of heaven in order to draw them into heaven.[111]

---

[109] Lane, *Hebrews*, 74.
[110] Cockerill, *Hebrews*, 158; Koester, *Hebrews*, 249.
[111] Cockerill, *Hebrews*, 158.

God's call to the believer from heaven is to persevere (hold fast, Heb. 3:6) in the face of temptation (Heb. 2:18). This call both warns and encourages the believer to continue the journey of faith while God builds his "house" of the faithful (Heb. 3:6). The listeners' responsibility is to hear the voice of God and not harden their hearts (Heb. 3:7). God also calls from heaven to believers on behalf of others. The faithful are to "exhort one another every day" (Heb. 3:13). This means the believer's heavenly calling includes helping build the house of God. God also calls believers into heaven. This is their reminder that they are children of God on a journey to the city of the living God (Heb. 12:22). This world is not their permanent address. They belong to the house of God (Heb. 3:6) because they have been provided access by Jesus, the one who brings "many sons and daughters to glory" (Heb. 2:10). The believers' responsibility is to continue their journey by holding fast to their confidence in the faith (3:6).

Prison is the land of unfinished projects. Our prison sentence is a trail of unfinished studies, books, courses, and ideas. We start on tasks and encounter difficulties or obstacles that keep us from reaching our goal. Sometimes we simply get sidetracked by new and more interesting projects. I personally have numerous composition notebooks which are half full of unfinished ideas. Their covers are labeled with titles like short stories, philosophy, and even exercise. Now they lay unfinished in my locker. I failed to "hold fast" to what I started. Somewhere along the way I lost "confidence." However, there is one project that no person can afford to leave incomplete: their journey with Christ. Our book of short stories can remain unfinished, but our story of redemption must be completed at all costs.

The titles apostle and high priest denote aspects of Jesus' ministry. While the term apostle is used nowhere else in biblical literature as a title for Christ, the title fits the mission of Jesus well.[112] An apostle is a messenger sent to proclaim a message. The author alludes to Jesus' apostleship in Hebrews 1:2 when he states, "In these last days he has spoken to us by his son." As God's final revelation, Jesus is both the message and the messenger. This correlates well with the author's upcoming comparison between Jesus and Moses. Moses was also a messenger sent from God. He was sent with a message of deliverance to Israel while in Egyptian captivity (Exod. 3), and to deliver the Law to Israel from Sinai (Exod. 19-20). However, Jesus is both the messenger, and the content of the message is superior. Moses was "to testify to the things that were to be spoken later" (Heb. 3:5). That testimony was the "good news" that was preached to Israel in the wilderness (Heb. 4:2), that "good news" was Jesus the message.

The author refers to Jesus' priestly duties by calling on his listeners to "consider" their high priest. Thus, not only is Jesus the bearer of a message from God to the people, but as priest, Jesus represents the people to God.[113] Jesus' dual role of apostle and priest is easily seen in his fulfillment of the Messianic Servant in Luke 4:18-19 taken from Isaiah 61. There are several parallels between the context of Hebrews and the role of the Messianic Servant. Luke 4:18-19 presents the servant as both an apostle and priest-like figure. First, Luke 4 refers to the anointing of the servant which is priestly language that parallels with Hebrews 1:9. The "oil of gladness" with which the Son is anointed in Hebrews 1:9 is the same "oil of gladness" the Messianic Servant will give

---

[112] Cockerill, *Hebrews*, 159.
[113] Cockerill, *Hebrews*, 160.

to the people to replace their mourning (Is. 61:3). The "good news" proclaimed to the poor (Luke 4:18) is the same "good news" delivered to the wilderness generation and the audience of Hebrews (Heb. 4:2). The message has not changed; God delivers his people from the captivity of sin and death. The Messianic Servant is sent (apostle) to proclaim liberty to the captives (Luke 4:18). The author of Hebrews describes Jesus as the one sent to "deliver all those who through fear and death were subject to lifelong slavery" (Heb. 2:15). Finally, Jesus directly connects the fulfillment of the Messianic Servant of Isaiah 61 with the beginning of his ministry (Luke 4:21). Jesus as the Messianic Servant of Isaiah 61 is both the apostle and high priest of Hebrews 3.

The listeners are to consider Jesus who is the content of their confession. This statement most likely refers to both a body of teachings concerning Jesus, and the act of proclaiming them to others.[114] The core understanding of the faith is the superiority of Jesus as the Son of God.[115] The Jesus of Hebrews 1:1-2:18 is the Jesus the listeners are to confess before others.[116] This is also a subtle reminder of the audiences' profession of faith at baptism.[117] The author is reminding his listeners of their initial commitment to Christ. This is the confidence to which the listeners are called to hold fast.[118] Their commitment is to mimic the work of their Lord. The believers' position in Christ requires them to fulfill the role of apostle and priest. The Christian is called to preach the Gospel and teach others concerning the faith (2 Tim. 4:2; Matt.

[114] Koester, *Hebrews*, 243.
[115] Lane, *Hebrews*, 75.
[116] Koester, *Hebrews*, 250; cf., Lane, *Hebrews*, 75.
[117] Guthrie, *Hebrews*, NIV, 127.
[118] Cockerill, *Hebrews*, 190.

28:20). Paul states that this is accomplished when believers are "sent," which is a form of the word apostle (Rom. 10:15). The believer also fulfills the role of priest. 1 Peter 2:9 refers to believers as a "royal priesthood" whose purpose is to "proclaim the excellencies of him who called [them] out of darkness into his marvelous light." Both the roles of the apostle and priest entail sharing the faith with others. When believers consider Jesus' faithfulness, they must also consider their role in the household of God as faithful stewards.[119]

The author now transitions into a comparison between the faithfulness of Moses and the faithfulness of Jesus. The author's point is not to degrade Moses or bring into question his faithfulness as God's servant, but to elevate Jesus' superior faithfulness.[120] The author describes Jesus as faithful looking back to his previous reference of faithfulness at Hebrews 2:17. The Son's faithfulness is in relation to the one "who appointed him" namely God. While Jesus is the eternal Son, he was made or was appointed apostle and high priest because of his faithfulness to God's plan of redemption. Here the author introduces Moses for the purpose of comparison by alluding to another Old Testament text, Numbers 12:7 (see below). While the author compares, he does not contrast. Throughout his sermon, he is careful not to degrade the Jewish religious tradition. This signals the author's understanding of unity between the Old and New Testaments. The New has not replaced the Old, it has simply fulfilled it in a superior way. As a result, the author highlights alongside Jesus, the

---

[119] Ibid., 162.
[120] Dana Harris, *Hebrews: Exegetical Guide to the Greek New Testament* (Nashville: B&H, 2019), 72; Koester, *Hebrews*, 248.

faithfulness of Moses. However, one's level of faithfulness is relative to one's level of responsibility.

In the body of Christ, one's faithfulness is generally rewarded with more responsibility. This is especially true in prison where positive leadership qualities are rare. A person can find themselves one day as the leader of a small Bible study, and the next, as a leader of a whole prison ministry. As their faithfulness is recognized, their responsibility grows, and growth of their responsibility requires more faithfulness. Jesus, in his parable of the talents, reminds his listeners that those who are faithful over little things will be given greater things (Matt. 25:23). Faithfulness and responsibility go hand in hand. Believers must remember to be faithful with what God has given them and to always be prepared to do greater things for the kingdom of God.

In verse 3, the author broadens his comparison. While both Moses and Jesus are faithful, Jesus is "counted worthy of more glory than Moses." To show this, the author appeals to common logic: creators (builders) are greater than their creation (buildings). This again is a reference to Hebrews 1:1-3. Jesus is appointed heir and is creator (builder) of all things (Heb. 1:3). The author also uses the term "glory" in order to compare Jesus and Moses' revelation of God. Moses experienced God in such a way that his face reflected the glory and shined brightly before the people (Exod. 34:29-30). Jesus on the other hand is the "radiance of the glory of God" (Heb. 1:3; John 1:14). Moses experienced the glory of God, Jesus is the glory of God.[121] In verse 4, the author once again alludes to Jesus' deity. If Jesus is the creator of all things (Heb. 1:2), and in Hebrews 3:4, God is called the builder (creator) of all things, then the conclusion follows that Jesus is

[121] Cockerill, *Hebrews*, 164-165.

God, the builder/creator of all things. Cockerill rightly notes, "Failure to accept this verse as confirmation of the Son's divine creatorship leaves it a foreign body in the text. When one accepts this verse as an affirmation of the Son's deity, it becomes a fitting introduction to the following verse which proclaims the divine Son's role over God's house in which Moses serves as 'steward.' "[122] Once again, the author easily transitions from the humanity of Jesus as high priest and apostle to the deity as eternal creator of all things.

The author now compares Jesus' and Moses' faithfulness by appealing to Numbers 12:7. In Numbers 12, Miriam and Aaron speak against Moses because of his marriage to a Cushite woman. As a result, "the anger of the Lord was kindled against them" (Num. 12:9). God calls Miriam and Aaron to account for their actions and states the following in defense of Moses: "Hear my words: if there is a prophet among you, I the lord make myself known to him in a vision; I speak with him in a dream. Not so with my servant Moses. He is faithful in all my house. With him I speak mouth to mouth clearly and not in riddles, and he beholds the form of the Lord. Why then were you not afraid to speak against my servant Moses" (Num. 12:6-8). God's speech emphasizes the special relationship that Moses had with God. Moses communicated with God in a way that other prophets did not. As a result of this, Moses was held in very high esteem by the Jews, and as Jewish Christians, the author's listeners too would have stood in awe of the man who spoke "mouth to mouth" with God. Moses' faithfulness as God's servant was second to none. However, the author qualifies Moses' faithfulness in two ways. First, Moses is faithful "in" God's house, and second, he is faithful

[122] Ibid., 167.

"as a servant." Moses' faithfulness was relative to his position and purpose in the house of God. As far as servants were concerned, there was none greater than Moses. His purpose was "to testify to the things that were to be spoken later." Moses' faithfulness was relative to his service to the Lord of the House, that Lord is the eternal Son.[123]

God's house during Moses' time was most likely the tabernacle; however, in a broader sense, God's house entailed all God's people, namely, Israel. Here, the author of Hebrews broadens the idea of house by including Christians. The author does not speak of two different houses, an Old Testament house and a New Testament house, but he speaks of the one house of God that is filled (fulfilled) with believers in Christ. Believers, along with the Old Testament saints, make up the one people of God. Finally, the author reveals the purpose of his comparison which is encouragement in the face of opposition. The listeners are to "hold fast" to their confidence and boasting in hope.[124] If Moses was once the great deliverer of the house of God during persecution and bondage, then how much more so will the new superior owner be concerned with His house?

Application

CONSIDER JESUS

Many Christians today fail to "consider" their relationship with the Lord. They go about their days busying themselves with countless tasks while never thinking about how they relate to their walk with Jesus. As a result, the believer often lives in two worlds. Monday through Saturday, they wear their secular hats and do all

---

[123] Moo, *Hebrews*, 100.
[124] For the conditional aspect of this statement see Moo, *Hebrews*, 101-103.

the things which serve the world. On Sunday, they put on their church clothes and serve God. However, to be a faithful servant in God's house requires one to "consider Jesus" in all they do. Take time today and examine all your activities. Ask yourself, "Am I considering Jesus in all I do?" Read Luke 14:25-33 and consider the cost of discipleship. Are you willing to put Jesus before all else?

HOLDING FAST TO JESUS

The believer's journey from faith to faith is a road of hills and valleys. On the mountain top, where we are closest to the presence of the Lord and our path looks so clear, it is easy to hold fast to our confidence. It is as if God hears our every thought and answers every prayer. From the mountain, nothing stands in our way, so we charge into the valley. Here things seem less clear and the Lord not so close. Like David, we cry out to God: "How long O Lord? Will you forget me forever?" (Ps. 13:1). The valley tests our confidence. Will we hold fast or let go? It is during these times of testing that our confidence must be tethered to the Lord. Jesus, our pioneer, has conquered every valley that we may find ourselves in. We must simply find the path which he has already cleared for us. Examine your walk with Christ and ask yourself: "Am I currently on a mountain or in a valley?" If you are on a mountain, prepare yourself for the next valley through prayer and study. If you are in a valley, search the Scriptures for a pathway out. Read Psalm 13 and meditate on the beginning and end of the Psalm. What does it teach about our walk of faith?

2. Remember the Disobedience of a People (3:7-19)

Prisoner's Insight for the Journey

Prison should be a journey to transformation. Let's be honest with ourselves, the majority of us were living lifestyles prior to our incarceration that were going nowhere. Somewhere along the way we had developed unhealthy habits which produced unhealthy relationships that ultimately landed us in this predicament. We did not set out to fail in life but somewhere along the way we went "astray" and fell in the wilderness of life.

So now that we are here, we might as well begin a new journey, a journey to transformation. But in order to do this, we must learn from our past mistakes. We must identify the obstacles in our paths that may trip us up. Old habits and unhealthy relationships must go. "Today" you must listen to the "voice" of reason and not "harden your hearts" to the process. We have begun a new journey seeking to enter the "rest" of God through transformation, and the good news is, we do not have to journey alone. We travel with others so that we can "exhort one another every day." But best of all, we have a pioneer that leads the way because "we have come to share in Christ."

The author of Hebrews reminds his audience that they are on a journey to enter God's rest. Therefore, they must listen to the "voice" of God "today" so that they do not harden their hearts. He calls on them to remember Israel's past and the eleven-day journey that lasted forty years because of disobedience and unbelief. If the author's listeners are to finally enter God's rest, they must not commit the same error by testing God on their journey.

Commentary

3:7-19

In this section the author does two main things, he warns his audience to persevere and provides them with an exposition of Psalm 95:7-11 which itself is a reference to Numbers 13-14. Verse 7 begins with a "therefore" which closely ties the author's explanation of Psalm 95 with the previous section. The two sections should be tied together as follows: "And we are his house if indeed we hold fast our confidence and our boasting in our hope (Heb. 3:6), therefore … (Heb. 3:7), take care brothers…" (Heb. 3:12). This means that Psalm 95 stands between the two sections as the author's example of what it looks like not to hold fast. While this may seem odd to the modern reader, the ancient reader would immediately recognize Psalms 95 as a reference to Numbers 14 where Israel rebelled against both God and Moses who led their journey to the Promised Land.[125]

The author introduces Psalm 95 by placing the words in the mouth of the Holy Spirit. By doing this, the author continues his theme of divine speech.[126] Furthermore, the author completes a "trinity" of divine speakers; the Father has spoken (Heb. 1:6), the Son has spoken (Heb. 2:12), and now the Holy Spirit.[127] While the official doctrine of the Trinity would not be fully formulated until 325 AD, here one sees that the early church viewed each person, the Father, Son, and Holy Spirit, as authoritative. The Holy Spirit reminds the people of God of their past, a subtle

---

[125] Cockerill, *Hebrews*, 176-77.
[126] Koester, *Hebrews*, 254.
[127] Harris, *Hebrews*, 77.

reminder of Israel's rebellion and subsequent failure to enter the Promised Land.

The author calls on his audience to hear the voice of God "today." All throughout this sermon, God has been speaking to his people. Now the author exhorts his audience to "hear" the warning of God. In Numbers 14/Psalm 95, the children of Israel are on the border of the Promised Land, the very goal of their exodus from Egypt. All of their struggles and toil have led up to this moment. Israel sent spies into the land to gather intelligence, and in their mind, what they found was not good. The spies returned with a negative report, and the people immediately began to grumble. They threatened to choose a new leader and return to Egypt. Their disobedience and rebellion were a result of unbelief. The children of Israel, who had witnessed God miraculously deliver them from slavery in Egypt, now in the face of opposition, threatened to return to that slavery. They did not trust that God would continue to fight their battles. As a result of their hardness of heart, God hardened his and swore in his wrath "they shall not enter my rest."

The author's audience is on the verge of the same mistake. The Son as their pioneer has led them from the slavery of "fear of death" (Heb. 2:17) and desires to bring them "to glory" (Heb. 2:10) if only they will "hold fast." He warns them not to commit the same mistake by falling "away from the living God" (Heb. 3:12). Paul in his letter to the Corinthians also reminds his readers not to follow the example of Israel. He states that Israel put Christ to the test, grumbled against God, and was destroyed by the destroyer. Paul reminds his readers that these events stand as an example of what not to do for the current generation (1 Cor. 10:9-11). Believers are called to learn from the mistakes of those who journeyed before them.

Prison is full of examples of what not to do. All a person must do is look around to find a lifetime worth of bad examples. Yet it is often strange how easily we fall into the trap of imitation. Some people come to prison and develop worse habits than they had before they arrived. They also convince themselves that somehow, they can carry these new habits to the world and be successful where no one else has ever been successful before. Some take the same hustle that landed countless people in prison, carry it to the world, and expect different results. To be successful in life, we must learn to take these examples for what they are, just plain bad.

In verse 12, the author picks up his "therefore" from verse 7. The author exhorts his audience to "take care," using a word in the original language that is normally translated as "see or look." By using it as a command, the author strengthens its meaning to entail "watch out for" or "keep on the lookout," or even "beware" of evil and unbelieving hearts.[128] Again, the author references Numbers where God points out the unbelief (Num. 14:11) and evil (Num. 14:27) of Israel. The author's listeners are to "take care" lest they allow the outside pressure to produce evil and unbelief on the inside. The author is concerned that the trials his audience face will cause them "to fall away from the living God." The idea "fall away" is probably best understood to mean "turn away" and mostly likely alludes to Israel's desire to return to Egypt. The author's audience faced a similar pressure to return to Judaism or possibly some other socially acceptable group. Furthermore, the phrase "living God" reminds them of the presence of God in the midst of their struggle. He is the God who speaks to them "today."

---

[128] Moo, *Hebrews*, 114.

In verse 13 the author emphasizes one believer's responsibility to another. He calls them to "exhort one another every day." This points to the importance of unity in the house of God. The journey to God's rest is not a solo journey because the pioneer leads "many sons and daughters to glory" (Heb. 2:10). Thus, believers are to be concerned about their heart condition and the condition of those they travel with. The journey to "rest" is ongoing and the length and time is unknown, so encouragement must continue "as long as it is called today." The hardness of heart and deceitfulness of sin can creep up at any time so constant vigilance is required. The author's point is that opposition should be expected but it is how believers react in the face of trials that determine their success. Will the Hebrews be like Israel and turn away from the living God after they have come so far?

There are two rules that almost every inmate learns immediately upon arriving at prison: mind your own business and look out for yourself because no one else will. We are taught to "do time" with our heads down, blinders on, and minds focused on ourselves. This is the convict way of doing things. But the Christian way calls for us to exhort one another, and to be our brothers' keeper. This means as a believer we cannot do time minding our own business. We must be aware of our brother's needs and struggles. We cannot only look out for ourselves. As a believer, we are called to meet the needs of our fellow man. This means at times, we will have to deny ourselves and put others before us. To live according to a Christian worldview means, we must reject the convict way of life.

In verse 14, the author emphasizes the common ground of the believer, "We have come to share in Christ." Christ shared in the flesh and temptation of humanity, now the author reminds his audience that they share in the victory of Christ.[129] What is the test for unity in Christ? Perseverance to the end. The listener's unity in Christ is made evident by the holding of their "original confidence firm to the end."

Many scholars have attempted to force these Scriptures to speak about the security of one's salvation. Is the believer eternally secure or can they lose their salvation?" First, the security of one's salvation is a theological debate that arose later in church history and most likely is not on the author's mind in this text. Second, in light of the Numbers 14 account, salvation should not be equated with entering the Promised Land. In Numbers 14:20, God clearly "pardons" the people's rebellion.[130] Even though they did not enter the Promised Land at that point, God still walks with them for 38 years in the wilderness. Moreover, if entering the Promised Land equaled salvation, then Moses would be excluded because he failed to enter. This is a position that most scholars would not take. Finally, the author most likely has perseverance in the face of opposition in mind. He emphasizes the commonality of the believer who has "come to share in Christ." This commonality is evidenced by their holding firm to the end.[131] The author does not say that if believers hold firm to the end, then they come to share in Christ. Their sharing in Christ is the reality of being called brothers and sisters by their Lord.

3:15-19

The author uses Psalm 95:7-8 so that he can highlight three points: Israel's hearing of God's voice, their hardness of heart, and

---

[129] Cockerill, *Hebrews*, 188.
[130] Allen, *Hebrews*, 269.
[131] Moo, *Hebrews*, 117.

their rebellion. First, the author emphasizes the hearing of God's voice, and the resulting rebellion of Israel. Most likely he wants to point out that hearing from God does not guarantee one will not rebel. This corresponds to his warning to "take care." Even in the midst of one's journey with God, rebellion remains a danger. This is further emphasized by alluding to Israel's deliverance from Egypt. Israel saw the miraculous works of God that freed them, but seeing God's awesome hand of deliverance, does not keep one from rebellion thus, "take care." Second, in verse 17, the author highlights Israel's hardness of heart even in the face of God's displeasure. The author again appeals to Israel's forty years in the wilderness. The careful reader will note the two different uses of Psalm 95:10 by the author (Compare the Old Testament use of Psalm 95:10 with the use in Hebrews 3:9). In the original use of Psalm 95:10, God in reference to the Exodus states, "For forty years I loathed that generation." Thus, the original context has a negative connotation. In Hebrews 3:9 the author places the emphasis on Israel's seeing God's work for forty years a positive use referencing God's providence. However, in verse 17, the author uses its negative sense.[132] Most likely he desires to draw a contrast between obedience to God's word and disobedience. For the obedient, the word of God results in provision as displayed in Caleb and Joshua's lives. For the disobedient, the word of God results in judgment as displayed in the lives of those "whose bodies fell in the wilderness." The author desires for his listeners to decide which they will be: doers of the word or hearers only (James 1:22). The author further categorizes those who did not believe or trust in the promise of God's rest as "those who sinned." The author's point is that sin is not simply disobedience to God's commands, but it is also a lack of trust in his promises. Finally,

[132] Moo, *Hebrews*, 118-119.

the author stresses the disobedience/rebellion that resulted in a failure to obtain the blessing of God. The children of Israel departed Egypt in search of freedom and blessing but along the journey they lost sight of their purpose. God had promised them rest and provision in a land they did not know, but before they could obtain the promise, their hardened hearts led them to rebel. The author summarizes Israel's failure as unbelief. Thus, he begins his exhortation with a warning to "take care" lest they be found with an unbelieving heart, and now, he concludes this section by reminding his audience that it was unbelief that barred Israel from God's blessing.[133]

Application

EXHORT ONE ANOTHER EVERY DAY

Encouragement in prison is hard to find. Prisons are naturally negative environments full of pessimists. It is easier to find the bad news than it is to hear the "good news." This negative environment over time begins to weigh heavily on one's shoulders. It has a way of affecting our hearts in a negative way which often results in bitterness. As believers we must resist the urge to become angry concerning our circumstances. The best way to fight off negativity is to surround yourself with positivity. This means that you must exhort others while also being exhorted daily. Even in this negative place there are always silver linings. You must simply change your perspective. Read 1 Thessalonians. 5:9-11 and share a word of positivity with someone who needs it, you may be surprised by their reaction!

---

[133] Cockerill, *Hebrews*, 173-195.

3. Strive for the Blessing of Obedience (4:1-11)

Prisoner's Insight for the Journey

You are in prison, but your life is not over. Your worst moment doesn't have to be your defining moment. The "good news" is that in this life, there are second chances, and "today," there remains an opportunity to do something worthy. So, your responsibility is to identify what that something is and "strive" to obtain your goal. Setting and achieving goals are like going on a journey; you must decide where you are going and how you are going to get there. If your goal is rehabilitation or education, then sign up for some classes. If your goal is simply going home, then you should be working on a parole plan. To arrive at any destination, you must begin the journey.

Furthermore, your lifestyle must serve as a means to your destination. This means you must live as if you have already arrived. You cannot expect to arrive at education without study, and you should not expect to go home by simply doing nothing. You must live every day of your incarceration as if you have arrived. Stop telling yourself that you will start tomorrow and start today. While your opportunity remains, strive to do something worthy with your life.

The author of Hebrews uses the story of Israel's failure to enter the Promised Land as a means to encourage his audience not to miss their opportunity to enter God's rest. Israel set out to obtain the promised rest of God in a land flowing with milk and honey; however, they failed because they did not live as if the promise was a reality. As a result of their faithlessness, and disobedience, Israel lost sight of their destination and fell in the wilderness. The author of Hebrews wants his listeners to know that the opportunity to obtain the promise of God's rest still remains for the people of God. However, if they are to reach their destination, they must strive to obtain his promise by living as if God's rest was a reality in their lives. They must live a life of faith.

Commentary

4:1-11

In verse 1, the author transitions from his explanation of Psalm 95, in relation to the wilderness generation, to its application for his current audience.[134] He aims to show that the rest God offered to Israel still remains for God's people today. Much like in the previous sections, the author stresses the continuity between the Old Testament people of God and the New.[135] Here both the promise of God's rest and the opportunity to enter it remains for the one people of God. The contrast should be seen in the various responses to God's promise. The people of old responded in unbelief and disobedience; therefore, the current generation should "fear" lest any of them seem to have committed the same error. The author desires that his audience arrive at their intended destination—the rest of God.

One of the most difficult aspects of this passage is the attempt to define the author's use of rest. In what sense can today's believer enter it? Is the rest of God a place or idea? Is one to enter now, or in the future? While difficult to decide, a look at the author's correlation between the Old Testament situation and the New Testament situation adds clarity.

---

[134] Moo, *Hebrews*, 126.
[135] Cockerill, *Hebrews*, 154.

First, in the Old Testament, God's rest was signified by entrance into the Promised Land. So, in this sense it was local. The people of God would obtain rest by entering into the Land of Canaan. Second, for Israel, entering the rest of God was a present reality. They simply had to cross the Jordan River, and the promised rest would be theirs. Of course, as the author has made perfectly clear, Israel failed to obtain the promise of God. However, the author states that both the promise of rest and the opportunity to enter still remains for his audience. So, in what sense could a first-century Christian far removed from the banks of the Jordan be able to enter God's promised rest?

In order to explain this, the author ties three biblical texts together. First, he uses Numbers 14 to provide the historical understanding of the promised rest. Second, he uses Psalm 95 as a further development of Numbers 14. Psalm 95 was written hundreds of years after the initial failure of Israel to enter God's rest. In this Psalm, the Psalmist appeals to his audience not to commit the same error as the Numbers 14 generation. This implies that at the time the Psalm was written the people of God still had an opportunity to enter God's rest. Finally, the author quotes Genesis 2:2 and ties it to the "my rest" of Psalm 95. The Genesis rest is God's rest that took place at the end of his six days of creation. This is the rest that God is currently experiencing. Therefore, the author implies that the ultimate rest for the past, present, and future people of God is the Sabbath rest of God instituted at creation. All other types of rest find their fulfillment in God's Sabbath rest. So, when and how does the believer enter into God's ultimate Sabbath rest?

For the Numbers 14 audience, the people of the Psalmist's Day, and the first-century Christian, the Sabbath rest of God is future and will be fully realized in the arrival of the New Heavens and Earth. Moreover, for all believers past, present and future, the attainment of God's rest is through faith in his promise. Therefore, in verse 2, the author states that the "good news" of God's rest was proclaimed to the people of old and is currently proclaimed to the present generation.[136] The failure of those who did not obtain the promise was a result of a lack of faith. The phrase "those who listened" most likely alludes to Caleb and Joshua in Numbers 14.[137] Both men believed the promise of God was obtainable even in the face of the bad report and opposition of the people. The author desires his audience to know that God still speaks "today" concerning his promise. The message has not changed. The people of faith inherit the promised rest of God. The first-century Christian is called to imitate Caleb and Joshua. They are to trust in God's unbreakable promise even in the face of opposition. This is why in verse 3 he reminds them of their future blessing.

Verse 3 in many translations appears to say that the believer has obtained rest through faith. However, this most likely should be read as: "For we who have believed are entering that rest."[138] This fits better with the overall picture of the author's emphasis on perseverance. He is encouraging his hearers to continue on their journey to God's Sabbath rest in faith. For the author, faith is living out the promise of God as if it is a reality. This means they are to live at rest in the face of opposition. In chapter 3, he has provided his listeners with an example of not living out the promises of God, in Chapter 11, he will provide numerous examples of people who persevered through faith.[139]

---

[136] Cockerill, *Hebrews*, 202.
[137] Moo, Hebrews, 128.
[138] Cockerill, *Hebrews*, 205; Pace Moo, *Hebrews*, 128.
[139] Cockerill, *Hebrews,* 183-84.

Moreover, in Heb. 3:3-4, as mentioned above, the author expands the concept of rest by combining Psalm 95 and Genesis 2:2. For the author, God's rest was seen in types and shadows throughout history. These types were meant to point back to the inauguration and forward to the consummation of God's Sabbath rest in the New Heavens and Earth. In this rest, man like God, will rest from his work.

In prison we are all in some sense moving toward our day of freedom. We prepare for this day as if it might arrive at any moment. I often tell people that I try to live as if I might go home tomorrow and strive every day like I am presently entering my future freedom. This means to live your life today as if your future is a reality. You cannot wait until it is time to go home to get ready to leave, by then, it will be too late to prepare. The same is true for God's ultimate rest. We must live every day as if that rest is a reality in our lives. This means pressing forward and persevering no matter what the obstacle. If we would not allow anything to stand in the way of our freedom, then why should we allow the cares of this world to stand in the way of God's rest!

4:5-7

In verses 5-7, the author again quotes Psalm 95:11 in order to emphasize the magnitude of Israel's failure. It was not simply a land that their unbelief barred them from but the very eternal rest of God.[140] This helps to heighten the urgency for his audience. In verse 6, the author summarizes the issue: some failed to enter God's rest due to unbelief, others are entering his rest through faith (v.3), and it remains still for some to enter. Because of this, God has appointed a "certain day" which the author emphasizes as the

---

[140] Ibid., 194.

"today" of the last days. His anticipation of this day was foreshadowed at creation, represented as a type in the Promised Land, prophesied as a future day by David in the Psalm, and will be consummated at the end of time. For his audience who contemplates a return to Judaism in the face of persecution, "today" has arrived. Therefore, they must not harden their hearts to the promise of God. There remains no rest outside of what Christ has provided.

4:8-11

In verse 8, the author anticipates an objection to his argument: "Did not Joshua enter the Promised Land?" Yet the author shows that the totality of rest could never have been realized in Israel.[141] If Joshua could have achieved rest, then there would have been no need for the prophetic "today" of Psalm 95.[142] What Joshua obtained was only a taste of what true rest in God could be. The "good news" is that despite the failure of Israel there remains a "Sabbath rest" for the people of God. The author employs a word here used nowhere else in Scripture: "Sabbath rest." He most likely coined this word to describe the end of age rest that the people of God would experience.[143] He could also have in mind the celebratory nature of the Sabbath, thus using the word to denote a rest defined by joyous celebration.[144] God's joyous future rest is further described as the completion of one's works. The author most likely alludes to the journey of life or the striving to enter God's rest. Just as God created, then rested, man will also finish his journey and enter God's rest.[145] However, in

---

[141] Moo, *Hebrews*, 130.
[142] Cockerill, *Hebrews*, 209.
[143] Moo, *Hebrews*, 134-135.
[144] Cockerill, *Hebrews*, 210.
[145] Ibid., 212.

the meantime, the believer must strive in faith. In verse 11, the author once again encourages his audience by exhorting them to "strive" to enter God's rest. The goal and destination of every believer must be the consummated rest that God will provide at the end of the age. For the author, his audience is on a journey much like Israel. As the day of this age draws closer to an end, the author desires his listeners to cross their Jordan in faith.

Application

SHARE THE GOOD NEWS "TODAY

The "good news" is that humanity who is guilty before God and separated from its Creator due to disobedience can be reconciled. Paul tells his readers in 2 Corinthians 5:19 that God was in Christ reconciling the world to himself, not counting their trespasses against them. This is "good news." However, there are countless people in the world who have never heard God's message of forgiveness. Take the time today and write out a Gospel presentation. Include Scriptures like the one above. Share this message with someone who you believe has never heard the message of forgiveness or someone who may be in need of some "good news."

4. Live by the Standard of the Word (4:12-13)

Prisoner's Insight for the Journey

For me, one of the most interesting practices that we inmates partake is the "heart check." Personally, I have always been amazed by this seeming rite of passage into the whole prison experience. One man, who is new to prison, reluctantly agrees to fight two or more men at the same time in order to test his willingness to stand up for himself. If the new guy survives the skirmish for a certain number of seconds without folding himself into a ball, then he is deemed to have heart—heart check complete!

I have been equally amazed at the inaccuracy of this practice to actually test the heart. In my years, I have seen numerous men "pass" their heart check but later refuse to stand up for themselves. I have also witnessed men ball up, scream during the check, and ultimately become the guy that you don't want to mess with. The test's inaccuracy results from the inability to measure the heart through seconds that lasted in a prison scuffle. True heart is evidenced by one's refusal to allow ***failure*** to fold them into a ball. If you want to know if a person has heart, "check" them at the end of their sentence and see how they spent their time. True heart is measured in one's ability to rise from the ashes of failure.

The author of Hebrews has methodically argued for the total superiority of Christ, the irrevocable nature of God's promise, and the necessity to persevere in the face of all circumstances. To accomplish this, he employed one tool, the living, active, Word of God. The author may write or speak the words, but it is the voice of God that gives them conviction and authority. The living God is proclaiming the authority of the living word over a living people. The word has the ability to check the heart and expose any weakness of faith. What the word exposes God sees, and for what God sees, the people are accountable.

Commentary

4:12-13

In verse 12, the author states explicitly what he has alluded to by his numerous uses of Old Testament texts, the word of God is living and active. Throughout his previous expositions and exhortations, he has placed the Scriptures on the lips of the Father, the Son, and the Holy Spirit. Thus, the word is not simply some dead text on an ancient scroll, but the very voice of God who speaks into the present. This reflects back to the introduction of his sermon: God spoke long ago … but in these last days … he speaks in and through his Son. Jesus is the fulfillment of the Old Testament message. The message of entering God's rest pointed to the Sabbath rest that Jesus would provide for all believers. Now the first-century church is receiving the same word.[146] The author describes the word as a sharp, two-edged sword that is piercing. Here he uses the metaphor of the sword to illustrate the words use. A sharp, double-edged sword is capable of cutting two ways, just as the word functions in two ways by providing blessing or judgment. The author illustrated this double use earlier with Psalm 95. The word of promise was proclaimed to all of Israel, but did not benefit all, because all did not believe. As a result, the word of promise became a word of judgment. The author reminds his audience that the word they are receiving "today" cuts both ways.

---

[146] Cockerill, *Hebrews*, 216.

The double-edged nature of the word is also piercing. It cuts deep and divides soul and spirit while discerning the thoughts and intentions of the heart. This means that the word not only exposes but also corrects. For the wilderness generation, the word exposed their hardness of heart and for the first-century believer it stands as the word of correction.

I often hear people in prison complain that they feel as if they are not growing in Christ. I immediately ask them two questions: "What does it mean to you to grow in Christ?" and "How often to do you study your Bible?" To the first question, I get a range of answers varying between character, change, and knowledge about God. Most people want to change and grow in the knowledge of the Lord. However, the answer to the second question often shocks me. Most people confuse reading their Bible with studying. They read a Psalm and Proverb a day and believe they have studied. They have been doing this same routine for years and wonder why they do not grow in the Lord. Reading the Bible is an excellent practice, but the Bible is not a bunch of individual statements of ancient wisdom. The Bible contains the story of redemption. Therefore, it must be read and studied with the whole story in mind. Every part of the Bible is closely tied to the rest. The good student should never pry the word from its context but seek to understand it in its original setting: the story of redemption. The more the person comes to understand God's redemptive work, the more the person becomes redeemed! The word helps to conform the believer to the image of Jesus.

The exposing nature of the word reveals the measure of a person's heart. The author's audience heard the word accompanied by the warning, now it was their responsibility to respond. David, in Psalm, cries out to God to search and know his heart to see if it contains any grievous ways (Psalm 139:23-24). This is what the word does for its reader. It examines the heart and enables one to keep his ways pure. It is the word that helps sanctify the believer. The author desires his listeners to know that they, like the wilderness generation, will be held accountable for their response. God is speaking his authoritative word into their present situation. The opportunity of rest remains; however, believers are required to hold fast to their belief in the promise while also striving in faith to obtain it.

Application

STUDY TO SHOW YOURSELF APPROVED

Paul writing to his beloved son Timothy tells him, "Do your best to present yourself to God as one approved, a worker who has no need to be ashamed, rightly handling the word of truth" (2 Tim. 2:15). In prison, we have ample time to learn many things. I know men who have learned languages, art, philosophy, and most any other discipline. We spend countless hours mastering chess moves and counting dominoes. However, when it comes to the word of God, we have very little time to spare. We open our Bibles, read a few verses, and convince ourselves that we have studied. Yet, in reality, we never scratch the surface of God's word. The Bible should be dissected and examined as if the person's life depended on it. Take the time today to read and study 2 Timothy 3:16, and 2 Timothy 2:15. What is the difference between reproof and correction in 2 Timothy 3:16? Consider what it means to rightly divide the word. What does the word complete mean in 2 Tim. 3:16?

II. God's Companion for the Weary Traveler (4:14-10:18)

Section Summary

The need for humanity to be reconciled to their Creator is evident from the numerous institutions which God provided mankind throughout time. The priesthood was meant to represent humanity before a holy God; however, the priesthood needed an advocate for themselves. Sinful humans could not advocate properly for sinful humans. The blood of animals was meant to cleanse worshipers of their transgressions. However, the blood of bulls and goats could not cleanse the conscience. The Old Covenant was meant to provide rules and guidelines, but these ultimately became a barrier that the worshipper could not overcome. If mankind was to be fully reconciled to their creator, then someone who could fully represent humanity and stand blameless before God was necessary. This is why God sent the perfect high priest to offer the perfect sacrifice to institute a perfect covenant. If humanity will finally have a true relationship with God, it can only be accomplished through a true relationship with Jesus.

Introduction to the Section

The author has brought his weary listeners from the throne room of God, where they considered the superiority of Jesus as God's ultimate message, to a call for perseverance through obedience to his living word (Heb. 1:1-4:13). Jesus is superior to all other forms of God's revelation, and in light of the importance of his message, the hearers must pay close attention lest they miss out on their opportunity for deliverance. Jesus has freed them from the fear of death and the power of the devil. He has provided for them a place in the household of God, if they trust in him, and hold fast to their confidence (Heb. 2:1-3:6). Now the author's audience must strive to enter God's rest by listening to his voice and not imitating the disobedience of the wilderness generation (Heb. 3:7-4:13).

The author has left his listeners with a high demand for obedience in the face of opposition. It is such a high demand that his audience is likely questioning their ability to be obedient to God's call: "How can anyone succeed?" The author comforts his listeners' fear by reminding them of their traveling companion. Jesus, their great high priest, has overcome the opposition on their behalf enabling them to draw near to the presence of God in confidence (Heb. 4:15-5:10). The listeners must leave behind their immature understanding of the faith and come to realize that they serve a superior high priest who has offered a superior sacrifice instituting a superior covenant (Heb. 5:11-10:18).

A. Jesus: The People's Great High Priest (4:14-6:20)

1. The High Priest who Sympathizes (4:14-5:10)

Prisoner's Insight for the Journey

As a Field Minister, one of my responsibilities is to tier walk. As I walk throughout the prison, I listen to the different needs and complaints of the population. Most of the time, people just need to "vent" their frustrations with someone who understands their situation. I generally listen to their complaints, offer some words of encouragement, and move on. At other times, I encounter men who have legitimate needs, actual issues that require actual solutions. In this instance, words will not suffice.

As a man who has spent over two decades in prison, I can sympathize with both the complaints and issues I encounter daily; I have encountered them myself. I also know what needs to be done, but because I am an inmate myself, I am powerless to actually solve the needs of the population. I cannot even solve my own needs. Like everyone, I seek help outside of my own ability.

The author of Hebrews transitions from his exhortation to enter into God's rest to an exposition of Jesus' priestly role. Here the author introduces a theme which will continue throughout chapters 5-10. His aim is to establish the priestly authority of Christ and show his superiority as a priest over the Levitical priesthood. Jesus is a more effective priest because he both understands the struggle of the people and is able to provide solutions in their time of need.

Commentary

4:14-5:10

Throughout his sermon the author has alluded to Jesus' priesthood (1:3; 2:9, 11, 17; 3:1), now he turns his attention to focus on what will be a major theme throughout chapters 5-10: Jesus' priestly office. In verse 14, the author begins by tying the argument of his previous section to that of his current discourse. The discussion of Christ's priesthood is related to all that he has previously said. As a matter of fact, it is essential to all that his listeners have heard. In Hebrews 4:13, he stated that all men are exposed before the eyes of God and will be accountable for what is seen by God. Therefore, it would follow that all men will need a mediator to advocate on their behalf. As a result, in verse 14, the author introduces more fully Jesus' mediatorial role on behalf of the people. The peoples' advocate is the great high priest, Jesus the Son of God. By use of the various descriptive titles found in his introduction (Heb. 1:1-4), the author is able to connect the previous themes of his sermon.

The phrase "great high priest" is redundant and is similar to saying high, high priest, or great, great priest. This serves the author's theme of Jesus' superiority by elevating him above all other high priests.[147] Jesus is the G.O.A.T. (the greatest of all time*)*. He is not just another high priest, but he is the divinely appointed high priest of God. The believers' great high priest "has passed through the heavens." The author employs language that depicts Temple imagery. The Temple priests would pass in to the Holy of Holies to offer sacrifice and then return when his duties were complete. Jesus is said to enter into the heavens which is the

---

[147] Cockerill, *Hebrews*, 223.

true Holy of Holies, the place where God dwells. The author's use of "passed through" here conveys the sense of entrance and remaining.[148] Unlike other high priests, Jesus has entered the presence of God to offer sacrifice on behalf of the people and remains to advocate for them. Finally, Jesus is also referred to as the "Son of God." This statement points to his eternal status as Son who rules at the right hand of the Father. The author's detailed description of Jesus in this section sets the tone for all he will say about Christ's role as priest, sacrifice, and mediator of a better covenant.

In prison, if you need to get something done, you better ask an inmate. Inmates are assigned to virtually every department in prison, and more times than not, the inmate is "unofficially" calling the shots. If you need your toilet fixed, find the inmate plumber and he'll make it happen. If you are trying to take a chapel program, then ask the chaplain's clerk, and you will be in the next class. The inmate is the inmate's best advocate. He stands between one's need and access to the solution. Instead of wasting your time filling out that request form that will probably never get answered, just find your inmate advocate and watch things get done!

To conclude verse 14, the author adds a brief exhortation to hold fast to their confession. Here the author "urges tenacious endurance in Christian profession."[149] The idea is to continually stand on what they believe in the face of opposition. If they believe that Jesus, the Son of God, is their mediator as great high priest, they are to live in that reality. In verse 15, the author supports his exhortation to "hold fast" by reminding them of the nature of their high priest. First, he employs a double negative "we do not have

---

[148] Allen, *Hebrews*, 303.
[149] Cockerill, *Hebrews*, 224.

… who is not able." This serves to emphasize the superiority and sufficiency of Jesus as priest. The author also aims to answer a possible objection to Christ's inability to sympathize with the struggles of the believer. Jesus might rule from heaven, but because he took on flesh, suffered and died, he can sympathize with the weakness of humanity.

Jesus' ability to sympathize is related to the trials he faced in the flesh. Jesus experienced every temptation known to humanity. While this includes all types of temptation, the author most likely has the audience's current struggle in mind.[150] The first-century Christian experienced a great deal of social pressure and was commonly considered a social outcast. Jesus, as the Jewish Messiah, who ate with sinners and tax collectors, could sympathize with the struggle of social pressure. The Son of man came to his own people, but his own people did not receive him (John 1:10). What separates Jesus from all other great high priests is his sinlessness. In the face of hate and opposition Jesus "held fast" and remained sinless. Thus, he serves as an example for the struggling first-century believer.

One of the more encouraging aspects of prison is the numerous formerly incarcerated men and women who return to prison to share their stories of triumph. These men and women who once wore prison white and endured the struggles of prison life are now examples for the currently incarcerated. Their messages are always well received because they have walked in our shoes and overcome our struggles. They serve as examples of what one day we desire to achieve.

[150] Ibid., 226.

In verse 16, the author exhorts the believer to act on the information he has provided them with. He tells them to "draw near to the throne of grace" in confidence. For the Jewish Christian, this was an awe-inspiring statement. Never before was the worshipper encouraged to boldly enter the presence of God. As a matter of fact, tradition holds that the priest would tie a rope to himself and attach bells to his robes just in case something went wrong within the Holy of Holies. If the bells stopped sounding for a period of time, others could use the rope to drag the priest out of the Holy of Holies. No one was to enter with confidence. However, because Jesus "has passed through" and remains, he now awaits the believer's entrance into the presence of God. In God's presence, the believer "may receive mercy and find grace." The mercy of God assures believers that they have received forgiveness and have been set free from sin. God's grace not only signifies the believer's newfound favor but also empowers the believer to persevere through every trial and tribulation.[151] The author exhorts his listeners to approach God for help during their time of need. Grace and mercy stand in contrast to the judgment and persecution which the believer receives from the world. In the presence of God, the believer finds the favor of God.

---

[151] Cockerill, *Hebrews*, 228.

In verse 1 of chapter 5, the author begins a comparison of Jesus' priesthood with that of the Levitical priesthood. His comparison begins in verse 1, continues through verse 10, and forms a chiasm:

A: The function of the high priest. (5:1)
  B: The person of the high priest. (5:2-3)
    C: The appointment of the high priest. (5:4)
    C: The appointment of Jesus as the great High Priest (5:5-6)
  B: The person of Jesus as great High Priest. (5:7-8)
A: The function of Jesus as great high priest (5:9-10)[152]

The author begins by establishing a common rule of priesthood. Every priest, without exception, is "chosen from among men." This statement emphasizes the solidarity of the priestly office with the people they are called to represent. This statement also recalls God's command to Moses to bring Aaron and his sons "from among the people of Israel" to serve God as priests (Exod. 28:1). Priests represent humanity because they are chosen from among the people. The author desires to drive home the humanity of "every high priest" in order to compare them with the humanity of Jesus the "great high priest." The Levitical priest is chosen "out" of humanity, but Christ's priesthood is founded on his taking "on" humanity.[153] The purpose of the priesthood was "to act on behalf of men in relation to God." This was a very high calling. Among the Jewish people, the office of high priest was honored above all others. So once again, the author does not aim to denigrate Jewish religious beliefs or practices but seeks to

[152] Harris, *Hebrews*, 114; Witherington, *Letters and Homilies for Jewish Christians,* 196-197.
[153] Cockerill, *Hebrews*, 232.

elevate Jesus' priesthood as the ultimate fulfillment of the priestly office.[154] The role of the Levitical priesthood was to offer to God gifts and sacrifices for the sins of the people. Here the author is likely alluding to the Day of Atonement where the sin of the people was atoned for through sacrifice.[155] The author does not intend a distinction between types of gifts and sacrifices. Instead, he wants to emphasize the many offerings of the Levitical priesthood in comparison to the one self-offering of Jesus (Heb. 9:12). Jesus is the ultimate sacrifice, "The lamb of God who takes away the sins of the world" (John 1:29).

The author continues his description of the Levitical priesthood by highlighting its inadequacy to solve humanity's sin problem.[156] The priest is said to "deal gently with the ignorant and wayward." The sense of "deal gently" is to curb one's anger and frustration against the sinner.[157] The priest simply tolerated the weakness of the people without sympathy. Christ, however, is said to sympathize with the weakness of the people (Heb. 4:15). The distinction here is important. The priest's role was to represent the people before God. Yet the condition of their heart prevented them from doing this adequately. A comparison between Moses' and Jesus' reaction to the people reveals the distinction. Moses cried to the Lord, "What shall I do with this people?" (Exod. 17:4). Jesus, however, saw the people and had compassion for them because they were harassed and helpless, like sheep without a shepherd" (Matt. 9:36). Moses looked on the people with frustration, Jesus looked on them with compassion. The different reactions flow from different perspectives toward the people and

---

[154] Witherington, *Letters and Homilies for Jewish Christians,* 192-193.
[155] Lane, *Hebrews*, 116.
[156] Cockerill, *Hebrews*, 234.
[157] Moo, *Hebrews*, 159.

natures of the priest. The author refers to the people as "ignorant and wayward." This highlights humanity's tendency to wander astray through ignorance. This can be willful disobedience, like that of the wilderness generation, or unintentional sins which flow from ignorance of God's will.[158] This emphasizes the hopelessness of the peoples' condition and their absolute need of a mediator. Yet the Levitical priest "appointed to act on behalf of men" can only tolerate the ignorance of the people because "he himself is beset with weakness." The priest cannot offer a true solution to the peoples' problems because he also struggles with ignorance and disobedience. The phrase "beset with weakness" conveys the idea of being clothed with or surrounded by weakness.[159] Here the weakness of the priest is a burden that hinders the proper administration of their office. The author has carefully compared the natures of the different priests. One is ignorant, wayward, and in need of help, the other is sympathetic, tested, and without sin.

Ministry is difficult mainly because it involves people. The church is made up of born-again sinners who continually struggle with the sins of the past, present, and future. The minister's responsibility is to "deal gently" with the countless personalities and problems that exist in the body of Christ. This is an extremely difficult task, especially, when the people of God just can't seem to "get it." It is easy to grow frustrated. The solution to one's problem is both so close yet so far. This frustration is compounded by the fact that every minister struggles with their own sins. Pastors are human and do not always follow their own advice very well. This is why everyone, people and pastors, need an advocate.

---

[158] Koester, *Hebrews*, 286.
[159] Harris, *Hebrews*, 117; Guthrie, Hebrews, NIV, 188.

No one is without sin. Yet, Jesus, has done for the believer what they could not do for themselves. Life threw every type of temptation Jesus' way. He faced them all and was without sin. He accomplished this even for those who do not seem to "get it."

In verse 3, the author highlights the result of the priest's weakness: "He is obligated to offer sacrifice for his own sins." Once again, the comparison with Jesus' priesthood is clear. Jesus is "without sin" while the Levitical priest is required to sacrifice for "his own sins." The author highlights the inadequacy of the Old Testament priest by emphasizing the priest's need to deal with his own sins before the sins of the people. In the Old Testament, the priest was commanded to offer sacrifice on behalf of himself and his household, then on behalf of the people. Jesus, on the other hand, being sinless, can focus solely on the needs of the people. He is able to "help those who are being tempted" (Heb. 2:18). The author desires for his audience to understand the full sufficiency of Jesus' ministry. They may be struggling with the temptation to turn away from the faith, but their advocate has already achieved victory over their struggles. The author's listeners must continue to hold fast to their confidence in the face of their personal trials.

Verse 4 restates the truth of verse 1. No one claims the honor of the priesthood for himself. The Old Testament testifies to the divine appointment of the Levitical priests on numerous occasions (Exod. 28:1; Lev. 8:1; Num. 16:5). To be called by God for any purpose was a great honor but to be called to the priesthood was considered the highest of honors.[160] The author emphasizes the necessity of divine appointment to the priesthood before explaining how Jesus was called. If an individual was a true priest of God, it was because he had received a call from God to that

---

[160] Koester, *Hebrews*, 287.

office. However, the author establishes the authority of Jesus' calling with his use of Psalm 110:4.[161]

In verse 5, the author states that Christ also was appointed by God. However, the difference between the appointments is seen in the status of Jesus before his calling. The Levitical priest was appointed from among men. Jesus, however, was appointed as the eternal Son.[162] Where the office of priesthood was seen as an honor, for Christ, it was an honor bestowed in humility. The author emphasizes the grandeur of this appointment. The eternal Son took on flesh in order to become humanity's great high priest. In order to stress Jesus' sonship, the author once again cites Psalm 2:7. Jesus, the Son of God is superior to the angels (Heb. 1:5), humanity (Heb. 2:9), Moses (Heb. 3:6), and the Levitical priesthood (Heb. 5:5).

In verse 6, the author further emphasizes the superiority of Jesus' priesthood by discussing its lineage. He accomplishes this by citing Psalm 110:4, the most cited and allude to Psalm in Hebrews.[163] By connecting Psalm 110:4 with Psalm 2:7, the author aims to prove that Jesus' "priesthood is founded on his sonship."[164] This helps to accomplish three things: (1) Jesus is a legitimate priest like Aaron; (2) Jesus' priesthood is superior where the Levitical priesthood is inadequate; (3) Jesus' priesthood is more sufficient as God's Son.[165] By citing Psalm 110:4, the author likely aims to address an objection to Jesus' priesthood. Jesus does not descend from the line of Aaron, a requirement for becoming a priest. Psalm 110:4, which will be explained further

---

161 Cockerill, *Hebrews*, 237.
162 Ibid., 239.
163 Lane, *Hebrews*, 118.
164 Cockerill, *Hebrews*, 238.
165 Ibid., 239.

in chapter 7, provides the scriptural authority for Jesus' priestly office. Jesus is a priest forever according to the line of Melchizedek. The special lineage and time frame (forever) likely serves to emphasize the inadequacy of the Levitical priests. As the author will later stress, Melchizedek's priestly line precedes the Levitical line, and the eternal nature of Jesus' priesthood, supersedes the temporal aspects of the Levitical line. The Levites were "prevented by death from continuing in office" (Heb. 7:23).

Verses 7-8 are some of the most difficult to interpret passages because of the author's ambiguity in structure and word choice.[166] In this section, the author discusses the sacrifice offered by Christ which contrasts the Levitical priest's offering in Hebrews 5:1. The priest offers "gifts and sacrifices" but the Son offers "prayers and supplication." The priest's offering was for his sins and the sins of the people. Jesus' offering was for the deliverance from the grave. Many commentators have seen a connection between verse 7 and Jesus' prayer in the Garden of Gethsemane: "Being in agony he prayed more earnestly" (Luke 22:44; Matt. 26:39; Mark 14:36). While this connection is possible, it is not necessary to connect this verse with Jesus' agony in the Garden.[167] One of the major obstacles of the Gethsemane interpretation is the author of Hebrews' phrase, "He was heard because of his reverence" (Heb. 5:7). This seems to imply that Jesus' prayer was answered. However, in the Gethsemane account, Jesus asked God to deliver him from the death of crucifixion (Matt. 26:39-44), a prayer that was not answered. Gareth Cockerill recognizing the difficulty states, "It is better to see this entire verse as a depiction of the dependence upon God

[166] Allen, *Hebrews*, 320-322.
[167] Lane, *Hebrews*, 120.

that characterized the son's earthly life and came to its climax in Gethsemane and on the cross."[168] The Son's whole life was an offering of prayer and supplication to do the will of the Father. Therefore, the phrase, "who was able to save him from death" is not a reference to save Jesus from the cross but most likely is an appeal to raise him from the grave.[169] This is the climax of the Gospel message. Jesus' "reverence" for the Father was displayed in his obedience to the cross. Paul also emphasizes this point when he states that Jesus was obedient to the point of death resulting in his exaltation to the right hand of the Father (Phil. 2:8-9).

As believers, many of our prayers go unanswered. This can be difficult to grasp, especially in the face of some trial or tribulation. We can begin to question the love of God and his will for our lives. It is during these times that we must remember that God is sovereignly working out "all things" for our benefit (Rom. 8:28). At times, we may not be able to see God's plan clearly, but this is when we must pray as Jesus did: "Father your will be done" (Mark 14:36).

Both verses 8-9 speak of Jesus' faithful fulfillment of his priestly duties. The author's statement that the Son "learned obedience" cannot be understood to imply a previous disobedience but should be understood in a similar way of being made perfect as mentioned above (see Heb. 2:10).[170] Allen states, "We thus conclude that Jesus entered into the high priestly office upon completion of the atonement made by his death on the cross and his resurrection ascension/exaltation to the right hand of

---

[168] Cockerill, *Hebrews*, 244.
[169] Koester, *Hebrews*, 288.
[170] Moo, *Hebrews*, 165.

God."[171] Thus as the incarnate Christ, the great high priest, he has added to obedience, a more perfect obedience. Jesus' obedience came while covered in the weakness of human flesh. Although he was a Son, he suffered the humility of the cross becoming the source of eternal salvation. The temporary, often repeated sacrifice of the priest, pales in comparison to the eternal one time offering of the Son. By qualifying the recipients of "eternal salvation" as "all who obey," the author reminds his listeners that obedience in the face of persecution is the example set before them. Christ who is the Son of God was obedient to the point of death. Their sacrifice of obedience pales in comparison. The author's emphasis of the obedience of Jesus and the obedience of the believer is vital to the success of his listeners. They may have grown weary in their journey of faith, but they must not lose hope. Jesus, their great high priest also grew weary but persevered. His suffering provided complete access to eternal salvation.[172] The believer's responsibility is to walk in his footsteps. This does not mean deliverance from the trials of this life, but Jesus' obedience guarantees a place for the faithful in the life to come. This is why Paul reminds his listeners of the importance of the death, burial, and resurrection. Since Jesus was raised from the dead, the believer has hope of eternal salvation (1 Cor. 15:1-19).

Finally, the author draws to conclusion his comparison between Jesus and the Levitical priesthood. Every priest is chosen from among men, but Jesus is designated "high priest" by God. The author intentionally changes the reference of Psalm 110:4 from simple "priest" to "high priest" to once again elevate the special status of the Son. Every simple priest descends from the

[171] Allen, *Hebrews*, 331.
[172] Cockerill, *Hebrews*, 250.

line of Aaron, but God's special high priest is designated after the order of Melchizedek.[173] The author appeals to Psalm 110:4 to justify the end of the old priesthood and establish the permanence and effectiveness of the new.[174]

Application

THE COST OF MINISTRY

As believers, we sometimes dive into the ministry with little thought. We do not consider the grave responsibility of caring for the needs of others. We set our expectations so high that it often hurts when we fall. The ministry is a special calling that requires the total commitment of the believer and the blessing of God. Without these two aspects, our ministry will not be successful. I have seen men totally committed to a ministry of preaching but lacked the blessing of God. Their true gift lied elsewhere. I have also seen anointed ministers who lacked total commitment. Their heart was not in it. Caring for God's people requires putting the needs of others first. Stop and consider the true cost of ministry. Read Luke 9:23-24 and Matt. 10:34-39. Ask yourself if you are prepared to forsake all to follow Jesus.

---

[173] Cockerill, *Hebrews, 250.*
[174] Ibid., 251.

TRUSTING IN THE WILL OF GOD

With our mouths we say, "I believe in the will of God for my life." Yet our actions often say something totally different. We pray that God will move in our lives, but when he does, we move in a different direction. I have met men who have prayed for an opportunity to go to Bible College, but when the opportunity arrived, they declined because they did not want to transfer to a new unit. This is why it is essential that believers search the Scripture to understand God's will for their lives. We must learn to trust in God's plan for our lives, so when doors open, we are prepared to step through them. Read James 4:1-3 and ask yourself if you are praying in accordance with God's will for your life.

2. *The Necessity of Spiritual Maturity (5:11-6:12)*

Prisoner's Insight for the Journey

Let's be real, living out one's Christian principles is difficult, especially in an unchristian environment. In most secular settings, Christians are seen as narrow-minded social outcasts with archaic, uninformed beliefs. Our faith is not seen as practical for the "real world." So sometimes, in order to be accepted we will compromise our principles, especially in the face of opposition. Failure to live out one's faith, regardless of the circumstances, is a sign of immaturity. The believer is called to live "in" but not be a product "of" the world. This means whatever the circumstances, believers are to stand on their principles.

This remains true even for believers held captive in this concrete jungle where anything can happen at any moment. In prison, the Christian's desire to live for Christ is often seen as a sign of weakness or fear. As a result of this, they become objects of ridicule and persecution. However, how believers respond to social pressure ultimately defines their level of maturity. Mature believers are able to discern the situation and act in accordance with their beliefs. Maturity will only come through practicing one's faith, or "holding fast" to one's confession. Believers cannot expect to mature if they resort to immaturity at every test and trial. If believers desire to "go on to maturity" then they must leave behind their immature principles.

In Hebrews, the believers are failing to "hold fast" to what they believe in the face of social pressure. As a result of persecution, they want to return to an immature understanding of the faith, they are acting like children. The author employs some of the harshest language possible to redirect their focus toward mature principles. The author knows that there is not a permanent solution in their former beliefs. He desires for them to move on to maturity in Christ.

Commentary

5:11-14

In verse 11, the author transitions from his exposition of Christ's priesthood to an exhortation geared toward maturity. He has spent a great deal of time expounding the superiority of Christ over all created beings and offices. He desires to continue his exposition but first feels the need to grab his listener's attention. The author achieves this by employing elements of shame and irony.[175]

The author's phrase, "much to say" anticipates the large amount of teaching on the priesthood of Christ still to come in his sermon.[176] The importance of this subject is evident by the amount of space the author dedicates to the topic. Up to this point, he has referenced Christ's priestly office and its many benefits for the believer at various stages in his sermon. However, beginning at chapter 7, he will go on an extended explanation of the priesthood of Jesus. The author also states that his teaching will be "hard to explain." This difficulty derives from two important aspects: the nature of Jesus' priesthood and the recipient's spiritual condition.[177] The idea of Jesus' priesthood finding its origin in Melchizedek instead of Aaron would be foreign to believers with

---

[175] Lane, *Hebrews*, 135; Witherington, *Letters and Homilies for Jewish Christians,* 204.
[176] Moo, *Hebrews*, 172-73.
[177] Moo, *Hebrews*, 173.

a Jewish background. However, in light of the author's previous allusions to this topic, it is most likely not the first time his audience has been introduced to the subject. Therefore, the greater difficulty is the listeners' spiritual condition.[178] The author states that they have "become dull of hearing." The idea here is that the audience had once been receptive but because of some change in circumstances they have stopped listening.[179] However, "dull of hearing" also implies a failure to heed what is said.[180] The hearers are displaying an unwillingness to act on or live in accordance with the truths the author has shared. He has already appealed to them to "pay much closer attention" to what they have heard (Heb. 2:1), now once again he calls for their complete attention. The author's continual call to listen reflects his emphasis on correct understanding leading to correct actions. When believers stop learning they stop growing and often regress. The disobedience of the wilderness generation is a perfect example. When they stopped listening to God and Moses, they remained in the wilderness.

In verse 12, the author employs an element of shame by appealing to the level of the spiritual maturity of his listeners. "By this time, you ought to be teachers" signifies that the author's subject matter is not new. The frustration of the author is evident: "How many times must I tell you these things before you will grasp them?"[181] They should at this point be sharing the truths of this sermon with others. The goal of all learning is the ability to share the blessing of wisdom with others. The listeners are not only hindering their personal growth but likely also stunting the potential growth of others. They should be teachers. Instead, they

---

[178] Cockerill, *Hebrews*, 255.
[179] Allen, *Hebrews*, 335.
[180] Koester, *Hebrews*, 301.
[181] Cockerill, *Hebrews*, 256.

are still in need of an instructor. The role of the teacher is to oversee the student's growth in knowledge and to serve as a guide along the journey of learning. Paul in the letter to the Galatians states that the Law served as a "guardian until Christ came" (Gal. 3:24). This means that the Law was guiding the people to a certain point, faith in Christ, but once that point is reached, the Law is no longer necessary. There is nothing further to learn under the Law. The same is true for "the basic principles of the oracles of God." Once the ABC's of the faith have been learned, it is time to move on.[182] However, due to their lack of application of the basics, the listeners are acting as if they need another lesson.

The basic principles are most likely listed in Hebrews 6:1-2 (washings, resurrection, eternal life … etc.). However, the author likely intends to include the audience's beginning instruction of the faith. He is telling them they are behaving as if they need to start at day one. "Basic principles" also contrast with the advanced teaching of Jesus' priesthood. The basic principles are milk designated for the immature believer. The priesthood of Jesus is solid food intended for mature believers who are capable of digesting doctrines of substance. Paul uses a similar phrase in 1 Corinthians 3:1-4 when he chastises the immaturity of his audience. The author employs shame in order to move his listeners to correct action.[183] This is evident because he never actually revisits the basic principles but moves forward to more mature teachings.[184] The author desires for his audience to live out what they have already learned. There is no need to move forward until they prove they can apply what they have previously received. The milk of basic principles keeps the believer "unskilled in the word

---

[182] Cockerill, *Hebrews*, 257.
[183] Ibid., 257.
[184] Witherington, *Letters and Homilies for Jewish Christians,* 206-207.

of righteousness." The word "unskilled" conveys the sense of inexperienced and "word of righteousness" alludes to the moral ability to distinguish right from wrong.[185] This phrase points to the listeners' failure to apply what they have learned. They are faced with opposition, and instead of standing firm in the faith, they are acting as if they have no faith at all. They must understand the full sufficiency of Jesus lest they revert back to former social and religious practices.[186]

The mature, on the other hand, digest teachings of substance which results in living out what they have learned. The author states that the mature have "powers of discernment" which enable them to "distinguish good from evil." The ability to discern between correct and incorrect behavior is essential for Christian living. The author's audience is reacting incorrectly by allowing social pressure to influence their actions. Cockerill states that mature believers "are able to discern and follow what is true and conducive to a life of faithful obedience while detecting and spurning every hindrance."[187] This is only possible if believers hone their abilities with training and "constant practice" by living in a constant state of readiness. The believer must "stay ready" to keep from having to "get ready." The idea of "trained" implies to train oneself. This means that it is the believers' responsibility to practice obedience.[188] True obedience is reflected in one's choice between "good and evil" or simply making the right choice when it matters most.[189] The author's connection between maturity and the ability to discern good from evil is reminiscent of Solomon's

---

[185] Allen, *Hebrews*, 337.
[186] Cockerill, *Hebrews*, 258-259.
[187] Cockerill, *Hebrews*, 259.
[188] Allen, *Hebrew*, 338.
[189] Guthrie, *Hebrews*, NIV, 203-204.

prayer for wisdom. Solomon compared himself to a child and asked God to enable him to discern between good and evil. God granted Solomon's request and he was considered one of the wisest men ever. (1 Kings 3:7-9). However, later in life, Solomon regressed. He failed to do what the author of Hebrews is calling his listeners to achieve; to live in a constant state of faithful readiness.

Prison is an unpredictable place full of unpredictable people. This means you must stay ready for any situation you might quickly find yourself in. I personally keep a lockdown bag of supplies just in case movement on my unit is suddenly restricted.[190] Preparations such as these are easy for most people. The more difficult challenge is staying both mentally and spiritually ready for whatever might come your way. This requires a little more preparation. I read, study, and pray every day to keep myself mentally and spiritually sharp. You may not be able to control certain circumstances, but you can absolutely control how you react to them.

A Note on Hebrews 6

Hebrews 6:1-4 contains some of the most difficult to interpret and passionately debated verses in all of Hebrews. The issue surrounds the eternal security/ loss of salvation debate.[191]

---

[190] The Texas Department of Criminal Justice institutes bi-annual "lockdowns" in order to search their facilities for contraband. During this time, the majority the inmates' movement is restricted, and they are fed sack lunches in their living area. The sack lunches consist of a PBJ sandwich and a mystery meat sandwich. Therefore, most inmates who have served any lengthy amount of time keep a bag stocked with extra food in order to supplement the poor meals they are forced to eat on lockdown. This is a "lockdown" bag!

[191] For a survey of the five major views of Hebrew 6 see, Allen, *Hebrews*, 370-77.

Historically there have been two main positions held by scholars with numerous variations. First, the loss of salvation advocates hold that Hebrews 6:1-4 is addressing genuine believers who are at risk of losing their salvation if they do not persevere to the end.[192] *Next, the eternal security group holds that these verses are not addressing believers but actually describe people who were never "really" saved which is evidenced by their falling away, or failure to persevere to the end. While both sides of the debate make strong points, they also most likely make Hebrews 6 say more than the author originally intended. The issue of the security of a believer's salvation is a later theological debate that many scholars read back into the text.*[193] *Here, the author addresses the maturity of the believer and perseverance in the faith, and both positions would agree that mature believers persevere to the end.*

A better way to approach Hebrews 6 is by attempting to discern what the author intended for his words to accomplish, after all, Hebrews is a sermon or word of exhortation intended for a specific audience with specific issues. Therefore, by understanding what the author was attempting to achieve, the modern interpreter/reader will be in a better position to apply this text to their current situation. Hebrews is a sermon written to a specific audience with whom the author is familiar. The letter appears to be addressing a group of Jewish Christians who were receiving persecution as a result of their faith possibly resulting in a desire to return to Judaism. Therefore, the author wrote to encourage believers to persevere in the face of opposition.

Several points can be drawn from the previous summary. First, Hebrews is an ancient sermon or word of exhortation that

---

[192] See Cockerill, *Hebrews*

[193] Moo, *Hebrews*, 184.

has no parallel in the New Testament. The sermonic nature of the letter is evidenced by its structure and content. Unlike other New Testament letters, it lacks an introduction, even though it was written to a specific audience. The literary style of the letter also shows that is was intended to be read aloud. Finally, its exposition of key Old Testament texts followed by exhortations fits the structure of ancient sermons.[194]

Second, Hebrews addresses a people and situation with which the author is familiar. This is supported by several internal pieces of evidence. The author reminds his audience of "former days" in which they were persecuted (Heb. 10:32). This shows he is familiar with their past. He also understands their current state of mind and their need of correction (Heb. 5:11). Finally, he mentions Timothy as "our brother" showing an intimate knowledge and relationship with the people of this community (Heb. 13:23).[195] *This supports the position that the author believed he was addressing a group of Christians. The author was fully aware of his audience's spiritual state. He is not encouraging them to enter the faith but persevere in the face of opposition.*

Furthermore, the author is addressing Jewish Christians who are struggling to break with Jewish practices. This point is one of the most important and difficult aspects to grasp, especially for the modern reader. First, a Jewish Christian is usually understood to be a person who was born a Jew or converted to Judaism and subsequently believed that Jesus was the Messiah. Thus, many of the earliest followers of Jesus like Peter, Matthew, and Paul would be considered Jewish Christians. Support for this view is seen in the author's assumption that his listeners will

---

[194] D. Guthrie, *New Testament Introduction*, 712-15.
[195] Ibid., 683-84.

understand the specifics of the Old Testament's religious practices. The author mentions the Tabernacle, priesthood, and sacrificial practices without feeling the need to further explain these rites.[196]

Moreover, there was not a clean break between the practices of Judaism and Christianity. The very need to compare Jesus to the practices of Judaism shows that there were at least still attempts at assimilation of the faiths. The author goes to great lengths to show the superiority of Jesus in regards to Jewish religious practices. This is why the author appeals to his listeners to go to Jesus "outside the camp" which is a reference of their need to separate from Judaism (Heb. 13:13). Once again, the author is not attempting to degrade Judaism. He does not offer an apologetic against Judaism but argues for the continuity of the faiths. The recipients are part of the one people of God. The author's emphasis is on the new way God has revealed himself through Jesus in the last days. Christianity is not superior to Judaism but stands as the fulfillment of all God desired to do under the Old Covenant. Therefore, Jesus is sufficient for all the people's needs, and an assimilation of Jewish practices is unnecessary.[197]

Finally, the purpose of the letter was to exhort believers to persevere. The audience was not hearing the author's teaching for the first time. They were familiar with many of the sermon's doctrines. Their issue was a failure to apply what they had heard to their current situation. They had failed to move on to maturity. Therefore, like many sermons, its purpose was to encourage believers to live out their faith. New Testament sermons usually

---

[196] D. Guthrie, *New Testament Introduction,*684.
[197] Cockerill, *Hebrews*, 23.

contain a few essential elements. First, an Old Testament text or story is presented. This is followed by an explanation of how Jesus fulfilled that text. Finally, the sermon ends with a call to action (Acts 2:14-39; 7:1-53). This structure is clearly seen throughout Hebrews. For example, Hebrews chapter 1 cites numerous Old Testament Scriptures and references how Jesus fulfilled them. Then in chapter 2, the author calls his listeners to pay much closer attention to what has been said. Sermons also use various types of rhetorical devices in order to grab their listener's attention: alliteration, similes, metaphors, hyperbole, shame, sarcasm, and irony.[198] *For example, the author employs five words in his first sentence that begin with the letter "P" in the original Greek (Heb. 1:1). This is an example of alliteration. The presence of these literary devices in Hebrews 6 is fundamental to discerning the author's intent. In the following verses, the author uses exaggerated speech in order to grab his listener's attention before focusing on the topic of Christ's Priesthood.*[199] *The author is telling them to stop being babies, grow up, and weather the storm.*

Commentary

6:1-12

In the previous section, the author has employed shame by comparing his listeners' spiritual state to that of infants in need of milk.[200] As Moo states, the author writes "to scold his audience for failing to progress."[201] The verses show that the author was employing exaggerated speech because now he encourages his

---

[198] Lane, "Hebrews," In *Dictionary of the Later New Testament and Its Developments*. Edited by Ralph P. Martin and Peter Davids. (Downers Grove: Intervarsity Press, 1997), 451.
[199] G. Guthrie, *Hebrews*, NIV, 207.
[200] Lane, *Hebrews*, WBC, 135.
[201] Moo, *Hebrews*, 170.

listeners to move on to more mature ideas by leaving behind "the elementary doctrine of Christ." If the author truly believed he was addressing babies in the faith then moving on to greater truths would be pointless. Their advancement to maturity is achieved by "not laying again a foundation" of basic instructions. The author understands that knowledge about Christ is not his listeners' issue. They are believers who know the basic gospel message. His audience struggles from an inability to apply what they know to their current situation. The foundation has been laid, now the author desires to build upon it a deeper understanding. The recipients are infants because they are living as if they only have a basic understanding of Christ. For the author, the more you know, the more equipped you are to deal with struggles.

"Repentance from dead works" most likely points to the syncretism found in early Christianity that resulted from Christians still adhering to Jewish practices. For Christianity, it is not what you "do" that provides access to God, but it is what you "believe" that defines the relationship. This is emphasized through the author's next statement: faith in God. One of the foundational truths of early Christianity was the transition from the works of the Law to faith in God. This was the emphasis of many of the Apostle Paul's letters. The early church struggled to break away from the practices of the Mosaic Law. Therefore, it would make sense that any group of believers, especially those of a Jewish background, would have been taught about repentance from dead works early in their instruction of the faith.

Prison can incarcerate more than the body it can also imprison the mind. This is why the penitentiary is full of gray-haired babies, men who in their 30's, 40's, and 50's still act like teenagers. They have failed to leave behind the elementary principles of their youth. This arrested development often results in the same behavioral issues which brought them to prison. They have not learned to embrace new and positive ideas which lead to success. They think and act the same way they did 20 years ago. However, in order to mature in any area of life, one must leave the old immature ways behind. This requires a person to acknowledge their immaturity and embrace a desire to change. A gray-haired child might be able to survive in prison where every decision is made for them and their daily needs are met, but the free world has no tolerance for gray-haired babies. So put away the bottles filled with the milk of immaturity and pick up a plate of the solid food of success.

In verse 2, the author lists four instructions that were "elementary teachings." The first is "washings" or "baptisms." This statement is difficult to understand and has led to a great deal of speculation. Most likely the author is referring to the various practices of ritual cleansing within Judaism and the teachings that distinguished them from the rite of Christian baptism.[202] This would be reminiscent of Apollos' instruction concerning baptism in Acts 18:24-28. Any Jewish convert would naturally be concerned with ritual purity. Jesus addressed this issue with the Pharisees in Luke 11:37-41. It is as if the author is telling his audience, "We have already addressed this issue, and we are not going to address it again." The mature believer is to look forward to the mature teachings of Christ. This would continue the theme of the author's desire to set Jesus and Christianity in a superior light in relation to Judaism. The mature would leave these issues behind and move toward a greater understanding of God. The author also highlights the laying on hands which is symbolic of

[202] Cockerill, *Hebrews*, 266.

the imparting of the Holy Spirit. This is often tied closely to the baptism.[203] Therefore, if the author had the superiority of Christian baptism in mind when he discussed "washings," the laying on of hands would closely follow in any foundational instruction. The next pair of teachings is also closely related. Resurrection of the dead was a major issue in Judaism and early Christianity. The Jewish sects of the Pharisees and Sadducees were divided on the issue. The Sadducees denied the resurrection which often became a point of contention in the New Testament (Matt 22:23; Acts 4:2; 17:18, 32; 23:6). In Christianity, the timing and manner of the resurrection was debated as seen in Paul's numerous attempts to address the subject (1 Cor. 15; 1 Thess. 4:14-18). Closely related to the resurrection is the idea of judgment. This most likely would concern the general resurrection of all people and the various fates between those in Christ and those that are not.[204] The previous list likely outlines issues with which the early church dealt, especially churches that consisted of Jewish Christians. The break from Jewish practices, a major part of the Jewish Christian's life, would have been difficult. Therefore, instruction in the differences would have certainly been foundational for the early church. The author had previously proclaimed the basic message of Christianity from beginning to end. They should be living out the basics of the faith. As Koester has noted, the author "spans the journey of faith from initial repentance to final judgment."[205] There should be no need to go backwards.

Verse 3 provides a statement that is often glossed over by many commentators.[206] However, from the standpoint of moving

---

[203] Moo, *Hebrews*, 180.
[204] Allen, *Hebrews*, 343.
[205] Koester, *Hebrews*, 311.
[206] Allen, *Hebrews*, 343.

on to maturity, this statement provides some clarity. Here the author acknowledges the sovereignty of God in the maturity process. The listeners' maturity comes through the power and will of God.[207] The Apostle Paul also confirms this process when he states, "I am sure of this, that he who began a good work in you will bring it to completion at the day of Jesus Christ" (Phil. 1:6). Those who take the loss of salvation position on Hebrews 6, must reconcile verses such as the ones above with their position. If God is active in the process of salvation, as these verses clearly teach, then who is responsible for the loss of salvation? The author of Hebrews is clear, if believers are to grow from infants to adults in the faith, it will be by the grace of God. If the Church is going to persevere in the face of opposition, it will only be by the power of God.[208]

It is baffling how some new believers seem to mature in the faith overnight while others often seem not to mature at all. New believers attend the same church and sit under the same teaching, yet their growth is vastly different. We often place the responsibility to mature on new believers and cast judgment when they fail to grow according to our standard. However, maturity is both the work of the believer and God. The believer is responsible for absorbing all that God gives, but God is responsible for how and when his lessons are applied to the believer's life. Have you ever come across a verse that you have read a thousand times, but suddenly in that particular moment it is exactly what you need to hear in order to deal with a certain issue. Furthermore, the verse now becomes a principle by which you live. This is what the Bible means by God's living, active word. God addresses the issues in

[207] Moo, *Hebrews*, 181.
[208] Lane, *Hebrews*, 141.

our lives in his time. So the next time you think about judging another's growth, remember God brings people along at his pace not yours.

Verse 4 begins the most difficult section in all the Hebrews. Understanding this section is vital to the interpretation of the whole letter. As previously mentioned, many biblical scholars have attempted to make these verses to say more than the original author intended and most likely more than any Christian would affirm.[209] The key idea of these verses is found in the statement, "It is impossible … to restore to repentance." Every other phrase in verses 4-6 modifies or adds meaning to this core statement.[210] For example, scholars who take the loss of salvation perspective hone in and emphasize the phrase, "it is impossible … for those … who have shared in the Holy Spirit … then have fallen away … to restore them again to repentance." They argue that the author is describing a true believer's "apostasy." However, this phrase should cause problems for all Christians.[211] At what point is a person unable to repent? The author of Hebrews views salvation as what takes place at the end of the believer's journey. So, the loss of salvation position, must answer the question, "At what point during the journey is it too late to repent?"

Other commentators argue that this section does not refer to true believers. However, this understanding is also problematic. They are a group of people who have "been enlightened." This means they have seen the truth of Christianity. They have "tasted the heavenly gift" and "shared in the Holy Spirit" (Heb. 2:4). They have "tasted the goodness of the word of God," and "of the age to

---

[209] Allen, *Hebrews*, 371.

[210] Ibid., 346.

[211] See Moo's "Theology in Application Section," *Hebrews*, 208-09.

come" which looks forward to the future resurrection. That these verses describe anything less than true believers is unfathomable.[212] Numerous commentators have pointed out, if this statement was found in Romans or Ephesians, then it would definitely be describing a true believer.

So, what is the author attempting to accomplish? Here the author uses hyperbole to grab his listeners' attention in order to encourage them to shake off their dullness of hearing and move on from immaturity.[213] He accomplishes this by giving a precise description of who they are. They have been enlightened, shared in the Holy Spirit, and tasted the goodness of the word of God. The listeners heard the author's description and said to themselves, "that's me." However, in verse 6, the author slaps his listeners with the phrase "then have fallen away." For the listeners who possibly entertained the idea of retuning to Judaism, the author had just stated the impossible possibility. How could any believer who fits the previous description fall away? It would be like suddenly trying to believe that 2+2=3. The author strengthens his hyperbolic language by inserting the unbiblical idea of the impossibility of repentance. Repentance was available even to the thief on the cross. Now the author employs shame by stating that to turn away would be to re-crucify Christ which is most definitely exaggerated language.

While many readers will scoff at this interpretation, any person who has ever delivered a sermon knows that at times the use of hyperbolic language is essential. As a minister inside the

---

[212] Cockerill, *Hebrews*, 269.

[213] The position presented here is similar to the "Means of Salvation View" in Thomas Schreiner and Ardel Caneday, *The Race Set Before Us: A Biblical Theology of Perseverance and Assurance* (Downers Grove: InterVarsity), 2001.

walls of a maximum-security prison, I know first-hand the effectiveness of a little hyperbole and shame. I preach to transformed criminals from the position of a man who has been transformed himself. I have used harsh language to speak to a group of once harsh men on numerous occasions. I have told my congregation that if they do not mature in prison, they will die in the streets. I tell them if they turn their back on Christ, one day, he will turn his back on them. When I say these things, my intention is not to teach Systemic Theology but to preach using rhetoric. I do not predict the death or final judgment of my congregation. I am not a prophet. I am a preacher; a pastor concerned for his flock. My father once told me that if I did not change my ways he would kill me! I never once believed his threat to be true, but it often caused me to correct my behavior.

In verse 7, the author uses an illustration to further emphasize his point. The people are like a piece of land that receives its blessing (rain) from God. People can naturally react to God's blessings in numerous ways. Here, the mature believer who has received the blessing of "solid food" produces the fruit of a mature believer. This person shows that they have moved beyond the elementary teachings of the faith based on how they live their lives in the face of struggles. The immature believer, who prefers the milk, produces the crop of the immature—thorns and thistles. The author continues his warning through his illustration by showing that both the mature and immature believer produces crops. One is a "useful" crop and the other is "worthless." His point is that those who are failing to produce the fruit of perseverance are in danger of "being cursed." Again, as the following section will show, the author is not saying that this is the reality of his audience but using hyperbolic speech in order to keep them on the right path.[214]

In verse 9, the author shows he is using hyperbolic speech by softening his language. "Though we speak in this way" is a clear reference to the hyperbolic speech of the previous section. However, instead of being apostates who bear thorns and thistles, the author refers to his audience as "beloved." A group of believers that he feels sure will receive "better things—things that belong to salvation." In verse 10, the author provides the grounds for his confidence in the believer; God is just. The Hebrews must remember that their faith and assurance rests in the character of God. This echoes the author's understanding from Hebrews 6:3. God is sovereign over the believer's maturity and ultimate salvation. It is the God of their fathers who started them on their path to maturity and final rest. It is the same God who will see them through to the end. They are not to grow weary in doing well but continue "serving the saints" as before. Their continual service is evidence of their maturity and proves that they have moved to "solid food" producing "useful" crops.

Pressure from outside the church can also cause believers to lose focus on their ultimate goal of entering God's rest. The author's listeners are suffering a new set of circumstances resulting in persecution. Therefore, he desires that they show the same endurance as before in all aspects of the faith. They must remain consistent regardless of their situation. The church always runs the danger of growing complacent waiting on the return of the Lord. The journey of faith is defined by hills and valleys, days of peace and days of tribulation, but it is the same God who accompanies the believer during all phases of life. In verse 12, the

[214] Moo, *Hebrews*, 196-99.

author concludes his section by returning to a theme from Hebrews 5:11. Previously, the author chastised his audience because they had "become dull of hearing." In Hebrews 6:12, the author employs the same phrase (dull of hearing) which the ESV translates as "sluggish." Thus, the author begins by shaming them for their sluggishness (Heb. 5:11-14), then moves to warn them through hyperbolic language (Heb. 6:1-8), and concludes by encouraging them to not to be sluggish "but imitators of those who through faith and patience inherit the promise" (Heb. 6:9-12).[215] As a result, it becomes clear that the author is not attempting to provide his listeners with a systematic understanding of the doctrine of salvation. The author's primary concern is to arrest any signs of faithlessness which this group may be experiencing as a result of outside pressure. The mature Christian who is fed solid food bears good fruit in their service to the saints. They are not to grow sluggish while serving the kingdom of God but are called to imitate the heroes of faith that have proceeded them in the struggle to obtain God's rest. The church should always remember that it is the sure character of a just God who enables them to receive the inheritance of his sure and just promises.

Application

MOVING ON TO MATURITY

Christian growth and maturity is often hard to measure. Sometimes believers appear to grow quickly, while at other times, they almost seem to move backwards. Take the time to consider your growth in light of what you have learned from this section. Have you grown "dull of hearing" as a result of some unfortunate situation or are you bearing fruit that is "useful" for the kingdom

[215] Moo, *Hebrews*, 169.

of God? Read the Parable of the Sower in Matthew 13 and consider how you have responded to the word of God. Is the word bearing fruit or are the cares of the world robbing you of your peace?

APPLYING WHAT YOU HAVE LEARNED

Maturity is about applying to your life what you have learned about the faith. Many times, believers are content with knowing just the elementary doctrines of Christ. However, the basic doctrines only prepare you to deal with basic issues. While you do not have to be a theologian to be a mature Christian, understanding the deeper things of God can help you weather greater storms. Take the time to dig deeper into the word of God. You will be amazed at how a full understanding of the sovereignty of God can help you deal with some of the greatest struggles that you will encounter. God's word is living and active. It has all the answers to all your struggles. But like any instruction manual, you must read what it says in order to assemble your life correctly.

3. The Reliability of God's Character and Promises (6:13-20)

Prisoner's Insight for the Journey

In prison we swear by anything and everything in order to validate the genuineness of our word. If we are honest, this most likely results from our dishonest pasts and our previous dealings with dishonest people; we have all lied and we have all been lied to. So, in order to counter the distrustful nature of ourselves and others, we swear on some of the strangest things. We swear by our mommas, our hoods, and on everything we love in order to convince our listeners that we are telling the truth. The problem is that mere oaths cannot bring about genuine action. We can swear by everything we love, but then in our next action break our oath. We are broken people trying to convince other broken people that this time we can be trusted. We believe our silly oaths can do this. We fail to realize that genuine action derives from genuine character, something we all struggle with. However, this is not the case with God. When God swears, he does not swear because of his dishonest past or dealings with dishonest people. God does not lie nor has he ever been caught off guard by a lie. God swears from his perfection, his genuine character. When God swears, his oath is sure and unchangeable, because his very nature is sure and unchangeable. God's oath does not validate his character; his character validates his oath. As a result, God swears so that a distrustful people, "might have strong encouragement to hold fast to the hope" that is set before them. God's oaths are our comfort.

The author is attempting to convince his listeners that God's promise of salvation has not changed. His audience has begun to question the promises of God for their lives in the face of persecution. They are failing to hold fast to the hope they once had and are in danger of turning away from the living God. The author encourages them to persevere by reminding them of the promises God made to Abraham. God promised to bless and multiply Abraham's descendants but then suddenly challenges Abraham's faith by requiring him to sacrifice the fulfillment of God's promise. The author wants his listeners to know that God's promises sometimes come with obstacles but if they will focus on the character of the one who promises instead of the character of their circumstances, they will have "a sure and steadfast anchor of the soul."

Commentary

6:13-20

The author ties verse 13 to verse 12 by reuse of the word "promise." The standard for how God's promises are obtained is exemplified in the life of Abraham. For the author, Abraham is the perfect example of what faith, patience, and God's just character looks like. The author begins this section by grounding God's promises in his very nature. When God swore an oath, he could only swear by himself because nothing greater existed. The author appeals to Genesis 22:16 and the account of Abraham's sacrifice of Isaac.[216] God had promised to give Abraham and Sarah a child in their old age. In the face of many obstacles, God upholds his promise and Sarah gives birth to Isaac. Isaac becomes the promised child through whom God would bless all people. However, in a test of Abraham's faith God commands Abraham to sacrifice Isaac his beloved son. Abraham moved by faith and obedience to God prepares to sacrifice Isaac. But before Abraham

---

[216] Moo, *Hebrews*, 214-15.

could continue, God stops him and states: "By myself I have sworn, declares the Lord, because you have done this and have not withheld your son your only son, I will surely bless you and multiply you" (Gen. 22:16-17). The author of Hebrews uses this story to highlight two important aspects of the believers' relationship with God: their faithful patience and God's unchangeable nature. Abraham after finally receiving the promise of God through Isaac was now willing to sacrifice the promise. The author states that Abraham so trusted in the promise of God to multiply his seed through Isaac that if he did sacrifice him God would be able to raise him from the dead (Heb.11:19). The listeners are called to imitate Abraham's faith and patience even when it is being tested by the inconceivable. They can rest assured that if God has provided the promise of an ultimate rest in his presence that this rest still remains and is obtainable even in the face of their trials. If Abraham obtained the promise, they can also.[217]

In verse 16, the author appeals to his audience's understanding of oath taking. Oaths in the ancient world were used "to bolster the veracity of one's claims."[218] So many people would swear by some deity. Jesus, in the Gospels, provides an example of people swearing by heaven which is the throne of God (Matt. 5:33-36). The author of Hebrews argues that oaths are always sworn on something superior to the oath maker. An oath made on someone or something greater was deemed "final for confirmation." There was no need for contracts and witnesses because one's honor was at stake and God was the ultimate witness. In verse 17, the author correlates this understanding with

---

[217] Cockerill, *Hebrews*, 285.

[218] D.R. McCabe, "Oaths and Swearing" In *Dictionary of Jesus and the Gospels* (Downers Grove: InterVarsity Press), 629.

God's oath making. The difference, however, exists in the ultimate nature of the one who is making the promise. The surety of God's promise rests on two unchangeable things: his character, and the oath itself. The author clarifies this by stating that "it is impossible for God to lie" (v.18).

I am reminded of a riddle I was once told: "Can God do anything? Yes. Can he create a rock so big he can't move it? No. Then God cannot do anything." This little mindbender actually teaches a valuable lesson. There are some things that God cannot do, not because he lacks power or ability, but because it would violate his nature as God. God cannot sin because his nature is holy; therefore, a God who sins ceases to be God. God cannot violate his promises because he cannot violate his truthful character.

God's unchangeable character provides for the believer an "encouragement to hold fast to the hope" set before them. So those "who have fled for refuge" in God can be assured that through faith, patience, and perseverance one can obtain rest. The author highlights the patience of Abraham in order to encourage his listeners to imitate his faithful example.[219] In verse 19, the author highlights the believer's security which is grounded in the nature of God. God's unchangeable character becomes an unmovable anchor for the believer's soul. Once again this highlights the sovereignty of God over the believer's journey. Those who are truly anchored to God have no need to worry about the trials of life. The storms of life may make the promises of God seem unobtainable but because believers are anchored to God's character, they must simply weather the storm. Access to God's ultimate rest is available to all those who place their faith in Christ

---

[219] Cockerill, *Hebrews*, 286.

who went before them as a forerunner. Jesus enables believers to enter into the "inner place behind the curtain" which is the presence of God. Once again, the author alludes to the tabernacle. A theme he will fully explore at a later time. Here the author reintroduces the theme of Jesus' high priesthood that he left off in Hebrews 5:10 in order to warn his listeners.[220] Now the author again picks up the subject of priesthood in order to provide a detailed explanation of the superiority of Jesus' priesthood. It is the security of Jesus' priestly office which will enable the author's listeners to persevere in the face of their trials.

Application

MAINTAINING HOPE IN THE FACE OF HOPLESSNESS

Prison is a very dark place where many people have the tendency to lose hope. As inmates, we attempt to place our hope in almost anything. We trust in lawyers to resolve what we often view as the injustices of the legal system. We look to the courts to offer relief for our sentences. We hope our loved ones will not ultimately abandon us over the years. Yet all these are inferior sources of hope. The justice system is broken, the courts are overburdened, and our families have more pressing concerns. If we are to maintain hope in a hopeless environment, then we must find a surer source. True hope can only be found in a relationship with Jesus. Take the time to examine your personal relationship with Christ. Read John 15:1-11 and consider your relationship to the true vine. Write out some of the things you once placed your

---

[220] Moo, *Hebrews*, 222.

hope in. Now consider how placing your hope in Jesus can help bear fruit in your life.

B. Jesus: A Superior Priesthood (7:1-28)

1. Melchizedek: A Unique High Priest (7:1-10)

Prisoner's Insight for the Journey

Everyone loves a good mystery. We are infatuated with the unknown. Prisons are full of books claiming to unveil the "true Jesus" or the "true Christianity" as if what we have is not true. We are all searching for that mysterious nugget of truth that will make all other things clear and less mysterious. If you were to survey the prison population and ask what biblical book they would be most interested in learning about, the majority would choose Revelation. To the average reader, the mysterious language and imagery found in Revelation must hold the key to the mysteries of the universe. However, to the informed reader the book of Revelation is not so mysterious. Especially when one considers that biblical books were not written to confuse but to clarify. What is so mysterious to us was most likely clear to the original audience. What is the point of writing a book no one understands?

So, when the author of Hebrews uses Melchizedek to support the priestly office of Christ, his point is not to make Melchizedek into some mysterious angelic-type figure. The author aims to use a historical priest of the Most High God who preceded the Levitical Priesthood in order to show that there existed a higher order of priestly office. This order was established in eternity and provided believers with a glimpse of it in Melchizedek before he fully established it in Christ. It was not

Jesus who resembled Melchizedek but Melchizedek who resembled the Son of God.[221]

Commentary

7:1-10

In verse 1, the author returns to the topic of Melchizedek's priestly office (Heb. 5:10, 6:20). For the author, this obscure Old Testament priestly figure will be central to his argument for the next three chapters. Therefore, in order to understand the author's point, a deeper examination of Melchizedek and the Old Testament priestly office is required. It is often emphasized that Melchizedek is the first priest mentioned in Scripture (Gen. 14). He is also the only priest king beside Jesus listed in the Bible.[222] These two points are significant for establishing the superiority of Jesus' priestly office. As the first priest mentioned in Scripture, Melchizedek's office both precedes and stands outside of the Aaronic/Levitical priesthood. This will be vital to the author's establishment of Jesus' right to the priesthood. Jesus descends from the line of Judah. As the eternal Son, Jesus also precedes and stands apart from the Levitical institutions. As a priest king, Melchizedek also stands in contrast to the normal practices of Israel. In the Law, there exists a separation between these two offices. Isaiah 6 alludes to the repercussion of attempting to act as both priest and king. King Uzziah died because he attempted to assume both roles (2 Chron. 26:16-21).[223] However, Melchizedek stands as an example outside the Law of one who assumed both roles. For the author, this establishes the precedent for a future

---

[221] Koester, *Hebrews*, 343.
[222] Albert Mohler, *Christ-Centered Exposition: Exalting Jesus in Hebrews* (Nashville, TN: Holman Reference, 2017), 99.
[223] Ibid.

priest king (Jesus) who will offer purification for sins and reign from a heavenly throne. Likely it also emphasizes the distinction between divine appointments versus hereditary ascension.

One of the main reasons Melchizedek is so mysterious for today's reader is that he is only mentioned in two other biblical places outside of Hebrews: Gen. 14, and Psalm 110:4.[224] He abruptly appears in the narrative as the priest of the Most High God and contrasts with the king of Sodom. Melchizedek comes offering blessings and receiving homage from Abraham.[225] The king of Sodom comes offering nothing but desiring the spoils of war. The author draws on his understanding of these two brief accounts in order to establish the greater priestly office of Jesus.

In Genesis 14, the book concludes with its account of Abraham's rescue of his nephew Lot. Abraham upon his return from the defeat of the kings is met by Melchizedek King of Salem, priest of the Most High God. Melchizedek offers Abraham bread and wine, then blesses him. As a result of this encounter, Abraham gives a tenth of his spoils from war to the priest Melchizedek in the form of a tithe (Gen. 14:17-20). The author of Hebrews draws on several parts of this account to support his argument. First, he establishes the office of Melchizedek who is said to be both priest of the Most High God and King of Salem. Next, he draws on the blessing of Abraham by Melchizedek. Finally, the author emphasizes that Abraham paid tithes to Melchizedek. In Psalm 110:4, the author pulls from a messianic Psalm which he has already depended on in numerous instances, but instead of focusing on Psalm 110:1, he combines it with Psalm 110:4. In doing so, the kingly figure from Psalm 110:1 is also a priestly

---

[224] See Moo's article on Melchizedek, *Hebrews*, 228-232.
[225] Cockerill, *Hebrews*, 306.

figure who ministers forever after the order of Melchizedek. The importance of Melchizedek's role as a priest/king is essential to the author's stress of Jesus' superiority. If Jesus is superior to the Old Testament institutions, then he must descend from a superior line.[226] This continues the author's theme of comparison and fulfillment that he began in chapter 1. Jesus is better because he provides a better priesthood. While this point may seem non-essential for today's readers, for the first-century Christian with a Jewish background, it was vital; it established their ability to access God.

In the Old Testament, the priestly line was to descend from the tribe of Levi. This was the tribe from which Israel's first two priestly figures Moses and Aaron descended (Exod. 28:1). While this was not always practiced perfectly, during the reforms of King Josiah and the scribe Ezra, the Levitical line of priests was reinforced. As a result, any person who did not descend from the line of Levi was not eligible to serve as priest. So essentially, the author of Hebrews is answering the question: "If Jesus is descended from the line of Judah, then how can he also be a priest?" The author's answer is: "He comes from a superior priestly line than Levi."

Verse 3 has produced different understanding from different interpreters. Some take the more mysterious route and understand verse 3 to teach that Melchizedek was an angelic figure, or possibly a pre-incarnate Christ. For example, the Qumran community located around the Dead Sea believed Melchizedek to be an archangel type figure.[227] They support this

---

[226] Stephen Alexander, "Melchizedek" In the *Dictionary of the Old Testament: Pentateuch* (Downers Grove: InterVarsity Press, 2003), 562.
[227] Stephen Alexander, "Melchizedek," 564.

understanding primarily with the statement: "He was without father or mother or genealogy, having neither beginning of days nor end of life" (v.3). This view, however, poses problems for the author's argument. If Melchizedek was a priestly angelic figure what need would there be for Christ to serve this priestly function? This argument would have challenged the authority of Jesus as a heavenly priest. Furthermore, the author does not feel the need to offer an apologetic against Melchizedek. If Melchizedek would have been an angelic priestly mediator, then the author would have likely needed to address Jesus' superiority to this angelic being as he did the other angels in Hebrews 1:5-14. The pre-incarnate Christ position also poses issues. Melchizedek is described as having no father or mother, the author of Hebrews references God as Jesus' Father on numerous occasions and the Gospel narratives attest to his virgin birth.[228] The biblical Jesus has both a father and mother.

Others understand this verse to teach that genealogy was not essential because Melchizedek is referred to as a priest with no mention of his ancestry.[229] This view is most likely correct. The Jews placed a great deal of emphasis on genealogy. This is especially evident in the reforms found in the books of Nehemiah and Ezra. Melchizedek stands as an example of a divinely appointed priest whose genealogy is not emphasized. Regardless of one's view, readers must remember that the author's point is not about Melchizedek, it is about Jesus. If Melchizedek was some eternal, angelic, priestly figure, then what need would there be for Jesus to later fulfill this role? In the latter half of verse 3, the author provides a clarifying statement that shows his emphasis is on Jesus

---

[228] Cockerill, *Hebrews*, 303-304.
[229] Koester, *Hebrews*, 343.

not Melchizedek: "But resembling the son of God he continues a priest forever" (v.3). This points to God's redemptive plan in eternity. From before the foundation of the world, God had planned to send his Son into the world to die for his people. Christ, in a priestly role, would offer himself to God providing complete forgiveness of sins and access to God. God called Melchizedek, a historical figure, to be a priest who preceded the Levitical priesthood and stood outside the Law of Moses in order to provide his Son a superior priestly line, thus, Melchizedek resembles the eternal Son.[230]

I am often amazed at the people's disappointment when I present to them a less mysterious interpretation of a biblical text. For some reason, many want to find mysterious codes and unsolvable mysteries on every page of the Bible. However, by attempting to remake Scripture into a riddle, they miss its very purpose. Paul, in Romans 15:4, states, "For whatever was written in former days was written for our instruction that through endurance and through the encouragement of the Scriptures we might have hope." The Bible was written so that believers may benefit from what it teaches. If everything was an unsolvable mystery, then believers would benefit from very little. Therefore, when we approach the text, we should first examine what it actually says rather than attempting to make it say something it never intended.

In verse 4, the author begins a comparison between Melchizedek and the Levitical priesthood. He introduces this section with the phrase, "see how great this man was" in order to grab his listeners' attention.[231] The author establishes

---

[230] Moo, *Hebrews*, 236.
[231] Allen, *Hebrews*, 415.

Melchizedek's greatness by reminding them that Abraham, one of Israel's greatest patriarchs and receiver of the promises of God, paid tithes to Melchizedek.[232] This verse highlights two important points. First, Abraham is described as "patriarch." This word acknowledges Abraham as the founder of Israel.[233] This means Abraham is thought of as the representative of the nation as a whole.[234] This solidarity of Abraham and the rest of Israel will be vital for the author's argument of Melchizedek's superiority. Whatever is implied by the relationship between Melchizedek and Abraham applies to all Abraham's offspring. Also, the author refers to Abraham's tithe as a "tenth of the spoils." This word likely signifies the quality of the offering. Abraham gave to Melchizedek the best of the best. This helps to establish the superiority of Melchizedek by emphasizing the quality of the gift and the dignity of the giver.[235]

Verses 5-6 compose one contrasting thought that can be summarized as, "On the one hand the descendants of Levi … but on the other Melchizedek.[236] This serves as a lesser to the greater argument. In verse 5, the author reminds his listeners that the Law established that all descendants of Abraham were to pay tithes to the descendants of Levi. The collection of the tithe set the tribe of Levi apart from all other tribes of Israel and constituted their inheritance (Num. 18:21-32).[237] This was the established order which God instituted for the children of Israel. In verse 6, the author provides his listeners with an exception to the rule. Melchizedek, who did not descend from Levi, receives tithes from

[232] Moo, *Hebrews*, 236.
[233] Koester, *Hebrews*, 343.
[234] Lane, *Hebrews*, 168.
[235] Cockerill, *Hebrews*, 307.
[236] Allen, *Hebrews*, 415.
[237] Guthrie, *Hebrews*, NIV, 254.

Abraham. This shocking exception highlighted by the author is further compounded by the statement "who had the promises." Abraham, arguably the greatest patriarch in the history of Israel; the man who received promises of God by which a nation would be established paid tithes to Melchizedek.[238] The Levites held their position based on the Law; Melchizedek's office is established by God's unchangeable oath found in Psalm 110:4. The Levitical priesthood was established on predecessors and successors, but Melchizedek's office which stands apart from the Law signifies the ultimate displacement of the Levitical institution.[239] The author's logic is sound. God promised Abraham a blessing (Gen. 12), then Melchizedek blesses Abraham (Gen. 14). If this pattern continues, then the author's hearers, who are heirs of the promise, should also expect a blessing from the one who Melchizedek foreshadowed.[240]

I grew up with two older brothers. We lived in a small town and went to a small school where everyone knew everyone. As I grew older, I would meet people who had gone to school with my brothers. They would recognize my name and immediately ask if I was "so and so's" little brother. Once I acknowledged that I was, whatever previous encounter my brothers had with these people reflected on me. Sometimes it came with favor, at other times, it brought drama. Whatever applied to my brothers ultimately applied to me. Our previous interactions with people will always have lasting effects.

In verse 7, the author highlights the significance of this action by clearly stating what he has been implying all along; "the

---

[238] Moo, *Hebrews*, 238.
[239] Lane, *Hebrews*, 171.
[240] Koester, *Hebrews*, 351.

inferior is blessed by the superior." Once again, the author uses a lesser to greater argument. This truth was not an absolute rule because at times the lesser would bless the superior as was the case of Melchizedek blessing God (Gen. 14:20).[241] By Abraham offering Melchizedek a portion of his spoils, he recognizes him as superior due to his office as priest of the Most High God. In verse 8, the author shows the superiority of that office by comparing the mortality versus immortality of its priests. The many men who served the Levitical priesthood show the mortality of the ministers; Levitical priests live and die. However, by omitting the birth, death, and genealogy of Melchizedek, the author is able to emphasize the eternal nature of the office. The author is not saying that Melchizedek reigns as priest forever. He allows the uncertain beginning and end of Melchizedek from verse 3 to testify to the everlasting nature of his priestly office. The Scriptures bear witness that the Melchizedek priesthood is everlasting; it has always lived and continues to live in the eternal Son.

In verse 9-10, the author adds a point to drive home the superiority of Melchizedek's priesthood by arguing that theoretically Levi who was a descendant of Abraham, paid tithes to Melchizedek because "he was still in the loins of his ancestor." This points back to the solidarity of Abraham and Israel.[242] What took place between Abraham and Melchizedek has implications for all of Abraham's offspring. The author signifies that he is using hyperbole when he states, "One might even say." This shows that he does not believe that Levi "literally" paid tithes to Abraham. His point is to show the representative nature of Abraham's actions. If Abraham, who is the greatest of Israel's patriarchs paid

[241] Moo, *Hebrews*, 238.
[242] Ibid., 239.

tithes, then Levi, who is lesser in status than Abraham would also have paid tithes.

Application

SOLVING THE GREAT MYSTERIES OF THE BIBLE

Scripture is full of difficult to understand sayings and teachings. This primarily results from the vast amount of time and difference in culture which stands between us and the original world of the Bible. Peter writing to first-century believers acknowledges this difficulty when he states, "Paul also wrote to you according to the wisdom given him, as he does in all his letters when he speaks in them of these matters. There are some things in them that are hard to understand" (2 Pet. 3:15). This is why background studies are vital to understanding the ancient world. Scholars and archaeologist have scoured the ancient world in order to help today's believer better understand the Bible. Take the time today and consider the first-century culture to which the author addressed his letter. Read an introduction to the New Testament or the introductory material in a commentary on the book of Hebrews. How does understanding the ancient world better equip you to understand the book of Hebrews?

2. Jesus: A Superior High Priest (7:11-28)

Prisoner's Insight for the Journey

God changes circumstances. In prison we have a tendency to believe things will not or cannot change. We develop these unbreakable routines that become sacred to our existence. Every day we wake up, read a Proverb and Psalm, watch the same T.V. programs, do the same exercise routine, and have the same conversations with the same people. Years, sometimes decades pass with no notable change to our sacred routines. Then suddenly, out of nowhere, circumstances change. God descends on our inviolable routines, our towers of babble, and confuses what we believe is unchangeable law. We soon find ourselves fighting against the change and unknowingly fighting against God. We fail to recognize that when God gets ready to do something new, he will bring about new circumstances. Change, even when it makes us uncomfortable, is God's way of causing us to grow. Our responsibility is to find God's plan in the midst of change. Even when the changes appear to be the work of the enemy, we must remember that God is still on the throne. The enemy is defeated, the war is won, but our daily battles against sin, and self must wage on.

The author reminds his listeners that change has arrived in the person and work of Jesus. The author's audience which descended from a Jewish background rightly held the Law of God in high esteem. To the Jew, the Law and all it commands was inviolable. They believed that the rituals and practices could not change. However, they never considered it to be incomplete and in need of further fulfillment. So, when God got ready to do something new in Jesus, they fought against the change and unknowingly fought against God. God had prepared in eternity a priesthood and a Law that would supersede what the Jews believed to be unchangeable. This new way would accomplish what the old could not. Jesus, our Great High Priest, would enact a better Law which made it possible for all people, Jew and Gentile, to approach God on equal terms. The author explains to his listeners that a better priest and a better Law provide better access and better worship.

Commentary

7:11-28

In the previous section the author has shown the superiority of Melchizedek and his office. Now he unpacks the implications of Melchizedek's superiority in relation to the Levitical priesthood. In verse 11, the author uses the word "perfection" in order to highlight the comparison between Levi and Melchizedek's priesthood. The idea of perfection in modern use almost always carries the idea of flawlessness. This generally implies some object or event's outward appearance. However, the biblical usage generally denotes completion. So here, perfection references the inability of the Levitical Law to provide access to God. The author poses the question to his listeners, "Did the Levitical priesthood accomplish God's purpose (7:11a)."[243]

The concept of perfection can be viewed here in two ways. First, some scholars argue that perfection references the Levitical priest's inability to access God. If priestly access to God would have been available through the Levites, then there would be no need for another priesthood. However, as Lane has noted, "The writer does not absolutely deny to the people of the old covenant

---

[243] Koester, *Hebrews*, 358.

the possibility of 'drawing near to God." He argues that the author's emphasis is on the inability of the Law to perfect the people.[244] This flows well with the author's argument in Hebrews 10:1-4. The Levitical system could not cleanse the conscience of sin.[245] The people continually felt the need to offer sacrifices. The security of forgiveness which the Levitical system lacked is fully realized in the believer's relationship with Jesus. The worshiper can now boldly enter the presence of God through the shed blood of the priest according to the order of Melchizedek. Other scholars appear to argue that the Levitical priesthood did not provide full access. In other words, it was mediated through cultic practices. The priest and Tabernacle stood between the worshiper and God. The believer was forced to rely on others for access. While this view is less likely, the author of Hebrews does at times place the blame with the Old Testament practices (Heb.10:4).

The author also draws a contrast between how the different priestly offices are filled. The Levitical priesthood is said to descend from the tribe of Levi. This means they inherited their position. The issue with the descent of the priesthood is easily seen in the behavior of Eli's sons. Some who inherited the office "were worthless men" (1 Sam. 2:12). However, God calls special individuals for special purposes. The priest according to the order of Melchizedek is said "to arise" to his office. This idea is often associated with the "coming of a great leader."[246] Jesus came to the priesthood by God's appointment in order to bring "perfection" to the believer's relationship with the Father.

---

[244] Lane, *Hebrews*, 181.
[245] Koester, *Hebrews*, 353.
[246] Cockerill, *Hebrews*, 316.

The author also closely ties the priesthood to the Law. For the Jew, those two concepts were inseparable. Moo states, "Having denied that God's purpose for humanity could have been attained via the Levitical priesthood, the author adds, as an aside, that this priesthood is inextricably tied to the law as a whole."[247] The priesthood was established by the Law and the Law was administered by the priesthood.[248] So the author argues that if the priesthood could have provided complete access to God, then there would be no need for another priest. The Greek language uses the word "another" in two ways. First, the word another can mean "another of the same kind:" Please give me another (same) drink. Second, the word can mean "another of a different kind." Please give me another (different) drink.[249] The author employs another in the second sense. Melchizedek is another "different" priest than that of Levi/Aaron. The support for this statement is found both by what was said before in Hebrews 7:1-10 and what will follow. The author is not arguing that no access was established through the Levitical Law, but that a full, more perfect access was provided by the new priestly order.

Ministry in prison is very political. Serving God within the church has as much to do with who you know as it does with what you know. Unfortunately, this means that many of the people in church leadership have descended to their position based more on their relationship with man than God. Church leaders choose their replacements based on friendships instead of gifts, abilities, and calling. This process leads to a lower quality of ministry. The people of God ultimately suffer because those chosen to serve

---

247 Moo, *Hebrews*, 248.
248 Ibid., 317.
249 Allen, *Hebrews*, 420.

them are unqualified. They cannot give the people what they do not have.

In verse 12, the author provides the logical conclusion of what he has previously said about the Levitical priesthood. If God had established the Levitical priesthood by law and foreshadowed another priesthood in Melchizedek (Gen. 14) by prophecy (Ps. 110:4), then naturally a change in Law would also follow. This statement would sound almost blasphemous to any Jew who held to the immutability of God's sacred law. However, immutability does not exclude fulfillment.[250] God, since the beginning of time, revealed his plan of redemption. The earlier parts of his redemptive story are made clearer by the latter. The perfection of his redemption is found in the person and work of his Son Jesus Christ. Thus, as the apostle Paul stated in Galatians 3:24, the Law was our guardian until Christ. The Law held the hand of the people of God until a perfect pioneer took the lead. In verse 13, the author clarifies the specific change in law that he had in mind by referencing the lineage of the priestly office. The Law dictated that only one from the tribe of Levi/Aaron could serve at the altar.[251] As a result, in order for someone from another tribe to serve, the Law would have to change. However, once again the change should not be seen as God's improvisation but as the unfolding of his eternal plan. God is not making it up as he goes, but reveals his plan as needed. In verse 14, the author continues his argument that Jesus' priesthood is unique when he states that Jesus descends from Judah, a tribe not connected to the priesthood. Most

---

[250] Cockerill, *Hebrews*, 317.
[251] Koester, *Hebrews*, 359.

translations say "descended from Judah" but the correct rendering is "arise" from Judah.[252] Moo states:

> More importantly, the verb and its cognate "rising" (ἀνατολή) are used in several Old Testament messianic passages: Numbers 24:17, where Balaam predicts that 'a star will come out [ἀνατελεί] in his place, and he shall build the temple of the Lord .... He shall bear royal honor and shall sit upon his throne and rule' (NRSV); and Jeremiah 23:5: "I will raise up for David a righteous Branch [ἀνατολήν], and he shall reign as king and deal wisely, and shall execute justice and righteousness in the land" (ESV).

This shows that God did something new by raising up a priest from a totally different line. Most priests descend which emphasizes their ancestry, but Jesus arises emphasizing power and authority. In Christ, God prepared to do something new. Yet this new work was planned from the beginning. God throughout his redemptive story provided hints and shadows of the glorious plan that we find fulfilled in Jesus.

In verse 15, the author closely compares the Levitical and Melchizedek priesthoods. First, another (different kind) of priest arises. Once again, the author used the word "arise" instead of "descend" to stress the appointment by God. God did not appoint the individual Levitical priest; they descended to the office usually by the son taking on the responsibilities of the father. However, "to arise" implies a priest established in a different way. This special priest appointed by God would not descend from

---

[252] Cockerill, *Hebrews*, 319.

Melchizedek but resemble the likeness of his priestly office.[253] Once again, the author does not stress the person of Melchizedek but the uniqueness of his office. Melchizedek's priesthood foreshadowed the priesthood of Christ. Melchizedek by the foreknowledge of God, established the precedent of Christ's priesthood.[254] In verse 16, he affirms the uniqueness of Jesus' priesthood by comparing the difference in how the office is received. The Levites received the priestly office based on the Law and family descent. Jesus takes the office "by the power of an indestructible life." This statement highlights the eternal nature of Jesus' priesthood while also looking forward to the author's discussion of the mortality of the Levitical priests. Jesus is a priest forever because he lives forever.[255] One of the main imperfections of the Levitical priesthood was its administration by sinful, mortal men. Where there is death in an office there can be no true stability. A look at some of the priests of Israel's past will reveal their inconsistency; some priests were better than others, but none were perfect. In verse 17, the author once again provides his biblical support for his argument. Jesus' priesthood is the fulfillment of Psalm 110:4. The words spoken by God through the Psalmist were directed toward Christ.[256] In verse 18, the author clearly states that the new priesthood has replaced the old with the strongest of terms.[257] The former commandment was weak and useless. The two terms (weak/useless) describe the Law's inability to perform its ultimate task—provide access to God.[258] Again, the author employs the word perfect denoting the Law's inability to

---

[253] Allen, *Hebrews*, 423.
[254] Lane, *Hebrews*, 183.
[255] Cockerill, *Hebrews*, 323-324.
[256] Allen, *Hebrews*, 424-425.
[257] Lane, *Hebrews*, 185.
[258] Moo, *Hebrews*, 254.

complete the person. The Law was to provide access to God mediated through priests, but the shortcoming of the people, priest, and sacrifices made it imperfect and unable to accomplish what it was designed to do.[259] Yet God, fully understanding the inability of the system, introduced a "better hope" in the foreshadowing of Melchizedek's priesthood. That better hope now provides the access and ability to draw near to God. No longer is sinful man reliant on sinful priests and inferior sacrifices. God sent his better hope (access through Christ) into the world to accomplish what no priest before him could—bring sinful humanity into fellowship with a holy God.[260]

By the time I am eligible for parole, I will have served 25 years in prison. Over the last two decades, I have witnessed vast amounts of change. The prison has changed, the people have changed, and I have changed. The world I left so long ago has passed on, and the people, places, and activities that are so clear in my mind no longer exist as I imagine them. I have learned that change is inevitable. Yet here, in our time capsules, we tend to resist change. We fear change. There are guys still rocking the same haircuts they were wearing 20 years ago. They still believe that things in the world still happen the "old way." Unfortunately for many of us, reentering society will be more like entering a foreign country for the first time. We will not speak the lingo, and the daily practices will be foreign to us. Thankfully for the believer, while practices may change, the God we serve does not. I know that the same God who has journeyed with me in prison over the last 20 years will also walk with me on the outside.

---

[259] Koester, *Hebrews*, 361.
[260] Allen, *Hebrews*, 426.

In verse 20, the better hope that the believer now has "was not established without an oath." The author uses a double negative (not/without) to emphasize the importance of God's oath.[261] The Levitical priests were established by Law and genealogy, but the new and better hope established by a superior priesthood is confirmed by an oath from God. God established Jesus as high priest with an unchangeable oath: "the Lord has sworn and will not change his mind; you are a priest forever" (Ps.110:4). The author once again cites his support. The fact that God established Jesus' priesthood with an oath is very significant. God's oath singles out Jesus as a superior mediator of a superior priesthood. The Law covered a multitude of the ancestors of Levi. Many priests served God under the Law, however, only one served God under oath: the "you" in "you are a priest forever" after the order of Melchizedek was specifically for Jesus. There were no past and will be no future "yous."

This unique appointment also established Jesus as the "guarantor" of a better covenant. The Old Testament priests were seen as mediators of God's covenant to his people. As a result, he stood as a representative between God and the people. Christ is also a mediator in this sense but here the author employs a stronger word for Christ's work of mediation. Jesus is not only the one who administers the better covenant but through the offering of himself has guaranteed that the covenant relationship will stand.[262] The forcefulness of the idea of "guarantor" can be seen in the covenant account of God and Abraham. God establishes a covenant with Abraham then put Abraham asleep and establishes the covenant on his own merit (Gen. 15). Christ's sacrifice has guaranteed the

---

[261] Cockerill, *Hebrews*, 328.
[262] Lane, *Hebrews*, 188.

believer access to God. The author also employs the word covenant for the first time. A concept he will unpack in the following chapter. Cockerill, stated "As eternal son and Guarantor he gives God's people all the reason they could possibly need to persevere through faith in the availability of God's power and the certainty of his promises."[263]

The author compares the mortality of the Levitical priesthood with the immortality of Jesus' office. The very fact that there were numerous different priests since Aaron points to the weakness of the office. However, Jesus' permanent priesthood proves its superiority. This looks back to the author's statement in Heb. 7:16 that Jesus' office was established "by the power of an indestructible life." He further supports this line of thought by stating that "he continues forever." This statement does not point to his continual service as much as it does his eternal nature.[264] Christ is superior because unlike all priests before him he lives forever. The author is able to provide his listeners with comfort knowing that they have a high priest who is always interceding on their behalf. In a time of persecution and uncertainty, his audience could trust in the security and stability that Christ's sacrifice provided.

The author further explains the benefits of Christ's priesthood. Jesus is able to save completely (uttermost, ESV). This phrase stands in contrast to the Law's inability to perfect anything. The author wants his listeners to understand that what the Law has been unable to perform Jesus accomplished absolutely. The author reminds his listeners that they can now draw near to God through Jesus. This beautiful statement is an invitation to enter into the

---

[263] Cockerill, *Hebrews*, 331.
[264] Ibid., 332.

presence of God. Cockerill states that before only the priests ministered before the altar in the Holy place and the people were denied this full access. However, now that distinction no longer exists, the people can go "directly to God himself through Christ and the sacrifice he has offered."[265] During their time of persecution, the listeners could find comfort in knowing that because Jesus is eternally in the presence of God, he makes "intercession for them." Jesus the great advocate is always before the Father providing believers full access to the presence of God so that they may receive the help they need during their trials.

The author now describes the splendor of the high priest. Jesus fits the description of what believers need. Jesus is everything fallen humanity is not. The author first describes him as holy. Cockerill states that this most likely references Christ's "covenant keeping," his obedience to the Father.[266] Jesus is also said to be innocent, untouched by evil, and unstained. This points to Jesus' moral purity and can be summed up as "sinless." Jesus was sinless in his outward obedience to the Law and his inward obedience to the Father.[267] The author also describes him as "separated from sinners and exalted above the heavens." The separation denotes Christ's exaltation. Literally his sinlessness has removed him from the presence of sinners into the presence of God. So separated denotes what Jesus has been separated "from" (sinners) and "exalted above the heavens" denotes where Jesus has been exalted "to." Jesus has been separated "from sinners and exalted "to" the Father.[268]

---

[265] Cockerill, Hebrews, 335-336.
[266] Ibid., 339-41.
[267] Lane, *Hebrews*, 192.
[268] Allen, *Hebrews*, 430.

Jesus is superior because he has no need to offer a daily sacrifice for himself. The above description excludes him from needing forgiveness for sins. His perfect obedience and pure heart enabled him to offer himself "once for all." Once again, the author highlights the weakness and insufficiency of the Levitical priesthood. They were sinners in need of forgiveness. This hindered them from fully mediating on behalf of the people. However, Christ's self-sacrifice "once for all" took care of the believers' needs. This is why they can "draw near to God through him" (v.25). In verse 28, the author sums up his previous argument.[269] The Law could only bring about imperfection through imperfect men. The Law was never meant to bring close fellowship to God. This is evident because it was mediated by another. But God's foreknowledge proclaimed through an oath, looked forward to a Son who would perfect the imperfect.

Application

UNLIMITED ACCESS

As believers, we often fail to consider the great privilege Jesus has granted us. We worry about things we cannot change and seek solutions in places where only problems are found. We forget that Jesus has provided for us an unlimited access to God. We can carry our concerns directly to the throne room. Not only this, but Jesus is there always making intercession on our behalf. The believer has both access and a faithful advocate. Today, read John 17, Jesus' high priestly prayer for believers. Meditate on what Jesus is asking the Father to grant you. Then ask yourself

[269] Cockerill, *Hebrews*, 343.

whether you spend more time in the presence of your problems or the presence of God.

C. Jesus: The High Priest of the New Covenant (8:1-10:18)

1. The Supremacy of the New Covenant (8:1-13)

Prisoner's Insight for the Journey

Living in prison has its own unique set of difficulties mainly because prison also has its own unique social rules. We live by a set of unwritten rules, an oral tradition that governs our daily routines. Most of the time, we may go years without ever questioning the established order. Yesterday, we celebrated our annual Christmas meal on my dorm. One hundred and eleven men were asked to contribute food, resources, and culinary skills to this labor of love. Black, white, and Hispanic men from different cities and gang affiliations came together to make Christmas in prison a little more bearable. Most everyone participated, but a few chose to sit out because of the unwritten rules.

In prison it is often frowned upon to eat with another race or people with certain types of crimes. So, when community meals are made, there are always a few who choose not to participate. On these days, they self-enforce this unwritten prison code; but what about the rest of the year? The same group, who segregate themselves on special days from certain classes of people, spend the rest of the year playing games, watching sports, gambling, and strangely enough eating in the chow hall with the same people they are attempting to avoid. These 364 days of inconsistency results from their attempt to live in a world and by a set of standards that is passing away. They are trying to hold on to a prison that ceased to exist two decades ago.

The author's listeners struggled with a similar issue. The culture and the rules by which they had lived for so long were changing before their eyes. For the Jews, the Law of Moses and the oral traditions of the religious elite governed their lives. But when Christ came, the established order was questioned. Jesus offered a different way to worship the Father. For many, this way was more inclusive, it destroyed the religious and social practices that had been in place. Jesus destroyed barriers. Yet there were those who were trying to enforce the old way by putting pressure on those who practiced the new. The Jewish Christians addressed in Hebrews are caught in the middle. The author writes to them so that they would understand that the old system was not meant to be permanent but that long ago God had promised that he would establish a New Covenant with the people of God. This New Covenant would make the need for the old obsolete.

Commentary

8:1-13

In verse 1, the author immediately gets to his point. All that he has said previously is summarized in: "We have such a high priest, one who is seated at the right hand of the throne of the majesty in heaven" (Heb. 8:1).[270] The author has boldly claimed that there exists a priesthood that is superior to the established order. He has stated that the new way has accomplished what the old could not and as a result the old is no longer necessary. Now he makes it personal. Jesus is not some obscure figure who ministers in a temple far away, but he is their priest who is seated at the right hand of the Father.

---

[270] Moo, *Hebrews*, 270.

In Hebrews 1:3, the author alluded to the priestly duties of the eternal Son when he stated: "After making purification for sin he sat down." He has been subtly preparing for his presentation of Christ's priestly office.[271] Both Hebrews 1:3 and 8:1 are clear allusions to Psalm 110:1.[272] This royal Psalm spoke about the reign of the Messiah. The Messiah would be placed in a position of authority at the right hand of the Father. The author uses this Psalm to help emphasize the reign and completed priestly duty of Jesus. No priest in the Old Testament "sat down" in the Holy Place. Their duty was to minister on behalf of the people and then exit the Holy Place after their duties were complete. Our author, however, takes this Psalm and shows that Jesus is superior because he has once and for all entered the Holy Place and "sat down." Therefore, this implies that the sacrifice he made was sufficient and acceptable to the Father. Jesus does not have to return daily or yearly with an unblemished offering because he offered "himself" the Lamb of God once and for all, this is seen in the fact that he is now "seated at the right hand of the throne." This also points back to the first chapter where the author stated that Jesus was "appointed heir of all things" (Heb. 1:2). The Son is the priestly king who rules over and ministers on behalf of his struggling people.

In verse 2, the author calls Jesus a "minister." The author uses this description of Jesus to achieve two goals. He asserts the superiority of Jesus while also making him the believer's personal advocate: "We have such a high priest … a minister." While the word minister can be synonymous with High Priest, the former focuses on the actions of ministering, the latter signifies the office.

---

[271] Cockerill, *Hebrews*, 350.
[272] Allen, *Hebrews*, 440-41

The author wants his listeners to understand that they have a personal minister who is continually advocating on their behalf. Jesus is "their priest."[273] The people of God now have a personal advocate, someone who understands their struggles yet is capable of providing a way of victory for them. Jesus serves in the "true tent" (a reference to heaven) established by God and not man. The Jews had become obsessed with the copy of the Holy Place while neglecting the original. The copy was always meant to be temporary and now that Christ, the true temple, had come there was no longer need for the old. The Jews had fell in love with their own handy work. But Jesus had predicted access to the original "true tent" there was no need to attempt to access God through the old; a place that was unable to perfect anything.

In verse 3, the author describes matter-of-factly the duties of the high priest. He "is appointed to offer gifts and sacrifices." While the author does not directly say it, the offering here is directed toward the forgiveness of sins (Heb. 5:1). This was the purpose of the Levitical Law; however, the author has previously made clear that the Law and sacrifices of the Old Testament priesthood could not "perfect" anything (Heb. 7:18). There was a weakness that existed in both the priest and offering (Heb. 7:18; 28).[274] The author establishes a point which he will return to later. If Jesus is a superior high priest, he must also offer a superior sacrifice.[275] While the duties of a priest naturally implied the offering of something, the author has withheld thus far exactly what Jesus offered. In verse 1:3, the author states that Jesus made purification for sins without explicitly stating how. In Hebrews 2:11, Jesus is referred to as "he who sanctifies" and in Hebrews

---

273 Koester, *Hebrews*, 381.
274 Guthrie, *Hebrews*, NIV, 281.
275 Cockerill, *Hebrews*, 358-59.

5:7 as one who offers up "prayers and supplications." Yet in both instances, an offering in comparison to the Levitical Law has not been offered. The author holds his audience in suspense until he reveals the superior offering in Hebrews 9:14.

In verse 4, the author anticipates his discussion of a new law. He states that if Jesus were on earth he would not be a priest because earthly priests are governed by earthly laws. The Levitical Law would have disqualified Jesus from the priesthood. Yet the author has already clearly stated in Hebrews 7:12 that a change in priesthood requires a change in law. The author will outline this change with the New Covenant.

The earthly priests serve in an earthly tabernacle. Once again, the author wants to show the superiority of Christ's office in ministry. The Levitical priesthood served as a copy and shadow of heavenly things.[276] This bold statement by the author points to the inferiority of the earthly temple. Neither copy nor shadow is the reality. They are mere representations or distortions of the real thing. The copy of the tabernacle did not look up to some heavenly eternal reality but looked forward to the day that Christ would sit down at the right hand of the Father.[277] The earthly temple was not a reflection of what took place in heaven but a teaching pattern pointing toward true forgiveness and access to God. In order to support his bold claim, the author references Exodus 25:40 where God instructs Moses to make everything according to the copy on the mountain. Here the idea of copy does not mean instructions but implies some objective "model that could be reproduced on earth."[278] Thus as Lane has stated; as a copy "the tabernacle was a

---

[276] Moo, *Hebrews*, 277.
[277] Cockerill, *Hebrews*, 360.
[278] Lane, *Hebrews*, 207.

rough reminiscence intended to suggest the idea of the original and to train the people of God to appreciate the heavenly reality itself."[279]

Prison commissary is stocked full of generic brands and products which are meant to compare in quality to those in the free world. We have Barbco corn chips and tortilla chips, vanilla crème biscuits (generic Oreos), and even Scobee tennis shoes. We have eaten and worn these products for so long that we often fail to notice their inferior quality. For us, these knock-offs have become the real thing. In 2022, TDCJ allowed us for a short period to make outside purchases for shoes. My family ordered me a pair of Adidas running shoes. The moment I tried them on, the inferiority of all the knockoffs I had been wearing for years was evident. The knockoffs are a poor representation of the real thing. On the bright side, these poor products are a daily reminder of the quality that awaits us on the other side!

The author continues his point from verse 4: "On the one hand, if Christ was on earth he would not be a priest (v.4) … but on the other hand, since he is in heaven, he has obtained a better ministry (v.6). The fact that Christ's priesthood is established is clear from the author's use of "has obtained." Jesus' ministry is "more excellent than the old" because it carries with it a permanence that the Levitical priesthood did not possess in types and shadows.[280]

Furthermore, his ministry is more excellent because "it is enacted on better promises." It has already been stated by the author that the Law was insufficient to make worshipers whole.

[279] Ibid., 260.
[280] Cockerill, *Hebrews*, 362-63.

However, the promises of the New Covenant look forward to God's desire to "remember their sins no more." The fact that the people and priests had to continually go before God for forgiveness showed the insufficiency of their acts. Christ's superior ministry fully established what the Levitical priesthood could not.

The author prepares for his discussion of the New Covenant by outlining the faults of the Old. Many readers fail to realize the significance of the first covenant versus the second covenant language found in this verse. The very fact that God foretold of a day he would establish a new covenant implies that the old would be replaced. Understanding the replacement of the Old Covenant with the new is akin to understanding the difference between Judaism and Christianity. There are numerous understandings of exactly how the New Covenant is actually "new." Koester provides four elements of the New Covenant: (1) God will put his laws within people and write his laws on their hearts. (2) The central theme of the New Covenant is the promise that "I will be their God, and they shall be my people." (3) All God's people will know him. (4) God will be merciful … and will remember sins no longer.[281] Some like Calvin have noticed the similarities between the Old Covenant and New Covenant and argue that the New is actually a renewal of the Old. G.K. Beale offers an interesting understanding of the author of Hebrews' use of Jeremiah 31:31-34. He recognizes the main difference between the Old and New covenants in their temporal versus eternal applications. The Old covenant was always meant to be temporary and necessitated the inauguration of a new more effective covenant. He argues that Israel always contained a faithful

[281] Koester, *Hebrews*, 391-92.

remnant who experienced individual salvation and the benefits of the Law written on their hearts. Therefore, these two aspects represent a continuation of the Old Covenant instead of the newness of the New. For Beale, the covenant's newness rests primarily in the "democratization of the teaching office."[282] This means that Jeremiah's focus was on the insufficiency of the priestly office. While Beale recognizes that this understanding does not naturally flow from Jeremiah 31:31-34, it appears to be implied by the author of Hebrews' use of Jeremiah's text.[283] He finds supports for his conclusion in the promise of the believer's ultimate forgiveness from sin; something the priestly office was meant to mediate but unable to deliver. Finally, Beale sees a relationship between the language found in Leviticus 26:9-12, Jeremiah 31:31-34, and Ezekiel 37:23-27. All contain a tabernacles/covenant theme which is also evident in the immediate context of Hebrews 8:8-13. Beale concludes that "in the end-time covenantal conditions all people will function as priests in the Tabernacle, being in God's direct presence."[284] This is made possible by their relationship to Jesus; the high priest according to the order of Melchizedek who resides in the presence of God. Because the believer now has total access to God's tabernacle through Christ, they also function as a royal priesthood in order to proclaim the excellencies of God (1 Peter 2:9-10). Beale's point is important to grasp. The office of the priesthood has ceased to exist and their role as instructors has been given to all believers. Koester highlights this when he states, "In the end it is clear that Hebrews assumes that Christ's heavenly ministry ... undergirds earthly

---

[282] Beale, *A New Testament Biblical Theology: The Unfolding of the Old Testament in the New.* (Grand Rapids: Baker Academic, 2011), 732-33.
[283] Ibid., 737.
[284] Beale, *A New Testament Biblical Theology*, 736.

Christian worship … and that his self-sacrificing gives rise to sacrifices of praise and good works among his followers (13:15-16). A place remains for leadership in the community of faith (13:7, 17), but Hebrews does not call these leaders 'priests.'"[285] While the existence of the similarities is obvious, the author's emphasis on difference is clear.[286] The author most likely has the idea of fulfillment in mind when he speaks of the New Covenant. The fulfillment of the Old Covenant in Jesus Christ is what distinguishes the Old from the New, Judaism from Christianity. The author throughout his sermon has emphasized that the story of God's redemption is one unified story. The audience/church is a continuation of the one people of God. As a result, Jesus fulfilled the requirements of the Old Testament enabling the people of God to draw near to his presence. Lane states: "The perception that the Mosaic and Levitical institutions have been fulfilled and superseded by the priestly mediation of Christ is the hallmark of the Jewish Christianity of Hebrews."[287]

In verse 13, the author once again highlights the weakness of the Old Covenant, God has rendered it obsolete. For those accustomed to the practices of Mosaic Law, this statement would have been shocking.[288] This means the practices are no longer necessary. The Old and New Covenants were never meant to coexist together.[289] This was vital for the listeners to understand. They could not access God through the old way of worship. God had inaugurated a new system and where the new had begun, the old was "ready to vanish away." While the author's statement that

---

[285] Koester, *Hebrews*, 380.
[286] Ibid., 340.
[287] Lane, *Hebrews*, xxxiii
[288] Beale, *A New Testament Theology*,
[289] Guthrie, *Hebrews*, NIV, 282.

the Law was obsolete would be shocking to his listeners, his understanding of the Law was in line with that of Jesus and the New Testament writers. Jesus emphasized his personal fulfillment of the law. What was old found new meaning in his person. Paul emphasized the temporary function of the Law as an instrument to reveal sin, bring death, and lead the believer to faith in Jesus. All recognized the temporary significance of the Levitical Law.

Application

LETTING GO OF OUR OLD WAYS

Many of us struggle with the idea of change. We cling dearly to our beliefs and practices as if our lives depended on them. We label new ideas as "worldly" and "liberal" without ever examining them for benefit or truth. We are all guilty of this. At one point, I would have scoffed at the rejection of Paul's authorship of Hebrews. Today, I believe the evidence points toward someone other than Paul. Take the time to examine some of your most cherished beliefs. Ask yourself whether these beliefs are based on a careful examination of the evidence or simply adopted from someone else. If they are found to be adopted and wrong, then be willing to change them. It is better to change than to believe an error.

2. The Failure of the Old Covenant (9:1-14)

Prisoner's Insight for the Journey

Prison is basically doing the same thing over and over again. It's like being stuck in a twisted version of the movie Groundhog Day. We wake up to perform the same rituals, put on the same white clothes, and go about a mirror image of our previous day; some of us do this for decades. We become "institutionalized" or "penitentiary" without even realizing it. A simple deviation from our engrained routine is devastating. Our routines afford us a small sense of control in an otherwise chaotic world.

Every Sunday for almost two years I helped lead and facilitate a Bible study in the chapel. That study and the encouragement of those faithful men, led to this book. However, one day, out of nowhere, the administration canceled the study. I was angry, frustrated, and wanting to fight against what I perceived as an unjust cancelation. Furthermore, I struggled to fill the void with another activity. For a while, I spent my Sunday mornings doing nothing until I realized that I had institutionalized my ministry. I learned that things change, even the things we do for God. As Christians, we must be willing and able to follow God in whatever direction he might go. As prisoners, we must remember that no matter how long we perform a daily routine, it is temporary. One day we will trade in these prison whites for something more comfortable, and on that day, the upending of our routines will be welcomed.

Old Testament Tabernacle worship was about consistent routines and rituals. The priest performed sacrificial duties on behalf of himself and the people daily. This practice was instituted by Moses and continued off and on with a few interruptions until AD 70 at the destruction of the temple. The sacrificial system for the Jewish people provided a temporary cleansing from sin and access to God. And as a result of the people's continuous need for forgiveness and access, the sacrificial system became an inviolable routine in the people's lives. However, God had a more permanent way: "When Christ appeared … he entered once for all into the holy place … securing an eternal redemption" (Heb. 9:11-12). What the people established as unalterable, God changed in an instant.

The author of Hebrews writes to his audience to show the changing of religious routines. As Christians, they were struggling to understand and embrace God's new way of worship. The author goes to great lengths to show that the old way was always meant to be temporary. The blood of goats and bulls could not perfect the conscience of the worshiper; therefore, as a temporary fix, it needed to be performed regularly. However, as Christians who had placed their faith in Christ, a new way governed by a New Covenant had been instituted for the believer, this secured an "eternal redemption" enabling them to fully "serve the living God."

Commentary

9:1-14

In the first ten verses, the author sets out to describe the structure and practices of the Tabernacle in the wilderness. Numerous observations have been made concerning the author's ordering of the items in the tent itself. Most likely the author follows a tradition of his time that reflects the rendering of the objects in the Most Holy place. Moreover, his intention is not to provide accurate detail of the objects but to signify the beauty and grandeur of the ministry that took place within.[290]

The author begins his description by linking the first covenant to an earthly sanctuary. This prepares the stage for the author to present the second covenant and its relation to a heavenly sanctuary.[291] For the author, anything that is earthly is ultimately growing old (Heb. 1:11-12). The first covenant and its regulations were a part of the system of worship which had been replaced by a more permanent structure of worship. The earthly tent was "prepared" a clear allusion to its construction by man and a comparison to God's Holy place not made by hands.

The author highlights the first section of the tent in order to emphasize its separation from the Holy of Holies.[292] In the first section stood the lampstand and the table with the bread of presence. No further description concerning the beauty of the items is offered. However, when the author prepares to carry his listeners into the Most Holy place "behind the second curtain" the items are described by their beauty. They are the "golden" objects so important to the history and religion of the Jewish people. The author paints for his listeners a picture of a room that no person but the High Priest was able to access. It is as if he is building anticipation for when he will invite his audience to draw near to the Holy place through the blood of Jesus (Heb. 10:19-22).[293]

The author now focuses his listener's attention on the Cherubim whose wings overshadowed the mercy seat. The mercy

---

[290] Cockerill, *Hebrews*, 376-77.
[291] Allen, *Hebrews*, 459.
[292] Moo, *Hebrews*, 303.
[293] Cockerill, *Hebrews*, 377.

seat represented God's earthly throne (1 Sam 4:4) and the place where the priest sprinkled the blood on the Day of Atonement. The author's description helps emphasize the people's inability to approach the presence of God to receive forgiveness. This description anticipates what he will later say about the all-inclusive access that Christ has provided the people. He chooses not to dwell on his description long in order to provide for his listeners an account of the activities performed by the priest and their insufficiency.[294]

In verses 6-7, the author describes the limitations of the ministry performed in the earthly sanctuary by emphasizing its repeated nature. The priest must go regularly into the first part of the tent in order to repeat his duties. This repetition will be contrasted with Jesus' permanent ministry in the heavenly sanctuary. The repetitive nature of the priest's actions show they were unable to achieve their purpose. Verse 7 describes the actions of the high priest. Once again, the author's description highlights the insufficiency of the priest's actions. "Only" the high priest is allowed to enter into the Most Holy Place. The author draws attention to the people's inability to access the presence of God. The High Priest access is also limited because it takes place only once a year on the Day of Atonement.[295] Furthermore, his access takes place only with a blood offering for his own sins and the unintentional sins of the people. The author emphasizes both the insufficiency of the minister and the offering in anticipation of his description of Christ's all sufficient ministry.[296] The author provides his audience with the Holy Spirit inspired implications

---

[294] Cockerill, *Hebrews*, 378.
[295] Moo, *Hebrews*, 305.
[296] Ibid., 379-80.

of his description.[297] If true access to God was impossible through the barrier established in the first tent, then how could it provide access to the heavenly sanctuary?

The author describes the earthly sanctuary as symbolic of the present age; the earthly tent was symbolic of the people's struggle to have true access to God. The repetitive nature of the rituals, the divided structure, and the shortcomings of the ministers all emphasize the problem of access. Moo states:

> As the author has just noted, 'the way into the Most Holy Place' was open to the high priest once a year on the Day of Atonement. But the author's point in this verse is that it was not open for all worshipers. Access to the Most Holy Place symbolizes access to fellowship with God himself, and the restriction of this access to only the high priest means that the tabernacle has a negative significance for the people of Israel. They learn that their state of unholiness keeps them from approaching the holy God.[298]

However, the negative aspect also points to the solution and the superiority of what Jesus accomplished. The author now describes why access to God was unavailable. The repetitive offering of various gifts and sacrifices were unable to cleanse the conscience of the worshipper. The people's issue stemmed from a disobedient heart; it was a problem of mankind's inner self. The regulations assigned to the earthly structure only addressed man's outer

---

[297] Allen, *Hebrews*, 465.
[298] Moo, *Hebrews*, 306-07.

purity.[299] Thus, the author relates the ritual to food, drink, and washings which are regulations for the body. Once again, the benefit of the New Covenant is implied. The Old Covenant was tied to external, ceremonial regulations that did not address the people's true issue of disobedience. The New Covenant directly addressed the issue by pointing to the need of man's evil heart. The heart of stone had to be replaced by an obedient heart of flesh (Ezek. 36:26).[300]

The author provides his audience with one of the many great "but Christ" statements in Scripture. He has previously described the insufficient ministry performed in the earthly sanctuary. They are repetitive and unable to accomplish access to God. The believer's conscience could not be perfected under the Old Covenant. The author now draws an important contrast: "but Christ has arrived as high priest." Jesus' appearing represents the inauguration of the New Covenant which pertains to "the good things to come." Some commentators translate this phrase as "the good things to come." The former translation focuses on the immediate benefits of Jesus' sacrifice namely the forgiveness of sins and access to God. The latter focuses on the "heavenly homeland" that the believer is called to strive toward. Both translations have valid support. However, as Cockerill has noted, "Present cleansing from sin and future entrance into the heavenly homeland are one inseparable whole. The pastor earnestly desires the second for his hearers and urgently presses the first upon them as the only adequate means for its attainment. Thus, the phrase 'good things to come' focuses on present cleansing from sin and access to God available for the faithful without excluding ultimate

---

[299] Ibid., 309.
[300] Cockerill, *Hebrews*, 383-86.

entrance into the 'heavenly homeland' opened by these present blessings."[301]

Prison is a lot like the Old Testament Tabernacle. It is full of processes meant to provide access and solutions which ultimately fall short. Much like God's Tabernacle, their failure resides more with the fallible people than the processes themselves. People, even God's priests, are error prone. Anyone in prison who has ever filled out an inmate request form (I-60) and received either an incoherent answer or more likely no answer at all knows the frustration of faulty processes. Request forms are meant to solve issues but instead often leave the sender more confused or uncertain than before. So, most of the time, if you want something accomplished, you must go straight to the source. Jesus has removed the need for the processes. As a believer in Christ, you now have direct access to the solutions to all your requests. The incarcerated believer's request form is a heartfelt prayer to God. The book of James tells us that believers do not have it because they do not ask, and when they do ask, they ask wrongly (James 4:3).

The author now draws attention to Christ's ministry in heaven. The Levitical priests minister in man-made temples. But Jesus ministers in "the greater and more perfect tent" not made by man. The author's main point is stated in verse 12, Jesus "entered once and for all into the Holy places." Now after highlighting the repetitive nature of the earthly priest's ministry, the author shows the finality of Jesus' heavenly act. Christ's permanent entrance was achieved through his own blood, not the blood of goats and calves. Once again, the superiority of his priesthood is emphasized. It was the blood of Jesus that provided for his

---

[301] Cockerill, *Hebrews*, 390.

hearer's permanent forgiveness of sins and access to God. The Levitical priests served at the mercy of the blood of animals, a sacrifice unable to achieve its intended results. The blood of Christ, however, achieved "eternal redemption." The word for redemption "signifies the paying of a price in order to obtain freedom from bondage for those redeemed." This is drastically superior to what the blood of animals achieved, a mere outward cleansing. Thus, Cockerill states: "This 'eternal redemption' provides something more than the 'purification of the flesh' (9:10) available under the old sacrificial system … That first redemption was temporal in both the benefits it provided and their duration. This second is 'eternal' in its effectiveness, benefits, and duration."[302] The author's statement in Hebrews 9:11-12 can be summarized as: "But when Christ appeared as High Priest, he entered once and for all into heaven, securing eternal redemption by means of his own blood."

The author once again reminds his listeners of the significance of the practices that took place on the Day of Atonement. The blood of goats and bulls, and the sprinkling of the ashes of a heifer served to purify the flesh. The author focuses on outward purity of the Old Testament acts in order to strengthen his argument for the achievement of the blood of Christ. Verse 14 completes his thought. If outward purity was achieved through those rituals; how much more would the unblemished blood of Christ provide inward purity for the people of God? The author also provides his audience with a beautiful picture of the God-head's work in redemption. The eternal Son offers himself through the eternal Spirit to the eternal Father. In verse 14, the author highlights the benefits of Christ's blood. The Levitical rituals

---

[302] Cockerill, *Hebrews*, 395.

purify the flesh, but Christ's blood purifies the conscience. He once again points to the promise of the New Covenant written on the hearts of mankind. "Dead works" references the sin of the people accumulated under the Old Covenant: "The wages of sin is death" (Rom 6:23). The blood of animals could not free the people of the penalty brought by sin. However, the blood of Christ purifies the believer's conscience freeing them of guilt. Their cleansed conscience now enables them to serve the living God.[303] The author moves from the inferior benefits of animal sacrifices to the superior redemption achieved through the blood of Jesus.

Application

PENITENTIARY WORSHIP PRACTICES

Since we all have the tendency to institutionalize some aspects of our relationship with God, take the time to examine all your worship practices. Do you perform the same actions day in and day out without much thought to their significance? Read Matthew 15:1-20. What was Jesus' issue with the Pharisees and Scribes' practices? Do your religious practices flow from a pure heart or religious obligation?

[303] Koester, *Hebrews*, 416.

3. The Mediator of the New Covenant (9:15-28)

Prisoner's Insight for the Journey

Dealing with our past is difficult. Most of us have done some terrible things. We have committed crimes that have destroyed the lives of others. This is a heavy burden to bear for any person, but especially so for the young Christian. As new believers we learn that God desires for us to love our neighbor and our enemy, ideas that are profoundly different than anything we have ever believed. So naturally we struggle with our pasts, and how much we have missed the mark that God has set for all of humanity. We cannot shake the feeling that our sins are beyond forgiveness. We ask; "Does God really forgive the murderer, the sex offender, and the drug dealer?" If you asked society, the answer would most likely be, NO! Thankfully, forgiveness is not about who deserves it (no one does) but about who seeks it. Jesus died to "put away" our past, present, and future sins. Forgiveness and redemption are available to all those who seek it. Our pasts have been dealt with in Christ so that we can live for him now and until he returns in order "to save those who are eagerly waiting for him" (v.28).

The author of Hebrews desires his listeners to understand the redemption they have in Christ. Jesus' "once for all" sacrifice paid for "the transgressions committed under the first covenant" something the blood of calves and goats could not do. Jesus' sacrifice permitted him to appear in the presence of God on our behalf. The continual offering of sacrifices is no longer necessary; the believer's sin has been put away. The recipients are now to live their lives as if they are eagerly awaiting his return.

A Note on Covenant versus Testament

Verse 15 introduces one of the more difficult sections of Hebrews. The difficulty stems primarily from the translation of the Greek word "diatheke." Some take this word to mean "will or testament" and others argue for "covenant." Both positions offer persuasive arguments. Therefore, an overview of the positions will benefit the reader.

Those who adopt the translation "will" argue that the ideas of "death" and "inheritance" support their position. In order for a will to be enacted and inheritance to be transferred a death must occur. They argue that this is not the case for a covenant. Covenants do not require the death of the covenant maker to be enacted. They also provide evidence that the primary meaning of the Greek word "diatheke" in the first century denoted "will."[304] *Koester summarizes the correlation between death, inheritance, and testament: "In human terms a testament is valid as a promise while the testator is still alive, but its provisions become valid when they are put into effect upon the death of the testator. In divine terms, God's new covenant was promised through Jeremiah, but was put into effect through Christ's death."*[305]

Those who adopt the translation "covenant" argue that the overall context and usage of the term "diatheke" in Hebrews supports their interpretation. In verse 15, the word "diatheke" is used in its Old Testament sense: "New Covenant." In Verse 18, the word is also used in its traditional sense. As a result, those who adopt the translation "covenant" argue that it is unlikely the

[304] Allen, *Hebrews*, 478.
[305] Koester, *Hebrews*, 425.

author of Hebrews would change the meaning of the word in verses 16-17. Moreover, of the 33 times "diatheke" is used in the New Testament this would be the only occurrence of its usage denoting "will or testament."[306] *Cockerill, also points out that theologically the term "will" does not fit. Christ does not transfer an inheritance to others as in the case of a will. He becomes the heir himself and shares his inheritance with the believer. A newer argument advocated by Scott Hahn seeks to strengthen some of the objections to the "covenant" position. Cockerill shares some of Hahn's insights: "Verse 16-17 are not describing how one establishes a covenant, but what must be done when a covenant is broken. These verses explain how the 'death' spoken of in v. 15 provides for 'redemption from the transgressions committed under' that First—and now broken—covenant. Thus, we might gloss v. 16, 'for where there is a [broken] covenant, the death of the covenant-maker' must be borne. God's people are the 'covenant-maker' who broke God's first covenant. Thus, they have invoked the covenant curse upon themselves and are subject to death ... According to vv. 16-17, the sacrificial death of Christ provided 'redemption' from the consequences that ensued from that breach."*[307] *Allen has noted that regardless of one's translation the author's point is a death had to occur in order for the covenant/testament to be ratified.*[308]

Commentary

9:15-28

The results of Jesus' sacrifice are summed up in his position as mediator. His blood has instituted the New Covenant

---

[306] Allen, *Hebrews*, 479.
[307] Cockerill, *Hebrews*, 405-407.
[308] Allen, *Hebrews*, 481.

and the better promise currently available. His sacrifice also ensures believers of the "promised eternal inheritance." Those who benefit from a purified conscience will also one day receive their heavenly home. Moreover, the author also points out that the penalty of death acquired under the Old Covenant has been paid "since a death occurred that redeems them from the transgressions committed."

Now the author describes how Christ's sacrifice achieved this redemption. Verse 16 references a general principle of covenant making and Cockerill offers a helpful gloss: "for where there is a [broken] covenant, the death of the 'covenant-maker' must be borne."[309] This verse describes the people under the Old Covenant's situation. For example, at Mt. Sinai the people entered into a covenant with God. This covenant was accomplished by animal sacrifices. The sacrifices represented the penalty of death for the covenant violator (Gen. 15). Israel broke God's covenant and the penalty was established. The author of Hebrews argues that the penalty must be paid. The covenant-maker is God's people and they are accountable for their transgression. The author argues that the covenant is not complete until the penalty of death is complete. This shows the importance of the statement in v.15: "A death has occurred that redeems them from the transgression committed under the first covenant." Jesus on behalf of the people paid the penalty.

The author concludes that the death of Jesus is the blood which completed the Old Covenant (v.19). He now illustrates the significance of the first covenant's sacrifices. First, he does this by incorporating or combining many of the Old Testament sacrificial accounts (Exod. 24:3-8, Lev. 14:4-7, 51-5, Num. 19:6). Next, the

[309] Allen, *Hebrews*, 406.

author describes Moses' pronouncement of the Law to the people and the subsequent sprinkling of blood on the book and the people. The author aims to show his audience that they were bound to the Law through the blood of the sacrifice. In verse 20 the author alludes to this by quoting Moses' words "this is the blood of the covenant that God commanded for you." The blood signifies the death of the covenant violator. To drive home his point, the author states that even the tent and the utensils were sprinkled with blood. Cockerill states: "The pastor has been building his case that the pervasive role of sacrificial blood in the Old covenant anticipated the cleansing power of Christ's blood."[310]

Under the Old Covenant "almost everything is purified with blood." This statement once again points to the purification process of the outer man. All things needed in worship to God must be cleansed outwardly.[311] However, as the author has stated this did not cleanse the inner man. Therefore, the author once again applies a general principle: "without the shedding of blood there is no forgiveness of sins." This general rule highlights both the need for forgiveness and the Old Testament's sacrificial systems' inability to achieve it. The blood which could bring about forgiveness of sins was the blood of Jesus.

Verse 23 presents another difficulty for interpreters. The author has already established the necessity for the purification of the earthly tent. Here he calls the earthly sanctuary a copy of its heavenly original. He argues if the copy required cleansing, then so does the original. He further emphasizes the superiority of the "better sacrifices" to accomplish the cleansing. First, it is difficult to understand the need for cleansing of the heavenly sanctuary. In

---

[310] Cockerill, *Hebrews*, 409.
[311] Guthrie, *Hebrews*, NIV, 311.

what way is heaven defiled? There are numerous explanations for the author's statement, some more probable than others. However, many commentators agree that the defilement is a result of the people's sins.[312] Cockerill argues that the sins of the people created "a barrier forbidding entrance" to both the earthly and heavenly sanctuary. The barrier erected in the heavenly sanctuary has now been removed by the blood of Christ.[313] The people now have access to God.

Verses 24-26 makes it clear that Jesus has not entered an ordinary man-made sanctuary but "into heaven itself." The author uses this statement to establish the exact location of Jesus' priestly duties. Jesus entered heaven in the presence of God "on our behalf." The author once again establishes the repetitive nature of the Levitical priest's sacrifices. Jesus does not "offer himself repeatedly" as do the Levitical priests. Jesus offers himself (his blood) while the Levitical priests offer blood not their own. If Jesus would have had to repeatedly offer himself, he would continually be suffering from the foundation of the world. This statement points to Jesus' suffering on the cross. If Jesus would have had to suffer the cross repeatedly then this would have begun at the beginning of the world. Sin has been around since the Garden; therefore, Jesus' suffering would have begun at that point. However, the author argues that Jesus "appeared once for all at the end of the ages." Jesus' one time sacrifice made possible forgiveness of sins past, present, and future. Thus, the author desires his listeners to understand that Jesus' offering is final. There is no other means of forgiveness.

---

[312] Cockerill, *Hebrews*, 416; Lane, *Hebrews*, 247; Guthrie, *Hebrews*, 315.
[313] Ibid., 416-17.

Much like the priests of the Tabernacle, my life in prison has been defined by repetition. I wake up, get ready, leave my dorm for work, and ultimately return to where I began my day. I have done this for decades: wake up leave and return. I often dream of when this repetition will finally end. I long for the day that I wake up and "once for all" leave never to return to my cell again. On that day, I will rejoice that my prison stay is complete and my penalty has been paid.

In verses 27-28 the author provides another general principle. Man is appointed to die once then judgment. This statement would have been readily affirmed by the author's audience. Just as people today, his ancient audience feared both death and judgment. As a result, the author links the onetime death of Jesus with the onetime death of the believer. The believer's death is a result of sin; Jesus' death dealt with sin. The believer will appear again to stand judgment; Jesus will appear again to judge. The author does not want to leave his audience in fear of death and judgment so he reminds them that Jesus' second coming will be "to save those who are eagerly waiting for him." This is a call for the author's listeners to persevere until that day. Christ has dealt with their sin problem, now they must walk in obedience awaiting his return.

Application

BIBLICAL FICTION

One of the strangest concepts often promoted by counselors and pastors alike is self- forgiveness. They proclaim that somehow, some way, people must learn to forgive themselves. However, I have searched the Scriptures high and low and cannot find this taught or even implied by the word of God.

As a matter of fact, if one considers the idea, it really makes no sense. Forgiving oneself is like owing oneself money. Forgiveness requires an offense to be committed. Where there is no offense there can be no forgiveness. So, the question is, can a person offend themselves? Can someone hurt their own feelings? Like I said self-forgiveness is biblical fiction. Instead of focusing on how we must forgive ourselves, we should be praising the glorious forgiveness that we have in Christ. Take the time today to praise God for the forgiveness that Christ achieved on your behalf.

4. The Superior Sacrifice of the New Covenant (10:1-18)

Prisoner's Insight for the Journey

As previously mentioned, a large portion of prison life is about repetition. In prison, in order to stabilize our often-chaotic environment, we develop routines. These then become the schedules of how we do time. Everyone's routine is somewhat different; it all depends on your focus. If your focus is exercise and fitness, then your routine is defined by a workout schedule. If your routine is education, then your schedule is dictated by school hours and study time. When we are focused on certain activities our routines rarely change. I can often tell you about what time it is based on who is currently working out under the stairs. Routines in themselves are not bad. They often display an individual's discipline and commitment toward attaining one's goals. The problem for us is that sometimes we change our focus without changing our routines. We want strong lower bodies, but we do chest, back, and arms all week. We move into the realm of insanity, doing the same thing over and over again expecting different results. It's like that video game where you die in the same exact spot every single time because you refuse to approach the problem from a different angle. This insanity often flows into other aspects of our lives. We convince ourselves that this time will be different only to find ourselves in the same spot, same results; our third case, or fifth fight over dominoes. We never try something different.

The author of Hebrews reminds his readers that the old routine of the Mosaic Law could not produce a change in results. The fact that priests had to continually offer sacrifices on behalf of the people showed that the routine was flawed. The continual practice of offering actually just served as a reminder of the problem of sin. Israel was performing the same routine getting the same results. The author of Hebrews says that Jesus changed the routine by offering a sacrifice that actually brought about forgiveness for sins. In his offering of himself, no other offering was required. In relation to sin Jesus' routine was the end of all other routines.

Commentary

10:1-18

The author focuses his attention on the Old Testament sacrifices. He uses the general word "law" in order to entail all that took place under the Old Covenant.[314] The law was but a "shadow," and just as the shadows are temporary and passing, the Old Covenant was also fading.

The author uses the imagery to show the temporary nature of the old system. Its sole purpose was to point to a more excellent way to access God. The new way would entail "good things" for the worshipper. The "good things" are the benefits currently offered in Christ and the promise of final rest at his second coming. This is important for the author's audience to grasp. Jesus provides "good things" for the believer. Regardless of how they view their current circumstances. Like Jesus, they must also endure affliction and reproach, and like Jesus, God will also reward their obedience through perseverance.[315]

---

[314] Cockerill, *Hebrews*, 428.
[315] Koester, *Hebrews*, 412.

Once again, the author focuses on the transitory nature of the Old Covenant. He states the "same sacrifices" of bulls and goats "continually offered every year" could never "perfect" the worshipper. The purpose of the Old Testament Sacrificial system was to provide the worshipper access to God by removing the stain of sin.[316] However, the blood of animals could not perfect the conscience of the worshipper and thus failed to achieve its intended goal. The children of Israel were engaged in the textbook definition of insanity, doing the same thing over and over expecting different results.

The author presents his listeners with a question meant to draw their attention to the sacrifices' inability to perfect the worship. He argues that since the sacrifices did not cease to be performed it proves that the worshipper was never "cleansed." After their offering for sins was complete there still remained a "consciousness of sins." The author's use of "consciousness" denotes the continual awareness that sin exists. He uses this word to contrast with his use of "reminder" in verse 3. After the ritual was complete, the worshipper was left with a feeling of its failure. It's like asking someone for forgiveness but never feeling truly forgiven. It leaves one with the urge to seek that person's forgiveness for the same offense again and again. The feeling of unforgiveness serves as a consciousness of the wrong committed, the very sight of the person is one's constant reminder.

The United States justice system has created a new class of people: the justice impacted citizen. In the U. S., the stigma which accompanies a felony conviction permanently scars a person's social standing. Even after their sentences are completed and their debts to society have been paid, the justice-impacted

---

[316] Cockerill, *Hebrews*, 430.

person is still marked. They cannot work certain jobs, live in certain places, or even vote for their representatives. This results largely from the distinction between paying a debt and being forgiven of an offense. While their debts have been paid by serving years and even decades in prison, every job or rental application denial, because of their past, shows they have not been forgiven. No matter how much they work in order to benefit society they still remain stigmatized. The only way to restore one's rights is to be pardoned by the Governor which is unlikely to happen. This is the beauty of the Gospel message. Jesus has both paid our debts and forgiven our offenses. In his kingdom, the justice impacted believer is a full citizen with all rights restored.

The author states that the temple sacrifices served as one's yearly reminder of their sinful condition. It is that dreaded monthly bill that deep down a person feels he cannot pay; that billboard that reminds one that taxes are due. When the worshipper leaves the temple, they carry with them the sense of an eventual return; the sense they failed to accomplish their objective. The author employs very strong language to convey the insufficiency of animal sacrifices: "for it is impossible for the blood of bulls and goats to take away sin."[317] He leaves no question of the ritual's failure to solve the worshipper's issue of a sinful and disobedient heart. The yearly performance of animal sacrifices proved the impossibility of their success. They could not even provide the worshipper with a sense of success but instead stood as a beacon of failure and the need to try again year after year.

The author's stress of the Old Covenant's insufficiency sets up his argument for the incarnation of Jesus. The blood shed

---

[317] Cockerill, *Hebrews*, 432.

from the body of the Son accomplished what the blood shed from countless bodies of animals could not. Jesus' blood made the impossible possible. In this section, the author explores the implications of Jesus' incarnation through the citing of Psalm 40:6-8. God's will was for the incarnation of his eternal Son to achieve what "sacrifices and offerings" could not. The author introduces this Psalm by placing on the lips of Jesus as the Son's words spoken to the Father. The listeners are fully aware that these words were originally spoken by King David. Thus, the author shows that "David's words of response in Psalm 22:22 and Psalm 40:6-8 find their truest significance as the Son's response to the Father."[318]

The exact backdrop of Psalm 40 is unknown, but it could have possibly been a reference to Saul's rash act of offering sacrifices on behalf of the people without waiting on Samuel (1 Samuel 15:22-23). If this is the case, the author most likely wants to highlight the act of submission and obedience in contrast to mere ritualistic offerings. This fits well with the author's use of highlighting Christ's obedience. "The Psalm represents the posture of obedience and resolute intention to die on the cross, embraced by Christ in the incarnation."[319] The apostle Paul echoes this sentiment in Philippians 2:7 when he states, Jesus "humbled himself by becoming obedient to the point of death, even death on a cross." The author uses this Psalm to drive home the following points. First, God was displeased with Old Testament "Sacrifices and offerings." This displeasure was most likely tied to the state of the worshipper's heart from which they were offered. Second, Christ's self-offering was both pleasing and in line with the will

---

[318] Ibid., 434.
[319] Guthrie, *Hebrews*, CNTUOT, 976-77.

of God.[320] Thus for a struggling audience, the message is clear. God desires the obedience evidenced through perseverance of faith.

The author returns to Psalm 40 and provides his own interpretation. First, he expands "sacrifices and offerings" to include "burnt offerings and sin offerings." He does this to encapsulate the whole Old Testament sacrificial system. Next, he ties these to the Old Testament Law. The author drives home the point that God does not find pleasure in these law mandated rituals. What pleases God is Christ's self-sacrifice and absolute obedience. The Son proclaims "Behold, I have come to do your will." Jesus is the Son with whom the Father is "well pleased" (Matt. 3:17). The author drives home God's displeasure by stating "he does away" (abolishes) the sacrificial system. Yet the very removal of the old system implies the establishment of the second. God has found fault with the Old Covenant so he will establish the New (Heb. 8:8). The New Covenant brings about what the Old Covenant could not.

The author now applies his interpretation to his hearers. Through Christ's obedience to the "will" of God "we have been sanctified." The author emphasizes the following. First, Christ's sacrifices achieved "sanctification" on behalf of the believer, something the past rituals were unable to accomplish. Second, "we have been sanctified" signals the completed aspect of Christ's work. This stands in contrast to the Old Testament sacrifices' failure to make perfect its worshippers. The author is not advocating some form of perfectionism but is ensuring his listeners that they have the ability to access God and thus

---

[320] Guthrie, *Hebrews*, NIV, 253.

"persevere in obedience."[321] This is a drastic reversal of the conscious reminder of sin under the Old Covenant. The New Covenant believer has been set apart (sanctified) so that they may now draw near (Heb. 10:1) to God with a purified "conscience from dead works to serve the living God" (Heb. 9:14). All the promises, both current and future, are ensured "through the offering of the body of Jesus Christ once for all."

The author returns to his main topic, which he began at Hebrews 8:1, the high priesthood of Jesus.[322] He makes one final appeal to the inefficiency of the Levitical priesthood by describing their ministry as standing daily and repeatedly offering the same sacrifices that never accomplish their goal. He aims to leave his listeners with one final impression of the futility of the Old Covenant rituals. The Levitical priest stands daily because his work is never complete. He offers the "same sacrifices" because this is all he has at his disposal. However, his continual work never accomplishes its intended goal to "take away sins." Verse 11 sets the stage for the author's major contrast he makes by using Psalm 110:1.

Every Levitical priest had continually offered futile sacrifices, "but when Christ had offered for all time a single sacrifice for all sins, he sat down at the right hand of God." The author contrasts several points. First, the Levitical priest "stands daily" which implies his unfinished work; Jesus sits at the right hand of the Father, signaling his work is complete.[323] The Levitical priest offers the same sacrifices which can never take away sins. However, the author's description of Jesus' single

[321] Cockerill, *Hebrews*, 443.
[322] Ibid., 446.
[323] Allen, *Hebrews*, 502.

offering and his sitting at the Father's right hand implies that Jesus' sacrifice accomplished its goal of removing sin. These verses describe Jesus' current session and accomplishments as the believer's high priest. Verse 13 looks forward to his second coming.

The author reveals that Christ is currently sitting as High Priest over the people of God. However, he also reveals that this is just the initial step in his ministry. Jesus will return again when his enemies will "be made a footstool for his feet." This is a vital point for the church to understand. The persecution and trials they are facing are only temporary. The enemy may look as if he is victorious but the fact that Jesus reigns from heaven, shows that he is already defeated. The author desires his hearers to persevere through their daily battles because Jesus has already won the war.[324]

The author drives home his point of ultimate victory in verse 14. The single offering of Jesus has accomplished what countless animal sacrifices could not; the perfection of the believer. This means that the stain of believers' sin has been taken away enabling them full access to the presence of God. The author also describes believers as "those who are being sanctified." The believer is both saint and sinner, both sanctified and continually in need of sanctification.[325] While the author's audience now has access to God through Jesus, they are called to live lives pleasing to God.

After introducing the New Covenant in Hebrews 8:1, the author now focuses on its specific benefits. He introduces those

---

[324] Cockerill, *Hebrews*, 450.
[325] Koester, *Hebrews*, 440.

benefits by placing them on the lips of the Holy Spirit. While Christ sits at the right hand of the Father as the High Priest and mediator of the New Covenant, it is the Holy Spirit that bears witness to its benefits in the lives of the believer. The author makes several notable alterations to Jeremiah 31 which was important for future generations. First, the author redirects the wording of the New Covenant recipients. He changes House of Israel and House of Judah to "them." This change in recipients has the effect of broadening the benefits of the New Covenant. The covenant is no longer focused on national Israel, but its benefits apply to all those who have faith in Jesus. Second, the author reverses the order of "heart and mind" to "mind and heart." This most likely is done to focus on the heart which the author emphasizes as the main issue of God's people. He used Psalm 95:7-8 in order to exhort the believers to faith and perseverance on numerous occasions (Hebrews 3-4). It is the "evil, unbelieving heart" which leads people to fall away (Heb. 3:12). Third, he alters "I will remember their sins no more" to their sins and lawless deeds. Adding lawless deeds helps emphasize God's total forgiveness.[326] Finally, the author changes verb tenses in the original Greek phrase to "I will remember." "God says definitely that he will no longer remember all of their former misconduct no matter how 'lawless' it may have been."[327] These subtle changes personalize the benefits of the New Covenant for the author's current audience and the faithful of future generations.

The author concludes his explanation of the New Covenant with a final reminder of the sufficiency of Christ's sacrifice. Since God, through Jesus, has once for all dealt with sin, "there is no

---

[326] Cockerill, *Hebrews*, 458.
[327] Ibid.

longer any offering for sin." The author closes the door on the Old Covenant sacrificial system. The implication for those wavering in the faith is clear. There is no turning back in hopes of finding forgiveness. Faith in Christ is the only means of access to God.

Application

FULL FORGIVENESS

Understanding the forgiveness of God provided to the believer by Jesus is essential for living in victory. The author of Hebrews continually reminds his listeners that Jesus has provided full forgiveness. This is evident in the believer's ability to approach God having their conscience cleansed. However, many today still live under the burden of unforgiveness. Take time and read Jeremiah 31:34, Isaiah 43:25, Psalm 103:12. How does the knowledge found in these texts help the believer live guilt free and in victory.

III. God's Examples of Faithfulness for the Weary Traveler (10:19-12:29)

Section Summary

In light of all that the author has shared with his listeners, they are encouraged to boldly approach the holy presence of God through the work of Jesus. He warns them of the danger of turning away from the grace of God because of their circumstance. They must persevere in the face of opposition. The author provides his audience with numerous examples of faithful men and women who through faith in the promises of God endured various trials and tribulations. The listeners must understand that God disciplines his children. Their current struggle shows that they are loved by God. They have not traveled this far to receive the judgment of Sinai, but through Jesus they have been brought to the city of the living God, a kingdom which cannot be shaken.

Introduction to the Section

In this section, the author transitions from exposition to exhortation. He began his teaching on the High Priesthood of Jesus in Hebrews 4:14 and examined its superiority and benefits until Hebrews 10:18. Now he transitions to exhortation signaled by three "let us" statements: "Let us draw near" (v.22), "Let us hold fast" (v.23), and "Let us consider" (v.24). These statements of exhortation build on all that the author previously said. It is the very benefits obtained by Jesus' sacrifice and present session that make the "let us" statement possible. This section serves to support the author's overall goal of encouraging his listeners to persevere in the face of all trials and tribulations. In the coming section of Hebrews 11:1-40, the author will provide his audience with numerous examples of perseverance of faith, beginning with creation and continuing until Jesus, who is the prime example of perseverance (Heb. 12:1-3). In Hebrews 12:4-24, the author addresses the circumstances of his audience, both their struggles (Heb. 12:4) and eventual triumph (Heb. 12:11). He concludes this section (Heb. 12:25-29) by reminding them of the impending judgment to come; their "God is a consuming fire" (Heb. 12:29). Thus, the author combines exhortation, example, and warning in hopes of encouraging his audience to persevere to the end.[328]

[328] Cockerill, *Hebrews*, 460.

A. Jesus: The Foundation of Perseverance (10:19-39)

1. Perseverance: Draw Near, Hold Fast, and Consider (10:19-25)

Prisoner's Insight for the Journey

In prison access is very limited. We need a "pass" or permission to go anywhere and everywhere. If we are hungry, we cannot simply go and eat. There are no restaurants or convenience stores for us to buy food from. We must wait on the officer to either call chow or bring our chow to us. We are at the mercy of the prison system, they tell us every day when, where, and what to eat. The inmate lacks access to some of life's most basic needs and comforts.

One of the most difficult places in prison to access is commissary. Every inmate has a particular day that he is assigned to go to commissary. He also shares this day with over 100 other inmates. Only so many inmates can access the commissary at one time, and the process is often disorganized and chaotic. We prepare our mission impossible plans to gain access to commissary on the previous day and as soon as the commissary window opens over 100 men begin to implement their plans.

One day I gained access to commissary three times and each time I was kicked out because I did not have permission. I finally grew frustrated and decided to give up that day. On my way back to the dorm, I happened to cross paths with the warden. He asked how I was doing and I explained that I had been kicked out of commissary three times and I was not doing very well. I guess that day he respected my tenacity because he gave me a pass. I immediately returned to the commissary window. I did not have to plan or sneak, I had access. I boldly approached the officer who had already removed me three times and presented my pass. He examined it with suspicion but gave me access. I had the authority of the warden to be in that line, and no one was kicking me out.

The author of Hebrews is reminding his audience that Jesus has provided them access to the Father. Once restricted by sacrificial rules and regulations, the blood of Jesus has now become their "pass" to enter the presence of God. The Hebrews can use their new access to draw near to God with assurance. They no longer have to worry about their plan or their pass. When Jesus has provided access, no one can restrict them because "he who promised is faithful." The greatest thing is that Jesus' pass has provided access for everyone, we simply receive his blessing.

Commentary

10:19-25

The author introduces this section with a "therefore" signaling its relationship to what was previously mentioned. Guthrie has found at least eight parallels between here and Hebrews 4:14-16.[329] All that the author has previously said stands as the foundation for the following exhortation. Apart from Jesus' priestly ministry, none of the following encouragement would be possible. Jesus has paved the way to finally enter the presence of God.[330] The Old Covenant worshipper's "Consciousness of sins" (Heb. 10:12) is now replaced by a "confidence to enter." This new

---

[329] Guthrie, *Hebrews*, NIV, 340-41.
[330] Cockerill, *Hebrews*, 465-66.

boldness is not a self-assurance, but confidence that flows from a true faith and understanding of what Jesus has accomplished. The boldness to enter the presence of God is made possible "by the blood of Jesus." By emphasizing the sacrificial offering of Jesus' body, the author was reminding his audience of both what was impossible under the Old Covenant and was now possible by the New.

The author strengthens his statement of access by referring to it as "the new and living way." Jesus' self-offering is not a modification of the Old Covenant, but the inauguration of a New Covenant. The "living way" also reveals that Jesus' work is not like the blood of dead bulls and goats. Jesus is the sacrificial mediator who lives to intercede on behalf of the people of God. His living and continual intercession is the means by which the hearers should have confidence. They are not entering the presence of God alone, but go there to meet Jesus, their pioneer and advocate.

The author employs a phrase "the curtain, that is through his flesh" which has "bedeviled Hebrews commentators."[331] This confusion stems from the previous understanding of the curtain as a barrier. Now the author describes Christ's flesh as the curtain by which the believer accesses the presence of God. Most likely one of the new aspects previously mentioned is the changing of the curtain from a barrier to a sanctifying entrance. This, once again, is a reversal of the old order. What was once seen as a restriction for the people, now is meant to establish confidence and assurance in the life of worshippers. The curtain of Christ's flesh beckons

---

[331] Cockerill, *Hebrews*, 468.

the worshipper to enter the most holy place as one who has been forgiven.

The author describes Jesus as the "great priest," a lesser description than "great high priest" used previously (Heb. 4:14). Jesus is the believer's "great priest" because he provides the believer with a great confidence through his great blood sacrifice. All that Jesus performed in the role as the believer's priest is both superior and sufficient. This priest reigns over the house of God. This is reminiscent of the author's description of Jesus in Hebrews 3:6. Jesus is the great priest who reigns over the house of God not as a servant but as a Son.

The believer's confidence in their great priest instills assurance enabling them to "draw near" to God. The word for "draw near" is meant to remind the listeners of the Old Testament priest's sacrificial duties. They would "draw near" to God in order to offer a sacrifice. The difference stands in the Christian's confidence and assurance, something the Levitical priesthood never had. The condition in which the believer is called to approach is with a "true heart" and "in fullness of faith." The true heart contrasts with the unbelieving generation's evil and disobedient heart (Heb. 3:12). This highlights the effects of the New Covenant on the lives of the believer. The Law of God has been written on their hearts enabling them to walk in obedience to his will. A true heart is displayed by the believer's willingness to live as if the promises of God are a reality in their lives.

The author also describes the means by which the worshipper must approach God: "hearts sprinkled clean from an evil conscience and our bodies washed with pure water." Here the author echoes Ezekiel 36:25-26 which outlines the blessings of the New Covenant. The author's use of the original language highlights both the completed aspect and the ongoing nature of God's redemptive work.[332] The washing of the body with "pure water" likely signifies the removal of the stain of sin from one's life. The author highlights that both the inner "heart" and outer "body" of man is wash clean by the blood of Christ. The whole man is now able to draw near to the presence of God. The believer's cleansed heart will enable them to walk in God's statutes and obey his rules. This is what the author's audience must keep in mind. A new heart implies new actions. They cannot waver in hope while walking in God's statutes. Perseverance and obedience to God's rules go hand in hand.

The author exhorts his audience to "hold fast" to their confession. The word "hold fast" in the original Greek denotes to "retain faithfully."[333] This word was also used as a technical nautical term which meant to "steer for" a desired course.[334] Either idea fits well with the overall context of Hebrews. The believer is to steer toward Jesus, the content of the believer's confession, while also holding fast to all that they have been taught. This means that the listeners are to remember all that the author has previously stated concerning Jesus. It will be the continual holding to these truths without wavering that will enable them to persevere in the face of tribulations. The confession also entails the promises of God. It is God's promise of final rest and ultimate victory over all enemies for which the people of God strive. The recipients are called to hold fast their faith in the promises of God because God is faithful. The believer's ultimate assurance must always rest in the very nature of God.

---

[332] Guthrie, *Hebrews*, NIV, 473.
[333] "κατέχω," in *BDAG*.
[334] Hanse, κατέχω, in *TDONT*.

Today is January 1, 2025, the start of a new legislative year in Texas, the start of a new year of hope. Every other year, countless Texas prisoners turn their attention toward Austin, the state capital, in hope of receiving some type of relief from the miserable prison conditions. We hope for a law that will force prison officials to air condition state penitentiaries so that men and women do not have to suffer the oppressive Texas summers. We hope that Texas will end its practice of slavery and finally pay its inmate workers. We hope that parole laws will change enabling men who have been incarcerated since they were juveniles to get a "second look" at freedom. We hope and we hope some more, yet relief fails to come. Once the legislative session is over and our hopes are crushed, we go back to our daily routines. Every other year, we build ourselves up in anticipation only to be let down again. This emotional rollercoaster ride is of our own making. Our hope is simply misguided. We have no reason to hope in a hopeless system. Our reasoning sounds like this: "I hope the law will change because I hope the law will change." It is having hope in hope which is hope in nothing. However, this is not biblical hope. Biblical hope is always grounded in something. The believer can "hold fast" to hope in the promises of God because of God's unchanging character. God is faithful and his promises are sure. Therefore, despite our circumstances, we can always "hold fast" to our hope because God cannot lie (Heb. 6:18) and what he has promised will surely come to pass.

The final exhortation in this section is focused on the believer's brothers and sisters in the faith: "Let us consider how to stir up one another to love and good works." The author appealed to his audience to be encouraged and encourage one another. This means that perseverance is not a solo operation but entails the whole body of believers. The listeners are to think on ways to show love to the people of God. During times of need, it is love that can enable one to endure their trial. Yet true love will always manifest itself through "good works." The author calls his audience to show their love by how they treat one another.

The author explains what love and good works look like. First, love and good works entail gathering together for worship and fellowship. Many scholars believe that some were no longer gathering for worship and fellowship due to a declining faith and outward persecution. However, the author desires his audience to know it is during difficult times that fellowship is most important. It is impossible to provoke or be provoked to love if one isolates themselves from the community of believers. The author also explains that love and good works are accomplished through encouragement, and encouragement becomes all the more important as the "day" draws near. The author has in mind the Day of Judgment and uses this final phrase as a reminder of the believer's anticipation of Jesus' return. This also serves as an eye-opener before he segues into his section of warning.

Application

BIBLICAL HOPE

There are many misguided views of biblical hope. Some attempts to understand hope are very close to the idea of luck, they are not grounded in any reality. The Bible presents hope in a drastically different manner. One author stated, "Hope to be sure, is not a kite at the mercy of the changing winds, but a 'sure and steadfast anchor of the soul,' penetrating deep into the invisible eternal world (Heb. 6:19)."[335] Read Job 13:15, Psalm 42:5, and 1 Peter 1:21. Who is the believer's hope grounded in? Think about the things you hope for, are your hopes grounded in the promises of God or your own personal desires?

---

[335] Tasker, "Hope" In the *New Bible Dictionary*. Eds. I Howard Marshall, A. R. Millard, J.I. Packer, and D.J. Wiseman (Grand Rapids: IVP, 1996), 479-480.

2. Perseverance: No Turning Back Now (10:26-39)

Prisoner's Insight for the Journey

As a young believer, I struggled to understand the tension that existed between the forgiveness that the Bible taught and the temporal punishment I was experiencing. I couldn't understand why God would allow believers to stay imprisoned. I had accepted Christ and cleaned up many of my obvious issues, but I still remained locked-up. If God truly loved me then why was I experiencing punishment and hardships? I remember many times that I would be doing so well, and suddenly out of nowhere, I would find myself in an altercation with another. These setbacks would often result in continual acts of bad behavior. It is as if I told myself: "Well you messed up again might as well mess up some more." I used these setbacks as opportunities to question the love of God and his work in my life. As I matured, I learned that my understanding of salvation was wrong. I had come to believe that salvation equaled no problems. The more I read the Bible and walked with God, the more I realized how wrong I had been. I finally had what I call a Psalm 73 moment. God pulled back the curtain and showed me what salvation really was. Salvation was not deliverance from all my worldly struggles in this life, but the ability to persevere despite them and the knowledge that they would not follow me into the life to come. Salvation does not equal no problems, salvation equals life and victory in Christ, and unfortunately life and victory in Christ will have problems.

The author's audience was struggling to understand their relationship with God in light of their persecution. Some were no longer fellowshipping with other believers. Instead of drawing near to God and his people during their time of need, they were isolating themselves. The author provides his listeners with another warning to correct their thoughts and actions. Salvation was not about avoiding their negative circumstances. They could not simply return to their old way of life and all would be normal. They had received "the knowledge of the truth." There was no turning back. All would be judged, even the uninformed, but the judgment would be far worse for those who knew and rejected the truth. Thus, the author reminds his listeners of their initial response to persecution when they first accepted Jesus. He reminds them that salvation is for those who, despite their struggles, have faith and preserve their souls.

Commentary

10:26-39

The author begins this section with a strong warning. For those who deliberately sin, there remains no sacrifice for sins. Once again, the rhetorical aspect of the author's statement is evident. Like a good pastor concerned for his flock, he includes himself in his warning: "If *we* go on sinning deliberately." In the original Greek, the author positions the word "deliberately" at the beginning of his sentence. This shows that he has in mind a specific type of sinner, one who willfully rejects the "knowledge of the truth."[336] An intentional sin in this sense is a premeditated action. It is as if the sinner is saying, "I know the consequences, but I am going to do it anyway."[337] The deliberate sinning also comes after receiving the knowledge of the truth. The knowledge the author has in mind is the sacrificial nature of Jesus' priestly office. If one ultimately rejects what Christ has accomplished, this

---

336 Lane, *Hebrews*, 292.
337 Guthrie, *Hebrews*, NIV, 335.

constitutes a willful dismissal of his gift of salvation. If, as the author has forcefully argued, Jesus is the only acceptable sacrifice, then there remains no further means of forgiveness. The author permanently closed the door of the Old Covenant sacrificial institutions. Even if they had been capable of providing forgiveness (which they weren't), the Old Covenant was now obsolete.

The only thing remaining for the one who rejects Jesus is "a fearful expectation of judgment." The person who rejects Jesus' sacrificial gift brings eternal judgment on themselves.[338] The author graphically depicts this judgment as "a fury of fire" that consumes the adversary. The one who once embraced the things of God temporarily (Heb. 6:4-5) is now referred to as the adversary of God. This points to the person's willful rejection. Those who heard the Gospel but despise what they heard now become the enemies of the Gospel.[339]

The author once again employs a lesser to greater argument in order to describe and emphasize the judgment of God. Under the Law of Moses, any person who "deliberately" set aside God's commands was condemned to die. However, the greater offense, and thus judgment, is over the one who sets aside Jesus. The author describes the rejection of Christ as trampling "underfoot the Son of God." This means to treat Christ with disdain.[340] The author's description contrasts with what he said about the violator of the Law of Moses. The Law is set aside, but Jesus, who is the Son of God, is trampled underfoot. The author also describes the rejection of Jesus as profaning "the blood of the

---

[338] Pace, Allen, *Hebrews*, 523.
[339] Cockerill, *Hebrews*, 486.
[340] Harris, *Hebrews*, 283.

covenant." This means to make the blood of Jesus common. Within the context of the two covenants, this is akin to making the blood of Christ less effective than the blood of bulls and goats. The purpose of the blood of Christ is for sanctifying believers, something that has obviously not happened in the life of one who rejects Christ's sacrifice. Any rejection of the work of Jesus is also a rejection of the work of the Spirit. One who has shared in the work of the Holy Spirit (Heb. 6:4) and yet rejects what they have witnessed outrages the "Spirit of Grace." This is similar to those in the Gospels who attributed the work of Jesus to Satan.[341] Lane states the attitude well:

> Taken cumulatively, the three clauses in v.29 define persistent sin (v. 26a) as an attitude of contempt for the salvation secured through the priestly sacrifice of Christ. Nothing less than a complete rejection of the Christian faith satisfies the descriptive clauses in which the effects of the offense are sketched.[342]

The one who rejects the goodness of God is destined for judgment. The author highlights this sure judgment by quoting Deuteronomy 32:35-36. The author quotes Deuteronomy 32:35 in order to reveal that God will have the final say over those who reject Jesus. This verse helps to reinforce the belief that judgment will come to those who reject God and persecute his people. To drive home this point, he separates Deuteronomy 32:35 from Deuteronomy 32:36. The author desires both the judgment of the unbeliever and the vindication of his people to be emphasized.[343]

---

[341] Guthrie, *Hebrews*, NIV, 357.
[342] Lane, *Hebrews*, 295.
[343] Cockerill, *Hebrews*, 491-495.

At the end of time, Jesus will return to judge those who rejected his gift and vindicate all those who persevered in faith. The author concludes his warning with a final reminder: "It is a fearful thing to fall into the hands of the living God." Judgment comes from none other than the one who laid the foundation of the universe.

The author now asks his audience to recall the days of former trials and sufferings. Hebrews does not specifically reference the occasions or time of the persecutions. Many scholars have noted the similarities between the author's description and the persecution under the Roman emperor Claudius in A.D. 49 when the Jews were expelled from Rome.[344] Regardless of the specific event, the author reminds his listeners that they had previously suffered and endured. He recalls the days after they had come to the truth. His audience had come to understand who Jesus was and what he had accomplished on their behalf. This new understanding enabled them to endure whatever trial came their way.

The author recalls four particular examples of their suffering. First, their faith in Jesus resulted in public shame. They were mocked, insulted, and even beaten for their newfound faith in Christ. Cockerill states: "It is difficult for modern readers to feel the full fury of the shame and public ostracism experienced by these first-century believers."[345] While he is correct that it is difficult, it is not impossible to relate, especially inside of prison where Christians are often treated with scorn by both the administration and fellow inmates.

---

[344] Guthrie, *Hebrews*, NIV, 359.
[345] Cockerill, *Hebrews*, 500.

The administration recognizes and promotes Christianity within the walls of the prison; however, they struggle to recognize the inmate's religious devotion. They see the inmate Christian as a second-class Christian at best, or one who is simply faking their commitment in order to receive some special privileges. The inmate's second-class status results in regular cancellation, and disrespect for worship services; things that would not be tolerated outside the walls of prison. Imagine an officer walking into a church on the outside and screaming a torrent of profanities at the congregation. The officer would be fired, no questions asked. However, in prison, this is a regular occurrence.

Furthermore, while Christianity is accepted within the confines of the chapel, it is ignored in every other area of prison. Prisons are controlled by gangs. As a result, they also establish the daily social practices of life inside prison. The law of drugs and violence rules the land, and the Christian struggles to live in two different worlds. In the chapel, he is taught to love his neighbor and do good to others. In his living area, he is taught to look out for himself and survival of the fittest. In the chapel, he is welcomed and embraced. In his living area, he is mocked and often asked to sit on the floor because he is unwelcomed at tables and benches.

The author also mentions being partners with those suffering afflictions. This means, while the individual might not have been specifically targeted, they suffered nonetheless by bearing the persecution of others. In a true community of believers, when one suffers, all suffer. Imagine living in a world where you are to blame for all life's problems. In the first-century, Christianity was often the scapegoat for both the Roman government and the Jewish religion. Their existence was often used as a cause for all bad events. If they preached Jesus as King, the Jews blamed them for the wrath of Rome on the Jewish people. If Rome burned to the ground, it was the fault of the Christians. This same issue exists inside prison. If an officer searches and finds contraband in a cell or living area, the Christian is blamed for snitching by his peers. Christians are often singled out as the cause for all change in prison policy.

The author reminds his listeners how they formerly responded to trials. They had “compassion on those in prison.” It was a common practice in the first century for Christians to be imprisoned for their faith. Those who remained free, bore the burden of those who were incarcerated. This is most clearly seen in the life of the apostle Paul. Timothy and many others saw to the welfare of Paul while he was imprisoned.

This same compassion is practiced inside the walls of prison daily. Those in the Christian community who have the ability to purchase food and hygiene share with those who do not. As a matter of fact, there is such an abundance of giving that it often overflows to those outside the faith in a form of evangelism. While this happens in the world also, the selfless giving of the inmate is quite remarkable. In Texas inmates do not earn wages for work. They rely solely on the giving of friends and loved ones. At times, due to hardship which the inmate’s family may be facing, they receive very little. Nevertheless, men and women give from their small blessing to those who have nothing. This is true Christian compassion. The inmate does not give from their abundance; they give from what they have (Mark 12:41-44).

The first-century church also suffered confiscation of their property. The belongings of those imprisoned were confiscated and sold and the money was given to the government. The author focuses on his listener's attitude during these times. He states that they "joyfully accepted the plundering" of their property. The author's audience understood they possessed a better inheritance than the one confiscated. The "better possession" of his listeners was an "abiding" inheritance. This means they looked toward what would be given to the children of God in the age to come. The possessions which were once confiscated are temporal and will perish, but what awaits the believer who endures is eternal and everlasting. The author calls his listeners to refocus on the heavenly blessing to come.

In prison, it is often difficult to see past the lengthy sentence, concrete, and steel bars. One's circumstances can appear so hopeless that pressing forward seems so pointless. However, hope and faith are the driving forces in one's walk in Christ. It is faith in Jesus' forgiveness that gets one moving forward and it is the hope of better days that keeps once striving. Regardless of the believer's sentence length, the Bible teaches that this world is not the goal. The Bible promises of a world to come where all Christians are first-class.

The author exhorts his hearers not to throw away their "confidence, which has a great reward." It was their confidence in the promises of God and hope of a future inheritance that kept them persevering in the faith. Now that they are experiencing new struggles, they must display that same confidence. The word confidence is also translated as boldness. He desires his listeners to display the same boldness toward professing Jesus in the face of an unbelieving world.[346] During trials and tribulations, the believer must double down on their faith.

---

[346] Cockerill, *Hebrews*, 504.

The trials of the incarcerated Christian can be difficult. They face struggles from two fronts. They have the difficulties of prison life and the struggles from the outside. Due to their incarceration, inmates often feel helpless in dealing with issues on the outside. The struggles and hardships of loved ones bear heavily on the confidence of one's faith. Relationships are strained and loved ones are lost during incarceration. The inmate often feels helpless, and then hopeless. However, the incarcerated Christian must remain bold in their faith for the sake of their families. Everyone needs encouragement in their walks with Christ, but sometimes they must also become the encourager of others. This will require them to remain confident of what they have in Jesus.

All that the author previously said supports his statement in verse 37; "for you have need of endurance." The author's exposition on the nature and work of Jesus, coupled with his warning to the believer, is meant to instill a spirit of endurance in his audience.[347] The audience has a High Priest who has achieved access to God and victory over their enemies. Now they must endure until these are total realities in their lives. The author desires his listeners to know that perseverance and endurance in the faith is the "will of God." This is opposite of the lifestyle of the disobedient generation of wilderness wandering Israel. Jesus, their pioneer, calls them to the obedience of faith evidenced through continual perseverance. The author reminds them that the promises of God are fully realized at the end of the believer's journey of faith. This section stands as a bridge between two types of people: those who failed because of unbelief (Heb. 3:7-4:11) and those who lived by faith (Heb. 11:1).

---

[347] Ibid., 505.

The inmate is also called to endurance. Daily they must ask themselves, "Which path am I following, the path of disobedience which leads to destruction, or the path of faith which leads to obtainment of the promises of God?" This is a reminder for the inmate to endure in the faith. Attempting to live in two different worlds (dayroom and chapel) is not an option. Doing the will of God means living consistently in the world of righteousness, the world defined by a life of faith.

The author now quotes Habakkuk 2:3-4 to support his position. He achieves several objectives with this verse. First, he reminds his audience of Jesus' imminent return and subsequent judgment. Second, he highlights the contrast between those who endure and those who "shrink back." The enduring believer is described by righteousness, the one who shrinks back is unpleasing to God. This also contrasts with the unbelieving Israelite generation from chapters 3 and 4. They shrunk back and failed to enter the promised rest of God. The heroes of faith in chapter 11 are those who lived "by faith" and endured while not receiving the promises. This provides his listeners with two potential examples. It will be his listeners' responsibility to decide who they will imitate. As Cockerill notes: my righteous one shall live by faith "is pregnant with meaning."[348] On one hand, the author is emphasizing the need for living a life of faith evidenced through persevering to the end. This places the emphasis on the believer's actions. On the other, the author stresses that faith in Jesus and what he accomplished is essential for perseverance. This places the emphasis on one's belief. In light of all the author has shared and his desire for his listeners to endure, both positions are important. Belief and actions are two sides of the same coin. Right

---

[348] Cockerill, *Hebrews*, 511.

living stems from correct beliefs and correct beliefs produce right living.

The author closes this chapter by emphasizing his faith in his listeners. The listeners are not those who shrink back, nor do they have "a fearful expectation of judgment" (Heb. 10:27). They are the faithful who have already suffered trials once before and overcome affliction. They are the faithful who had compassion on their fellow sufferers. They are the faithful who display boldness in the face of persecution. Thus, they are the faithful who "preserve their souls." The author's claim concerning his audience sets the stage for his lengthy exposition on the people of faith. His listeners are called to display faith as those who preceded them.

The incarcerated believer should consider his walk in the Lord. While all believers will ultimately suffer some trial of faith, it is those who press through that will be victorious. They must not allow the cares of the world to quench their desire for the next. One day, "in a little while" the Lord will return for his people. On that day, he will separate the ones who endured from the ones who shrunk back. In which group will you be?

Application

PAST TRIALS FOR FUTURE REWARDS

We have all been through some things and our past experiences color our present realities. We are who we are because of where we have been, and we didn't get here overnight. The same is true for our future success, it will be colored by our present circumstances and not happen overnight. So, we must always carry our past lessons with us, they are valuable teachers. Read 2 Corinthians 11:16-33 and consider how Paul's trials shaped his ministry. Now take the time to list three past experiences which will enable you to serve the Lord more effectively in the future.

B. Jesus: The Goal of Faith (11:1-40)

Section Overview

In the following section the author provides his listeners with numerous examples of faithful living. This section aims to highlight some of Israel's greatest heroes and recalls the stories of their struggles and victories. The author's goal is to encourage his current audience to live faithfully to the will of God waiting on the full reality of his promises, just as those before them. The author is telling his listeners that if the heroes of faith could do it, so can you.

The author opens this extended section with a definition of faith (Heb. 11:1-3). What he says here will be illustrated through the lives of Israel's heroes. Verses 4-7 take listeners from the time of creation to the days of the flood. Verses 8-22 tell of the life of Abraham, the bearer of the great promises and Israel's greatest patriarch. Verses 23-28 describe the life of Moses and his struggles in Egypt leading to the deliverance of Israel from Egyptian captivity. The following section highlights some of the aspects of Israel's wilderness wandering (Heb. 11:29-31). The final section recalls the period of the faithful during the time of the Judges, David, and the Prophets. He reminds his listeners that the faithful of the past had also been persecuted. Yet they were commended because they persevered through their trials and lived their lives "by faith" in the promises of God; promises that would not be fully realized apart from the author's current audience (Heb. 11:32-40).

This section serves to further strengthen the unity of the biblical story. The people of old were living in anticipation of the promises that the current generation were experiencing. God's former covenant is fulfilled in his current covenant creating one people of God who live "by faith" in his Son. Those who preceded the author's listeners are cheering them on as they run their race of faith (Heb. 12:1-3).

Prisoner's Insight for the Journey

In 2005, at the age of 28, I received a 50-year aggravated sentence of which I would have to serve at least 25 years. I thought my life was over. I was only 28 so I could barely understand the concept of 25 years. At first, I believed it was a mistake. I couldn't believe that people actually spent that much time in prison. However, once I arrived at my unit I met hundreds of men in my position. I was crushed, the reality of my predicament set in. I met a Christian brother one day named Gaylon. He was a leader in the church and had been locked up for 20 years. I started to watch how he did time; I literally studied his walk. I knew if he could do it so could I. I submitted my life to the Lord and began my journey of faith. When I would struggle with my circumstances, I could look to the many men of faith who preceded me. I told myself if God enabled them, he can enable me. By faith I have reached my 20-year mark and by faith I will also arrive at 25. The journey has not been easy, but God has been faithful.

The recipients of Hebrews are struggling to understand the promises of God while suffering persecution. If God had truly promised rest, why were they not experiencing rest? One of the author's themes throughout his sermon has been perseverance. Therefore, in order to encourage his listeners, he provides numerous examples of faithful men and women who overcame struggles while awaiting the promise of God. The author begins his section by describing faith and ends it by reminding his audience of what they are striving for. If they are to overcome their struggles they must trust in God and look to the example of those who went before them.

Note on Biblical Faith

How do you define faith? This is one of my favorite questions to ask both young and old believers. Generally, you will receive one of two answers. From the young believer, you will get something along the lines of believing or trusting in Jesus, and from the old, seasoned Bible scholar, you will get a quote from Hebrews 11:1. But is either of these adequate definitions of faith? Does not simply believing or trusting in Jesus seem to lack substance? Does not Hebrews 11:1 beg to be unpacked a little? After all, James tells us that the demons believe (faith in Greek) and shudder (James 2:19). And in Hebrews 11, what exactly does the author mean by "substance" of things hoped for or "evidence" of things not seen?

Because of the reemphasis of salvation by faith alone, scholars during the Reformation sought to define biblical faith more clearly. I have personally found their definition helpful when reading the Bible and also for understanding how God works in our lives. The definition adds content to believing and trusting in Christ while also unpacking the standard definition of Hebrews 11:1. Upon examining the Scriptures, the Reformers came to see a three-part meaning for faith: knowledge, assent, and trust.

Faith is always grounded in the knowledge of someone or something. I cannot have faith in nothing or even faith in faith. This idea is nonsense and nowhere found in Scripture. When the

Bible tells us to believe, our belief always has an object.[349] *In the book of Acts, Paul and Silas tell the Philippian jailer to believe (faith in Greek) in the Lord Jesus and he would be saved. One of the go to texts for leading men and women to salvation is Romans 10:9-10, where v.9 tells one to believe in their heart that God raised Jesus from the dead. Both of these texts highlight that faith/belief must be grounded in knowledge. The first text tells us that our faith must be grounded in the person of Jesus. Therefore, if you had never heard of Jesus and I told you that you must believe in him to be saved, I would hope your next response would be, "Who is Jesus? Tell me about him." Yet I fear that in many instances this is not the case. Our Romans text tells us that there are some "facts" that we need to know about Jesus. Here, specifically, the Bible tells us that we must believe in the resurrection of Christ. Paul states the same truth in 1 Corinthians 15:17 when he tells us that if Christ has not been raised our faith is futile. Futile means pointless, meaningless, or without purpose. The point here is that faith is grounded in the knowledge of the historical person and work of Jesus. I cannot simply believe whatever I want to about Christ, I am required to believe and affirm what the Bible teaches about him. This brings us to the second aspect of faith—assent.*

Assent means to agree to or affirm something especially after thoughtful consideration. In Acts 26, Paul addresses both King Agrippa and Festus telling them of his conversion experience on the road to Damascus. After laying out his account, King Agrippa asked Paul, "In a short time would you persuade me to be a Christian?" (Acts 26:28). In essence, King Agrippa was asking Paul if he expected him to assent to the account that Paul

349 Allen, *Hebrews*, 543.

had just provided. The King was given the facts but now it was up to him to agree or disagree with Paul's story. After all, the Jews also had their account of the events that mostly disagreed with Paul's. Another example of assent is found in the Gospel of Matthew. Jesus asked the disciples, "Who do the people say that the son of man is?" They answered, John the Baptist, Elijah, Jeremiah, or one of the prophets. Then Jesus asked them: "But who do you say that I am?" (Matt. 16:13-16). Again, Jesus was asking them if they agreed with the assessment of the people. Of course, they did not and Peter made his good profession of faith: "You are the Christ, the son of the living God. This goes back to the first point, our knowledge about Jesus is important. It is not acceptable to believe that Jesus is simply a prophet. Our faith must be grounded in the truth of the word of God. However, every believer must also make their own personal profession of faith. So the real question remains: "Is Jesus your messiah?" This brings us to third part of faith—trust.

Trust is defined as assured reliance on the character, ability, strength, or truth of someone or something. Trust is different from both knowledge and assent, it is personal. I cannot change the facts of Christianity. The knowledge that Christ lived, died, and rose again are historical facts that have been attested to for over 2,000 years. Whether I agree or disagree does not change the facts, but the facts alone will leave my faith incomplete. I must also trust that the facts are for me. Let me illustrate. I can have infinite knowledge of chair making. I could know all the types and styles of the different chairs and their various purposes. I could assent that chairs are made for sitting. I could even go as far as agreeing to the fact that a particular chair can hold up my 180 pounds, but until I submit my weight to the chair, I have not trusted in it.[350] *There is a difference between knowing that God forgives sin and trusting that he has forgiven mine. I fear that many today are lacking one of the vital elements of faith. Their faith is not grounded in a correct understanding of Jesus, or they do not know him personally. Either way their faith is incomplete. The Bible is full of stories of trust. Jesus told the woman with the issue of blood that her faith had made her well (Mark 5:34). Jesus pronounced forgiveness on the paralytic lowered through the roof because he saw their faith (Luke 5:20). Jesus tells blind Bartimaeus that his faith has made him well (Mark 10:52), and marvels at the faith of the Canaanite woman and grants her request (Matt. 15:28). All these people came to Jesus "knowing" who he was, "assenting" to his ability to save, and "trusting" that he would save them. This is biblical faith.*

1. Faith Defined (11:1-3)

The author begins this section by providing his listeners with a definition of faith. Faith is more than mere "assurance" on the part of the believer. Faith is the "substance" of what is hoped for. As Cockerill has noted, "faith is living as if the things hoped for are real."[351] Thus, the author reminds his listeners that faith is living as if the promises of God are a reality in their lives. Saints do not endure in hope of heavenly blessings, they endure because the inheritance is already theirs.

Faith is also more than a conviction of things not seen. Faith is evidence based. This means the believer experiences the proofs of what the eye cannot see: "Through trust in God the faithful experience his power in their lives and receive his

[350] This illustration was adapted from R.C. Sproul.
[351] Cockerill, *Hebrews*, 521.

approval. Thus, they confirm his reality."[352] The author's hearers had experienced the goodness of God, they had witnessed the work of the Holy Spirit, now they must rely on the evidence of past experiences to help them endure present trials.

Among scholars there is some debate over the meaning of the Greek word *hypostasis* (assurance ESV). Some English translations understand this word in a subjective sense and translate it as "confidence" or "assurance." They hold that faith is the believers' confidence of what is promised in the future will ultimately come to pass. Faith then is more forward oriented and focused on what is to come.[353]

Others understand the Greek word in an objective sense and translate it as "essence" or "substance." This means faith makes real what is hoped for in the future. Faith is present-oriented and focused on experiencing future blessings in the present.[354] Koester argues that the author could have both the subjective and objective meanings in mind.[355] Faith is both one's present anchor which grounds the here and now and one's sail which carries them swiftly into the future. While a dual meaning for faith appeases both sides of the debate, it should be noted that the Greek word *hypostasis* was never used subjectively in ancient literature.[356] Therefore, here the objective understanding should be favored. Faith is like a title to a car you do not currently possess. The title is your "substance" which points to a future reality of ownership. The title says the car is yours today even though you may not be in possession of it. For believers, faith is the title to their future

---

[352] Ibid., 521.
[353] Moo, *Hebrews*, 2024.
[354] Lane, *Hebrews*, 328-329.
[355] Koester, *Hebrews*, 472.
[356] Harris, *Hebrews*, 298.

blessings. Likewise, the Greek word *elenchos* (conviction ESV) could be understood either objectively or subjectively. If understood subjectively, the focus is on believers' inner "conviction" of future blessings.[357] If understood objectively, faith is the "proof" of things not seen.[358] Whichever position taken, it is best to stay consistent in one's translation. Together, both words should be understood either subjectively or objectively.

In verse two, the author introduces his heroes of faith by referring to them as "the people of old." This phrase points back to the history of Israel's great leaders. The men and women the author will describe received the approval of God through their faithful lives. As Lane has noted, God's approval of their faithfulness is evident through his inspired record of their acts.[359] God moved men by the power of the Holy Spirit to record the faithful lives of his people so that today's believers can benefit from their testimonies (2 Pet. 1:20-21).

In verse 3, the author highlights the creation of God. Believers see the creation and by faith understand its origin. That which is visible did not derive from itself. Here, the author emphasizes the orthodox view of *ex nihilo* creation; God created the universe out of nothing.[360] As Koester has noted, the visible creation finds its source in the invisible word of God.[361]

Living as if the promises of God are a present reality results in the commendation by God. A faithful life bears witness to the life of the faithful.[362] The author, through the example of

---

[357] Moo, *Hebrews*, 410.
[358] Harris, *Hebrews*, 298.
[359] Lane, *Hebrews*, 330.
[360] Moo, *Hebrews*, 412.
[361] Koester, *Hebrews*, 474.
[362] Guthrie, *Hebrews*, NIV, 375.

creation, provides his listeners with an illustration of faith. Faith is like understanding that the world was created by the Word of God. While no one was present at creation, the creation itself is evidence of a Creator (Ps. 19:1-2). God's nature is present everywhere in his creation (Rom. 1:20).

For the incarcerated believer living as if the promises of God are a reality is essential for one's faith. One can lose sight of the objective. The trials of prison life and the cares of the world all compete for the believer's attention. However, living as if the promises of God are a reality helps to keep one focused. It's similar to the way one does time waiting on their parole date. The believer can do this time with either a "if I make parole" mentality, or a "when I make parole" mentality. The first reflects the person who is just doing time, the second reflects the person who is preparing for freedom. Believers can weather the trials and tribulations in hope of relief, or they can weather the trials and tribulations because they know relief is just over the horizon. The believers' faith should flow from the victory they have in Jesus, not in some misplaced hope that all will work out. Victory is the believers' reality; it is their inheritance.

As believers endure the trials that life throws their way, they give witness to the power of God in their lives. Moreover, the believers' ability to weather the storms of faith is God's witness to his grace. Countless men and women live faithfully for the Lord every day in jails and prisons around the world. One must simply open their eyes to find a faithful servant of God. They are everywhere. Sometimes the believer must follow the lead of another. When one finds themselves unsure of which direction to travel, follow the example of another believer who is walking "by faith."

2. *Faith From Creation to Flood (11:4-7)*

The author begins his exposition of the faithful with Abel. He states, "By faith Abel offered to God a more acceptable sacrifice than Cain." The author appeals to the Genesis account of Abel's acceptable sacrifice in order to show that, at times, the people of faith may suffer because of their commitment to God.[363] God's acceptance of Abel and rejection of Cain, moved the latter to kill his brother. However, the author points to the fact that his faith still speaks. Abel stands as an example of those who believed in the promise of God yet did not receive what was promised. The author contrasts Abel's trial and suffering with Enoch's victory. Genesis describes Enoch as a man who walked with God (Gen. 5:21-24). This statement signifies Enoch's obedience to the things of God. Enoch's commitment is rewarded through his translation into the presence of God. The author states that Enoch did "not see death." This description of Enoch points to the other side of the believer's walk of faith. Those who persevere have the reward of eternal life in the presence of God.

The author summarizes both Abel's and Enoch's lives. Both were commended for their commitment to God. Abel, through his offering, and Enoch, through his walk. Their faithful lives pleased God. They stand as examples of Habakkuk 2:4: "My righteous one shall live by faith."[364] Abel's commitment to God was rewarded through becoming a continual witness to a life of faith. Long after his death, "he still speaks." Abel's ability to speak into the audience's current situation is a result of his faithful offering which is recorded as an example in Scripture.[365] Enoch's

---

[363] Moo, *Hebrews*, 414.
[364] Moberly, Walter, "Exemplars of Faith in Hebrews 11: Abel." *The Epistle to the Hebrews and Christian Theology*. Grand Rapids: Eerdmans, 2009.
[365] Moo, *Hebrews*, 413.

faithfulness was rewarded through a continual life. He was taken so "he should not see death." Both serve as examples of the believer's future reward, a continual witness, and eternal life in the presence of God. The believer's ability to persevere and please God flows from a faith that is grounded in both the existence and goodness of God.

The author expands his definition of faith from verse 1. The "things not seen" is the existence of God. The knowledge that God "is" drives the life of the believer. The "things hoped for" flow from the knowledge that "he rewards those that seek him." Once again, the author desires his listeners to mimic the life of faith displayed by Abel and Enoch. They must live as if the promises of God are a reality in their lives.[366] Cockerill notes "sometimes, as in the case of Abel, people suffer for their faith without temporal deliverance. At other times, as in the case of Enoch, God brings great deliverance in response to faith. For most, the life of faith is a mixture of suffering and triumph."[367]

In verse 6, the author provides his listeners with a general truth. Faith is fundamental to a right relationship with God. Apart from faith, an intimate relationship with God is impossible.[368] The author highlights the close relationship between faith and action. True faith encourages one to seek what cannot be seen with the naked eye. Biblical faith requires believers to affirm both the existence of God and his providence over their lives.

The author uses Noah as his next example of faithful living. Noah stands as an example that God will deliver his people from judgment. The author states that Noah was warned of a

---

[366] Ibid., 530-31.
[367] Cockerill, *Hebrews*, 526.
[368] Moo, *Hebrews*, 414.

coming judgment "yet unseen." Once again, the author appeals to a faith which flows from reality. Noah was not constructing an ark in case the flood might come. He was building and preaching because judgment was sure.

The author also states that the ark was "for the saving of his household." Through Noah's faith, he provided a means for his household to escape judgment. Cockerill notes that Noah's righteousness is declared by God at the completion of the ark. He states, "close attention to the text shows that Noah 'condemned the world' and 'became an heir of righteousness' by being delivered from the universal judgment of the flood." Cockerill's point is that Noah is deemed righteous "because of the way he conducted his life."[369] While Cockerill does not make this connection, the idea of perseverance is easily seen in Noah's construction of the ark. Noah's reward of deliverance stands at the completion of his journey. There are several correlations between the author's examples and Jesus. Abel represents Christ's suffering to the point of death. Enoch represents Christ's victory of exaltation. Noah represents Christ's salvation of the household through obedience.[370]

Noah provides incarcerated believers with a beautiful example of patience and perseverance in the midst of an unbelieving world. God called on Noah to build an ark in order to preserve life after the flood. Noah obeyed God and followed his command even in the midst of an unfaithful generation. The incarcerated Christian is also called to do the will of God in an ungodly environment. This means at times they may be mocked and ridiculed because their faith is a condemnation of the

---

[369] Cockerill, *Hebrews*, 533.
[370] Ibid., 534.

unfaithful. Their obedience highlights other's disobedience. Nevertheless, if the believer will remain faithful to God, he will bring them through any storm and place them once again on solid ground.

3. Abraham's Faithful Journey (11:8-22)

The author uses Abraham and Moses to stand as the centerpiece of his examples of faith and perseverance. Once again, the author recalls the Genesis account of his heroes reminding his listeners what faith in action looks like. Faith for Abraham was answering the call of God to leave his homeland and travel to a place unknown to receive an inheritance possessed by other people. The author describes Abraham as living in a foreign land with no permanent dwelling for generations. He describes Abraham, Isaac, and Jacob as wanderers in their own land.[371] The author uses this story to illustrate for his audience that while the promises of God are sure, they are not necessarily immediate. Like Abraham, Isaac, and Jacob, the believer must persevere through various trials until the promises of God become a reality.

Abraham's nomadic life living in tents enabled him to look toward a "city that has foundations." The idea of "looking toward" is a continuous expectation derived from an absolute confidence.[372] Once again, the author recalls his definition of faith. Abraham is not following God in hope of a promised land, but because a "Promised Land" exists. What is unseen in Abraham's present is a reality in his future. The city to which Abraham looked is none other than God's heavenly home. The tents in which Abraham and his descendants dwelt were temporary and destructible. The city of God is eternal and everlasting. The author

---

[371] Lane, *Hebrews*, 350.
[372] Ibid., 351.

aims to remind his listeners that their ultimate possession is not of this world. The persecution and potential loss of property in this life will be offset by the rewards of peace and prosperity in the presence of God, the true Architect of the believer's life.

The author now introduces Sarah, Abraham's wife, to his examples. The author's example of Abraham highlights God's faithfulness concerning his future promises. Now he uses Sarah to illustrate God's present power over one's circumstances. Sarah, who was advanced in age, past the point of childbearing, is promised a son. In the Genesis account, Sarah actually laughs at God's messenger (Gen. 18:11-13) because of the seeming absurdity of the promise. Nevertheless, she bears Isaac to Abraham in her old age. The author uses Sarah to illustrate to his present audience, that God is able to overcome their current circumstances. The God who promises is faithful to produce a whole nation from a couple advanced in age. Koester states the struggle of faith well:

> This presented them with a contradiction between the divine promise, which said that they would have children, and ordinary experience, which said they could not. In such a context trusting experience means abandoning God's promise while trusting God's promise requires overcoming experience.[373]

From one old man came a people as numerous as the stars of heaven and the sands of the sea. The author once again points to God's power over man's weakness.[374] God produced through

[373] Koester, *Hebrews*, 496.
[374] Cockerill, *Hebrews*, 546.

Abraham the countless faithful who persevered in faith. The author calls his listeners to mimic faith in God's promises and in his present power. God is able to bring the believers through their current struggle into his final rest.

The incarcerated believer is also on a journey of faith in a foreign land. It does not take long for one to realize that prison is no one's final destination. The believer, like Abraham, is called to follow God to a future kingdom while relying on his power to persevere. The journey is not easy, and the tests of one's faith are around every corner. Following God requires one to know that life must be lived as if the promises of God are a reality. The believer's faith is grounded in the character of God and his power to deliver in one's time of need.

The author describes the saints from the previous section as having "died in the faith." This means that they went to the grave believing in the promises of God; however, not one received "the things promised." For the author, the ultimate promise that all others pointed to was the heavenly country which signified eternal rest in the presence of God. The Old Testament saints received temporal blessings such as land and descendants. However, through faith they knew these were only samples of what God had to offer.[375] As a result, "they were strangers and exiles on the earth." Their true home was the heavenly Jerusalem (Heb. 12:12) of which God was the designer and builder (Heb. 11:10).

The author uses strong logic and reasoning to show that the patriarchs were anticipating something better than the earthly Promised Land. First, he refers to the saint's description of themselves as exiles, strangers, and sojourners. He argues that

---

[375] Moo, *Hebrews*, 431.

people who call themselves these names as "seeking a homeland." They are travelers on their way to a destination. The author rules out their previous home as a desired destination. If they had been sojourners, exiles, or strangers of their initial homeland, they could have simply returned. The author draws his conclusion in verse 16. Since his first and second points are true, then it follows they were desiring "a better country" than they had experienced. This better land transcends all earthly countries because it is the heavenly city prepared by God for his saints.[376] The patriarchs' faith in God's promises and their perseverance in the faith resulted in divine approval. God is not ashamed to be their God. This echoes the blessing of the New Covenant: "I will be their God and they shall be my people" (Jer. 31:33). God has prepared a home for his weary travelers. Access to this heavenly city is made possible through the sacrifice of his Son.

For the incarcerated believer, much like the patriarchs, God has in store greater blessings than this life has to offer. Inside the walls of prison are many faithful men and women who will never again be physically free. However, their lives testify to their current freedom in Christ. A man once testified that he is freer today than he ever was outside of prison. This understanding of spiritual freedom while incarcerated points to a day in the future that all men in Christ will once again also be physically free.

The author now turns to one of the most significant acts of faith in all of Scripture. In Genesis, Abraham is commanded by God to offer Isaac as a sacrifice. The author highlights several aspects of this story to drive home his example of true faith. First, the author points to the testing of Abraham's faith. By faith, Abraham left his homeland, now the offering of his only son will

---

[376] Cockerill, *Hebrews*, 551-52.

stand as the final test of faith. This points to the believer's need to live a life of continual faith. It is faith which places one in the household of God and it is faith which enables them to persevere to the end (Rom. 1:17). Second, the ordering of the words in the original Greek emphasizes Abraham's obedience. Abraham does not hesitate to obey the command of God. Third, Abraham is described as "he who received the promises." Abraham was fully aware of the implication of sacrificing Isaac. It was as if Abraham was sacrificing the promise itself, and thus his future: "Through Isaac shall your offspring be named." Nevertheless, the author describes Abraham as "in the act of offering up his only son." Abraham's willingness to risk all is explained in the next verse.

Abraham's willingness was grounded in his faith in God. If God had promised that through Isaac would come Abraham's descendants, then even if Abraham sacrificed his son, God would make a way. Abraham believed that God could raise him from the dead.[377] The author states that in God's sparing of Isaac, Abraham figuratively received him back. The author highlights Abraham's faith by implying that Abraham was so committed to offering Isaac, that the act might as well have taken place. As a result, Isaac points to God's ability to raise all the faithful from the dead. Isaac became a type of believer's future resurrection.[378]

Abraham illustrates the absolute commitment of faith for the incarcerated believer. Abraham left behind all he knew in order to follow God. Sometimes we will also be called to leave behind former associations and relationships. In my journey of faith, I am constantly reminded of the words of Henry Blackaby, "You cannot go with God and stay where you are." Yet Abraham

---

[377] Koester, *Hebrews*, 499.
[378] Cockerill, *Hebrews*, 557.

also illustrates how to live faithfully. We must also be willing to surrender the blessings of God when called to. This reminds me of Job's statement, "The Lord gives and the Lord takes away blessed be the name of the Lord" (Job 1:21). We must always be prepared to give God what is rightly his. Lane states this beautifully, "When Abraham obeyed God's mandate to leave Ur, he simply gave up his past. But when he was summoned to Mount Moriah to deliver his own son to God, he was asked to surrender his future as well."[379]

Now the author emphasizes Isaac's faith by stating that he "invoked future blessings for Jacob and Esau." Isaac's faith is seen in the words "future blessings." Isaac was passing on the promises of God to his children. He was so sure of their reality, it was the most significant inheritance he could leave for his children. Even when Isaac failed to receive the promises himself, he remained so committed to God that he was sure they would eventually come to pass. The author also accomplishes a subtle warning by referencing Esau who sold his birthright; "future blessings" belong to those who persevere. The author uses Esau in 12:16-17 as one who sought to inherit the blessing but was rejected.

Again, the author continues his examples of faithfulness with Jacob's blessing of Joseph's sons. Jacob is described by "dying" yet "bowing in worship." This is a beautiful picture of faith until the end. He also believes in the promises of God and passes them on as an inheritance to his descendants. He is described as bowing "over the head of his staff." He is a sojourner and an exile, and the staff represents that his journey is incomplete.[380] The author shows his audience that faith perseveres

---

[379] Lane, *Hebrews*, 360.
[380] Moo, *Hebrews*, 436.

to the point of death. The author concludes this section with Joseph. Joseph looks to a day when Israel would once again set out to obtain the promises of God. He commands his people to carry his bones out of the foreign land. This reveals his faith in God's promises.

The incarcerated believer must be willing to forsake all to follow God. The believer cannot grow complacent in their offerings to God. God desires 100% of the believer's commitment. This means at times "sacrificing" one's personal comfort in order to achieve great things for the kingdom. Two men once chose to give up the benefit of living in the safest, most comfortable part of the prison in order to move to the most dangerous and violet housing on the unit. Their goal was to carry Jesus to where he was needed most. They believed if they were faithful to what God was calling them to do, that God would be faithful to his mission. The faith of two men who were willing to sacrifice their comfort helped transform the lives of many others.

4. Moses' Faithful Leadership (11:23-31)

The author turns to Moses' life as an example of faithfulness. He begins by discussing the faith of Moses' parents. The king of Egypt, fearing the growth of the Hebrew people, commanded that all Hebrew boys were to be killed at birth. However, when Moses was born he "was hidden for three months" from those who would harm him. The author states that Moses was rescued because he "was beautiful." This most likely references God's special purpose for the life of Moses.[381] The parents recognized God's special plan for Moses, so they

[381] Cockerill, *Hebrews*, 566.

disobeyed the king's edict. They would rather fear God than fear man.

The author now describes Moses' adulthood. Moses as a child was rescued by Pharaoh's daughter and raised as her own son. He was given the best privileges Egypt had to offer. The author states that he "refused to be called the son of pharaoh's daughter." In the Exodus account, Moses comes to the defense of the Hebrew people resulting in the death of an Egyptian. Through his choice to defend his people, he chose to reject the house of Pharaoh.[382] The author states that Moses would have rather suffered than benefit from the sinful pleasures of Pharaoh's household. The author uses Moses to drive home an important point to his listeners. They are also being asked to choose sides. They are being asked to suffer with the people of God and reject the comforts of their former lifestyles. The author reminds them that those comforts are "the fleeting pleasures of sin." The temporary and soon to be passing pleasures of this life pale in comparison to the eternal blessings God has for his people in the next.

At times, blessings are only realized through suffering. For Moses, by identifying with his people, he became the enemy of Egypt. He would rather suffer with God's people than benefit from the riches of sin. The author calls Moses' trials "the reproach of Christ." Some translate this phrase as "disgrace for the sake of Christ" (NIV). The author desires his listeners to know it is better to suffer for Christ than to reap the pleasures of sin. The author identifies Moses' suffering as "the reproach of Christ" signaling that all those who persevered and endured striving for the promises of God were persevering, enduring, and striving for

---

[382] Lane, *Hebrews*, 371.

Jesus.[383] The Old Testament saints looked forward to the cross, and the New Testament saints looked back on its benefits. Thus, Moses "was looking to the reward" in Christ by faith. This "looking" is a habitual concentrated attention on a goal.[384]

Commentators are divided over the author's reference of Moses leaving Egypt. Some hold that this points to Moses' first departure into Midian after killing the Egyptian. While this fits well chronologically, the Exodus account specifically states that Moses fled in fear (Exod. 2:14). Here, the author states, "he left, not being afraid of the anger of the king." This would be a departure from the Old Testament account, a move the author would unlikely take. Other commentators argue that this is a reference to Moses leading his people from Egypt.[385] While this fits well with the author's statement of Moses' fearlessness, it does not fit chronologically. In the next verse, the author mentions the Passover which occurred prior to the Exodus. This would be a chronological departure, something the author has avoided in his recounting of God's faithful.

While not perfect, a possible explanation could be that the author is summarizing the two events.[386] No one individual in Hebrews 11 is defined by any single act. While Moses feared Pharaoh, his life is defined by fearlessness. This supports the author's next statement, "He endured as seeing him who is invisible." Moses' life is defined by fearlessness because his focus was on God.

---

383 Allen, *Hebrews*, 560.
384 Lane, *Hebrews*, 373.
385 See Allen, *Hebrews*, NAC, 560-62 for an extended explanation.
386 Koester, *Hebrews*, 504.

The author now highlights Moses' faith in the establishment of the Passover. The faith it required to command the children of Israel to observe the Passover, condemning the first-born of Egypt, while delivering the first-born of Israel was remarkable.[387] The imagery of sprinkled blood and deliverance brings to the minds of his audience the accomplishment of the shed blood of Christ. Just as God had previously delivered his people from physical captivity, now, through a better offering, he has once for all set them free from all captivity.

The author focuses on Israel's crossing of the Red Sea. By faith, they crossed on "dry land." The author highlights Israel's initial level of faith; however, their subsequent disobedience cannot be far from his mind. Those who began their journey in faith are the same who fell in the wilderness because of unbelief (Heb. 3:19).[388] However, one of the author's main focuses since beginning with Moses has been God's power. It was faith in God's enduring power that caused baby Moses to be spared, adult Moses to reject Pharaoh, and ultimately deliver God's people. It was God's power that parted the Red Sea and closed it over the Egyptian army. The people's faith was grounded in the powerful manifestation of an unseen God.

The same power was evident in Jericho through the people's faithful obedience. God is able to remove the obstacles of his people. They are called to live as if the promises of God are a reality and the obstacles of their faith do not exist. The author closes this section with Rahab. The author pulls no punches by describing her as a prostitute. While that nameless generation departed Egypt by faith and ultimately fell in the wilderness,

---

[387] Ibid., 510.
[388] Cockerill, *Hebrews*, 582-83.

Rahab the Canaanite prostitute, has her name etched in the hall of the faithful. Many rejected the promises of God and perished, but Rahab obediently received God's blessing in the persons of the spies. God's mercy is evident in Rahab's life. Her past lifestyle does not define her present faithfulness.[389]

The incarcerated believer is called to rely on the power of God for endurance. Many times, Christians believe they are capable of making their own way. They start in faith following the plan and power of God but grow weary in waiting for the plan's fulfillment. As a result, they take matters into their own hands. This is often the mistake of the person who, after release, returns to prison. I have seen many people faithfully follow God to be released and suddenly stop. It is as if they have convinced themselves that they no longer need the support of the God who enabled them to endure years of incarceration. The Christian's success is defined by their level of dependence on the power of God. The same God who brings one out of Egypt (prison) is the same God who sustains the believer in the wilderness (world).

---

[389] Cockerill, *Hebrews*, 584-85.

5. The Triumphs and Trials of the Faithful (11:32-40)

The author introduces this section with a rhetorical question: “And what more shall I say.” This signifies the sufficiency of his previous examples.[390] The lives already discussed are more than enough evidence for the faithfulness of the believer and the power of God. In the following nine verses, the author picks up the pace of his description. He quickly moves from the time of the Judges to the days of the Prophets. He lists their victories and triumphs; they conquered kingdoms and lions alike. They are remembered for being “made strong out of weakness” and putting “foreign armies to flight.” The power of God was present when “women received back their dead by resurrection.” However, he also describes their trials and afflictions. Some were tortured, refusing to give in, because of the hope of a better life. Others were mocked and imprisoned for their journeys of faith. Many ultimately died horrible deaths and were forced to wander this world without clothing or shelter. And because of their great faith, the world was not worthy of them.

The author concludes his exposition of the faithful by recalling verse 2. The saints of old were commended for their faith. However, he now adds that though they endured all manners of trials and tribulations, they did not receive what was promised. Their reward for obedience would have to await the arrival of Christ. The author returns to his theme of the one people of God. All believers, past and present, receive the blessing of the New Covenant in Jesus.

---

[390] Cockerill, *Hebrews*, 587.

Application

LIVING FAITHFULLY REGARDLESS OF THE CIRCUMSTANCES

Living as if the promises of God are a reality is difficult even for the faithful. The believers read the word, memorize the promises of God, but fail to walk them out. This difficulty derives from a breakdown between faith and action. One can know every Scripture in the Bible but not know how to live them out effectively. True faith is evidenced by how one lives. James makes this point in his epistle. Faith without works is dead (James 2:26). A faithful lifestyle will naturally flow from a true faith. Take some time and examine some of the promises of God that you hold dear. Ask yourself, "Am I living as if theses promises are a reality in my life?"

C. Jesus: The Example of Endurance (12:1-29)

1. Staying Focused on Jesus (12:1-3)

Prisoner's Insight for the Journey

Exercise is one of the many ways we pass time in prison. We design grueling workout regimes in order to whip the body into shape. We spend countless hours, weeks, and even years doing burpees, push-ups, crunches, and if you're fortunate enough to have them, lifting weights. As a result, there are some true "monsters" living in prison; men who have reached levels of strength, stamina, and endurance which are almost super-human. I am not one of them.

When I first got locked up, working out was not on my radar. I spent most of my time playing dominoes, scrabble, chess, and reading books. As a matter of fact, my favorite pastime was reading long novels while laying on my back. Not one of my hobbies required physical exertion. However, one day during a prolonged lock-down, my cellie, who was a self-proclaimed fitness guru, talked me into doing some push-ups with him. On a normal day, he would rip off sets of thirty and forty push-ups like it was nothing. Somehow, I convinced myself that I was capable of the same numbers, at least until I barely completed my first set of ten! I quickly learned that I had the understanding and the strength to doing a push-up, but I lacked the stamina and endurance to do very many. Stamina and endurance are built through discipline and continual effort. The same is true of our walk in Christ. Living for Jesus is not a sprint, it is a marathon.[391] Playing for team Jesus is not about one game, it's about the whole season. Christianity is not only a moment at profession and baptism; it is a lifestyle.

The author of Hebrews spent the entire eleventh chapter providing his listeners with examples of people who lived a life defined by stamina, endurance, and discipline in the faith. Moses dealt with his own personal struggles but also the struggles of an entire nation. He reminds his audience of Rahab, an unlikely instrument of God, who risked her life for the promise of God. He recalls prophets who were despised by their own people but, nevertheless, called their people to repentance. Yet despite their shortcomings, mistakes, and outright sins, not one of these people was defined by any single moment of success or failure. They are listed in the hall of the faithful because they persevered in spite of themselves. Their lives were defined by stamina and endurance.

Now the author of Hebrews is telling his listeners that regardless of their current struggles, they must also run with endurance. Every set of push-ups begins with the first repetition and every walk with Jesus begins with the first step of faith.

Commentary

12:1-3

The author begins this chapter of exhortation with a "therefore" that closely ties his previous exposition of the faithful with what he is now going to say.[392] He reminds his audience that

---

[391] Moo, *Hebrews*, 468.

[392] Moo notes: "The author uses a strong inferential conjunction … [therefore] to indicate the transition from exposition to application, from describing faith

they are not alone in their trials. They have been preceded by countless faithful followers who also suffered trials and persecution. As a result, the author depicts all those who previously struggled in the faith as witnesses or spectators to their current struggles. Cockerill notes a dual meaning of the word witness; "The pastor has chosen the term "witness" because it enables him to affirm that the heroes of old are both 'witness' *to* and *of* God's contemporary people."[393] This means the faithful of old have provided the author's listeners with an example to live by.

Tom Brady played football for the University of Michigan. During his college career he was told by many to give up on hope of ever playing in the NFL. However, despite the weight of negative opinions, Brady was drafted in the 6th round. He went on to defy all odds by winning 7 Super Bowls and solidifying himself as the greatest QB of all time. Yesterday was Super Bowl Sunday (2-9-2025), Tom Brady was in the press box calling the game. On the field was Patrick Mahomes a young man who many believe may one day surpass the great Tom Brady. Whether or not this ever happens (Mahomes lost) Tom was in the box as a witness to the greatness of a young NFL QB and a witness of the greatness possible through hard work and perseverance.[394]

The heroes of chapter 11 are also watching (witnessing) to see how the current generation will live. The saints are a great "cloud of witnesses" watching to see what the author's audience will do with the promises of God. The current hearers had received

---

to urging his readers to exhibit the endurance that faith produces." Moo, *Hebrews*, 468.

[393] Cockerill, *Hebrews*, 602.

[394] Thanks to Cole Tucker for the Tom Brady illustration.

all the promises that the Old Testament saints anticipated. They were beneficiaries of the New Covenant blessings. They were experiencing the indwelling of the Holy Spirit and accessing the presence of God through the shed blood of Jesus. Now they were being watched to see what they would do with their blessings.

Now most inmates have had a bad experience with witnesses. As a matter of fact, we don't like people watching us. Rule number one in prison is minding your own business. But accepting Christ is also accepting that others will be in our business. We open ourselves to accountability. We have eyes on us constantly. Now, some are watching because they want to see us fail. They are looking for an opportunity to discourage our faith and hinder our growth. These are the type of discouragers that moved the author of Hebrews to pen this letter. The author's audience needed encouragement because they had haters rooting against them, causing them to question their commitment to the faith.

But there is another type of witness. They are the ones watching to see if we succeed. These are the believers' fans, cheering for their success. This is the type of witness that the author is referring to. The author's audience is surrounded by the heroes of the faith, and they are cheering for their success.

The author also reminds his listeners that Christianity is a long-distance race. Therefore, in order to run without restriction, they must "lay aside every weight." In the first century, men wore long robes with multiple layers. Moving without hindrance was virtually impossible, especially for the athlete. Therefore, the competitor would strip to the bare minimum before competing.[395]

---

[395] Koester, *Hebrews*, 522; Witherington, *Hebrews*, 326.

The author's audience was allowing trials, persecutions, and the cares of the world to cling closely to them. They were overweight with the sin of uncertainty.

The author does not explicitly state what sin he has in mind, but in light of the context it would appear that he is speaking of apostasy, turning away from the faith. His audience was in danger of reverting back to their former lifestyles. For some, this would mean embracing the Law of Moses and all its rituals and practices. For others, this meant embracing some Roman deity. For the author, neither path was acceptable. He was clear in his presentation of Jesus. Faith in Christ was the only way forward. His audience just needed to lay aside their weakness of faith and "run with endurance" on the path that has been set before them.

The author's listeners were growing weary in their walks with Christ, but the author exhorts them to run even harder. In Hebrews 10:32-39, he had reminded them of the previous trials through which they endured. Now they must once again persevere in the faith. He is calling them to strive so that they can obtain the ultimate promise of God, eternity in his presence. However, the audience is not alone in their struggle. The great cloud of witnesses cheers them on from glory and Jesus has paved the way. The author calls his listeners to "run while looking to Jesus." Jesus has provided the believer with the perfect example of perseverance in the face of trials. The idea here of "looking" is better understood as "fixing" one's eyes on Jesus. This implies intentional focusing without distractions.[396] The author's listeners were being distracted by the many obstacles of faith. Distractions will also hinder one's performance. Jesus must be the object of all faithful runners' focus. Christ is the believer's founder and

[396] Moo, *Hebrews*, 470.

perfecter. This means that as founder, Jesus has established the new way by doing away with the old. Furthermore, he is the perfecter because he demonstrates for and enables the believer to run in the face of trials.[397] Jesus endured the cross with joy. This is a shocking and difficult concept to grasp. How does one suffer with Joy? How does one not despise the shame of such a shameful death? It can only be accomplished through the knowledge of ultimate victory. Jesus endured suffering and shame because he knew it was temporary.[398] His rightful place was to be "seated at the right hand of the throne of God." The author's audience must also run as if the race is already won. The great cloud of witnesses cheers them on from glory and Jesus leads the way into the presence of God.

Now the author calls on his hearers to "consider him who endured." Jesus is to be their example of endurance. The author is not simply asking the listeners to compare their sufferings to Jesus' suffering, but he is calling on them to consider the totality of Jesus himself. He is the perfect example of perseverance, but he is also the example of victory. The audience should focus on what will be the final outcome. Just as the believers were pressured by those outside the faith, Jesus also endured hostility from sinners. The cross was the conclusion of Jesus' suffering, but his life was defined by opposition from his opponents.[399] Believers are to focus on the whole of Jesus' life so that they "may not grow weary or faint-hearted." The listeners are to dig deep into the reserves of the inner man in order to find the strength to win the race. Cockerill states: "The race is not lost in the legs, but in the

---

[397] Ibid, 471.
[398] Cockerill, *Hebrews*, 610.
[399] Cockerill, *Hebrews*, 611.

runners inmost being."[400] The benefits of the New Covenant provide the believer with all the tools necessary to be a successful runner; however, it is the believer's responsibility to continue to run. The listeners had the power of the Holy Spirit, the glorified saints as fans, and Jesus as their running coach. If they would focus on the victory ahead instead of the current lap, then they would also achieve the prize of God's final rest of his eternal presence.

Application

THE ENDURANCE OF THE BELIEVER

As inmates we often come across many hindrances. Our weights come in many different forms such as family, friends, contraband, and even simple conversations. The good news is whatever weight your life may hold or how heavy it may be you can lay it aside and look to Jesus as you run with endurance. Read Philippians 3:13-14 and examine the weights you may be carrying. In what way can you shed some of your unnecessary burdens and run more faithfully?

---

[400] Ibid, 612.

2. *The Discipline of the Father (12:4-13)*

Prisoner's Insight for the Journey

Most all inmates struggle with or have struggled with discipline. Much of the struggle stems from being raised in an overly corrective, or many times, abusive environment. Any simple infraction was met with a severe punishment. To compound the issue, the very person who was the punisher was meant to be a protector, a father. So, when the Bible teaches that God is a loving father who disciplines his children, the inmate struggles to relate. The discipline they received from their fathers was anything but loving. For them, discipline always equals punishment. As a result, any simple correction is most often met with absolute rebellion. The prisoner struggles to reconcile discipline with benefit.

However, this is both a distortion of fatherhood and discipline. Fathers are called to be loving providers and protectors of their families. At times, this requires them to discipline those they love. But true discipline is always meant to flow from a father's desire to provide and protect. Its goal is also meant to bring about a beneficial change of circumstances. Discipline from a loving father should never make the situation worse. Earthly fathers are imperfect, at best, but this is not the case with the heavenly Father. God's discipline always flows from his loving character and desire to benefit his children. Receiving the correction of God means you are blessed to be one of his many cherished sons and daughters.

The author's audience is struggling with their current trials and tribulations. They feel as if they are being punished for their faith. However, the author reminds them that what some mean for evil, God will use for good. They must simply run their race of faith and fight against anything that may hinder them. The victory is theirs; they must run to the finish line and fight to the bell.

Commentary

12:4-13

The author now provides insight into his audience's circumstances. They are struggling against opposition, but it has not resulted in bloodshed. The author accomplishes several things with this statement. First, he contrasts his listeners' current suffering with the suffering "Christ endured for sinners" (v.3). Christ suffered to the point of death on a cross, but their suffering has not reached that level. His listeners were most likely experiencing shame and alienation from society. However, he is also preparing them for the potential heightening of their suffering. He previously mentioned those who suffered to the point of death in faith (Heb. 11:37). Jesus also suffered by the hand of sinners. Therefore, they should prepare themselves to possibly suffer likewise. The author employs boxing imagery with his use of the phrase, "shedding your blood." The listeners' struggles could possibly become a fight for survival. Finally, this statement sets in perspective the author's discussion on discipline from God. Some struggles are for the believer's development.[401]

In verse 5, the author quotes Proverbs 3:11-12 to introduce his discussion of God's discipline. He switches from the imagery of the athlete's struggle of running and boxing to the picture of a father's desire to correct and instruct his children. This reveals the two perspectives on suffering in the faith. Trials and persecution

[401] Cockerill, *Hebrews*, 618-19.

from the opposition are meant to inflict suffering and harm. However, God can use the same trials and persecutions as a means for strengthening his sons and daughters. This is reminiscent of Joseph's statement to his brothers in Genesis 50:20. What some intend for evil, God uses for good. The author's use of Proverbs 3:11-12 emphasizes the distinction of struggling as an enemy of God and struggling as a child of God. The child of God should not "regard lightly" the correction of their Father. God's intention is not to punish his children, but to strengthen them for the future trials of life. God's discipline in this case is meant to produce endurance, not repentance.[402] The believer's goal is to learn and benefit from all the trials of life. If one can learn obedience and endurance in the lesser problems of life, then they will be more equipped to deal with the greater struggles.

The author also wants his listeners not to grow weary from their struggles. Having the proper perspective concerning trials and tribulations is essential for endurance. The believers must train themselves to ask: "What is God attempting to teach me through this trial?" Viewing trials as instruments of instruction instead of destruction distinguishes the mature from the immature believer. The mature believer has "forgotten the exhortation" (v.5) that as a loving Father, God desires the best for his children, even when the trial is difficult.

Thus, the Proverb reminds the author's audience that "the Lord disciplines the one he loves." God's discipline is not about punishment, but about growth. No loving father enjoys punishing their child, but all loving fathers want to see their child grow to maturity.[403] This means living in the household of God comes with

---

[402] Harris, *Hebrews*, 366.
[403] Moo, *Hebrews*, 475.

times of correction. No believer is beyond the correction and discipline of God. The author's listeners must realize that their trials flow from the desires of a loving Father and not the anger of a wrathful God.

In verse 7, he provides his listeners with precise instructions: endure. The discipline which they are experiencing is for their improvement; therefore, to reap the benefits, they must endure the trials. The author appeals to reason: God is a loving Father; loving fathers discipline their children; they are being disciplined by God; therefore, they must be God's children. He also states the reverse of this truth. Where there is no discipline from God, there is no claim to sonship. Discipline as instruction is part of being a child of God. Thus, the author emphasizes that his audience's current struggles prove they are loved children of God.[404] This aims to comfort his listeners in their time of need. No believer desires to endure pointless trials and there are no pointless trials in the household of God.

The author continues his discussion of discipline by comparing one's response to their earthly father's discipline versus the discipline of their heavenly Father. If the believer respected the discipline of their earthly father, how much more should they respect the discipline of their heavenly Father? The instruction of earthly fathers aimed to produce respect. The correction of the heavenly Father aims to produce obedience that leads to life. The author emphasizes the diverse manner of instruction by denoting the diverse character of the fathers. One is earthly and the other spiritual; one disciplines for a "short time," the other disciplines for the purpose of eternity. In verse 10, the author highlights the shortcomings of an earthly father's

[404] Lane, *Hebrews*, 422.

discipline. It is described as a "short time" and as what "seemed best to them." As Cockerill notes, "Even if well intentioned, the discipline of earthly fathers is limited by their judgment and prejudices." God's discipline is never limited nor misapplied but always aims at the benefit of his children.[405]

God's goal for his children is to "share his holiness." This means that trials and tribulations serve the believer's sanctification. The Christian is called to be conformed to the likeness of the Son (Rom. 8:29). This means the believer is called to follow Jesus' example of obedience, even in the face of persecution. The believer becomes more Christ-like by becoming more Christ dependent.

The author concludes with a final reflection on the nature of divine discipline. All correction "seems painful" and unpleasant. The author does not downplay the difficulty of his listener's circumstances. Their trials are real and painful. However, he reminds them that they are temporary. "But later," after the trial has passed, it is replaced by "the peaceful fruit of righteousness." The goal of the believer's suffering is to train them for a future life of peace. Anyone who has ever lived through a storm of life is naturally more prepared for the next. This is the author's message. God is preparing the believer through current trials for a peaceful future. The author's audience will either allow their struggles to break them or to make them.[406]

The author returns to the imagery of the boxer and the runner. He calls his listeners to lift their "drooping hands" and strengthen their "weak knees." His hearers are being beaten by the

---

[405] Cockerill, *Hebrews*, 626.
[406] Moo, *Hebrews*, 477.

blows of all those who oppose Christ. Nevertheless, they must keep their guard up and continue to move. If they lower their hands, the enemy is sure to land a knock-out punch. Yet much like the boxing match, their fight will not continue forever. The believer's bout has also already been won by Christ; they simply need to remain standing until the bell.

The believer as a runner must "make straight paths" for their feet. The race of faith is a journey that, at times, is difficult. However, they must, by their example, clear a path for those who follow behind. The reality of life is that some run better than others. There are those who will run with endurance the race set before them, laying aside whatever hinders their success (Heb. 12:1). However, there are also those who will run with difficulty. While every believer is called to run their own race, they must also run in a community being cheered on by the great cloud of witnesses who ran before them. Jesus ran on behalf of all believers. Now, all believers must run by example for their brothers and sisters in faith.

There are numerous takeaways for incarcerated believers. While the inmate is generally incarcerated due to their own poor decisions, once they are in Christ, prison life becomes part of the struggle. Living as a believer in prison has its own unique set of circumstances and how one approaches these circumstances influences how one serves their time; it's all about perspective.

For example, most people on some level hate every day of prison life. They have been stripped of their freedom and many of life's most basic needs. Becoming a Christian does not change any of this, however, it should change one's perspective. Many inmates have shared how prison taught them to appreciate the things they once took for granted. Family visits and phone conversations suddenly have become more meaningful and important. Through the trial of separation, the inmates learn the value of time spent together.

The imagery of the boxer and runner is also important. The inmate cannot allow their circumstances to beat them down. They must fight every opponent for every round. This includes the hardships of loved ones lost, failed appeals, and parole denials. Life in Christ does not remove these opponents, but it can enable one to endure their blows.

The inmate is also like the runner. They run over and around every obstacle life puts in their way. They are called to run from victory to victory. They follow those who ran before them and lead the way for those who follow. They run successfully by keeping their focus on Jesus. The longer one runs and the harder one fights, the more prepared one is for the next bout.

Application

RESCUED NOT ARRESTED

Discipline is not always a bad thing. Sometimes what we first believe is painful and evil ultimately works out for our benefit. Take the time today and honestly consider your time of incarceration. Can you see any way that God has used your prison experience to mold you into a better follower of Christ? List some of the most important ways your incarceration has benefited you.

3. Esau's Failure to Endure (12:14-17)

Prisoner's Insight for the Journey

The inmate's greatest enemy is self. We moan and complain about what we do not have while failing to acknowledge all that we forfeited. We once had furloughs until someone, while on leave, committed a new crime. We had free weights and canned food until someone decided to use them as weapons. Most importantly, we once all had freedom but traded it for some temporary satisfaction that landed us in prison. Now many of us long for our freedom to be returned; however, we lack true repentance. Freedom without repentance is short lived.

The author desires his audience to know that when facing opposition, they must remain cautious on their journey. There exist obstacles from without and within which aim to hinder their obtainment of "the grace of God," and if all possible, cause them to sell their birthright and forfeit their ability to enter the heavenly Jerusalem.

Commentary

12:14-17

The author transitions from his instruction on the discipline of God to a warning concerning perseverance in community. He calls his listeners to "strive for peace" with their brothers and sisters. Opposition from without can often cause division within. The author previously reminded his audience not to neglect meeting together (Heb. 10:25). Therefore, they must diligently seek peace among the people of God. The adversary's tactic is to divide and conquer; a house divided will not stand.

"The peace of the community must be maintained by diligent pursuit of the God-given, Christ-provided 'holiness' that is its source."[407] By pursuing the peace that flows from the holiness given by Christ, believers ensure their access to God. Those who do not seek peace show they have no part in the holiness of God.

The word "strive" denotes the continual pursuit of an object or goal. In this sense, it is something the faithful are to zealously pursue. Paul, in his numerous letters, encourages believers to strive for faith, love, righteousness, and peace (1 Thess. 5:15; 2 Tim. 2:22; Rom. 14:19).[408] The author ties the command to strive into the Christian's moral obligation to be conformed to the image of Christ. By striving for Christlikeness, believers ensure they "will see the Lord." The peace which the author encourages his listeners to obtain is only achieved by the standard of holiness. This is vastly different from the culture's definition of peace. Peace for most secular cultures simply means "problem free." This implies that peace can be achieved by any standard. The world often employs compromise in order to obtain peace. This is why worldly peace is never lasting; it is not grounded in holiness.

As once worldly people, we know what it means to pursue our desires. We once pursued drugs, alcohol, money, and even violence. We were hard people pursuing a hard lifestyle. In my addiction, I remember waking up and immediately thinking about how I was going to strive for my next drink of alcohol or hit of dope. I woke up with my mind set on sin. As born-again believers, we must strive for the things of God in the same way; however,

---

[407] Cockerill, *Hebrews*, 634.
[408] Oepke, "διώκω" *Theological Dictionary of the New Testament*. Ed. Gerhard Kittel (Grand Rapids: Eerdmans Publishing, 1964).

now our standard is holiness. Instead of waking up with our minds set on sin, we must now wake up with our minds set on the things of God. We must actively pursue what God desires for our lives. God is able to take our willingness to go above and beyond to get what we desire and sanctify it for his glory so that we will go above and beyond to be in his presence.

The author continues his warning by encouraging his listeners not to fail to obtain the grace of God. Grace signifies the favor of God bestowed through the inheritance of God's blessings. The believer in one sense is currently experiencing God's grace, but in another, is yet to experience its full benefits. Therefore, the author continually throughout his sermon calls his audience to endure the struggles of the journey and obtain the full benefits of God's grace. Failure to pursue the peace which flows from holiness is to reject God's ultimate offering of grace. "One can 'fall short' of Christ's provision [grace] from lassitude, from discouragement or the rigors of the race, or through attraction to the rewards of an unbelieving world."[409] This call is not simply a subjective reflection on one's inner person. The author exhorts his listeners to "see to it that no one fails to obtain the grace of God." This "no one" implies that believers are called to watch out for their fellow believers. The body of Christ is meant to function in unity. This means caring for the spiritual wellbeing of their brothers and sisters. Distractions vie for believers' attention. They come from without and from within and like a "root of bitterness" they spring up and cause trouble. The author's listeners likely are allowing the cares of the world to steer them off course. Those who reject God's ultimate blessing become defiled and possibly lead others astray also. The author is not only concerned for the

[409] Cockerill, *Hebrews*, 637.

individual believer but also for the whole community of faith. The root of bitterness can spring up and spread throughout the body of believers like a cancer.

He further describes those who reject God's grace as "sexually immoral or unholy like Esau." The author relates Esau's forfeiting of his birthright to a sexual sin. Both Esau's sin and sexual sin spring from a desire of immediate gratification. Those who reject God's blessing, like Esau, forfeit their inheritance for immediate pleasure. One of the dangers of sin is its ability to ensnare its victim almost without warning. Thus, Esau, "afterward" desired to undo his sin: "he desired to inherit the blessing." However, no opportunity for repentance was available even "though he sought it with tears." This is a difficult passage because it appears to teach that one's inability to repent is possible in this life. However, Esau's failure is likely a result of his unrepentant heart. First, repentance is always possible in this life (see section on Hebrews 6:6). Second, Cockerill notes that "sought with tears" refers to the blessing and not repentance. Thus, it was the loss of his birthright and not the sin that Esau mourned.[410] This is like being sorry for getting caught, instead of being sorry for what one did.

The author's concern is that his audience does not become distracted by either what is happening outside the body or the sinful pull from within. They are to stay focused on the race ahead while depending on the grace of God to see them through. It is God's grace that draws one into fellowship with him and it's God's grace which enables believers to fight to the bell.

---

[410] Cockerill, *Hebrews*, 641.

The incarcerated believer can learn a very valuable lesson from the example of Esau. The living conditions in prison have a way of increasing one's desire for the most basic comforts. Countless brothers and sisters have fallen to the allure of the contraband cell phone or quick buck made from some other activity. However, giving in to the immediate gratification of communication or money always results in the forfeiture of other blessings. The prisoner already has so very little, so is it really worth giving it up so easily?

Application

RIDDING YOUR LIFE OF BITTERNESS

Many people confuse the concept of regret with that of repentance. Regret is feeling bad about the loss of a former blessing or privilege. There are many men and women who regret committing their crimes. They are sorry that they got locked up. Repentance is feeling remorse for the action which led to the loss of the blessing. Repentance also implies a change in thought and behavior. This is why the author of Hebrews tells his listeners to strive for peace and holiness. Those who strive show the change of their character by seeking to think and behave differently. Read Matthew 5:21-24 and consider the relationship with your brother and sisters in the faith. Are you harboring some root of bitterness toward someone?

4. The Goal of Endurance (12:18-24)

Prisoner's Insight for the Journey

The prison chapel is the home of the untrained preacher. It seems as if every church from the surrounding community sends their untrained lay preacher to practice their skills, or lack thereof, on the unsuspecting inmate population. As a result, most sermons consist of "half" the gospel message.

Some preachers arrive at service convinced that every inmate is a lost sinner who is unaware of their sinfulness. So, they deliver fiery sermons aimed to convict the wretched inmate of their transgressions. While the need for the acknowledgement of sin is vital for salvation, the untrained minister often leaves his audience standing at the foot of Mt. Sinai in fear of a judgmental and demanding God. His sermon makes "the hearers beg that no further message be spoken to them" (Hebrews 12:19). The sermon ends and the listener is never presented with the way to Zion. They leave the chapel scratching their heads wondering who is able to fulfill such a demanding requirement.

To the other extreme, the untrained preacher fears to use the words sin and judgment. They believe that the prisoner's circumstances call for a message of love and prosperity. There are no calls for repentance or need to persevere. God loves you just as you are; unfortunately, this includes dead in trespasses and sins. The untrained minister delivers the unrepentant sinner straight to the "heavenly Jerusalem" and a "festal gathering" (Hebrews 12:22) without ever explaining the need for Jesus.

Thankfully, the author of Hebrews is no untrained preacher. He does not bring his audience to Sinai and leave them trembling in fear. He brings them to Sinai to reveal the holiness and majesty of God. He allows them to hear the order that could not be endured and come to understand their sinfulness in the presence of God's holiness. He reveals the problem and the need. Yet, he also shows them the solution. Jesus and his sprinkled blood speak a better word than judgment. Because of Christ's sacrifice, they do not have to remain at Sinai. Jesus, their pioneer, has paved the way to Zion, the heavenly Jerusalem. The author shows his listeners both the judgment of the Old Covenant and the grace of the New made available through the sacrifice of Jesus.

Commentary

12:18-24

The author continues his pattern of warning followed by assurance. His listeners have not inherited judgment as Esau did, but instead, through Jesus, have inherited a heavenly home. In this section, the author uses Mt. Sinai as a picture of judgment for those who reject Christ (Heb. 12:18-21). Mt Zion on the other hand represents the blessings of the believers' access to God's presence (Heb. 12:22-24). Thus, the author is not merely interested in contrasting the two covenants, or two time periods. He focuses on the distinction between "belief and unbelief with apostasy and faithfulness with judgment and blessing."[411]

The author introduces his contrast with the phrase "for you have not come" in verse 18 and concludes the contrast in verse 22 with "but you have come." The author's point emphasizes that his listeners are not like Esau because they already possess their inheritance. They must simply strive to obtain its reward.

---

[411] Cockerill, *Hebrews*, 642-43.

The author begins his picture of judgment with a fearful description of God's presence on Mt. Sinai taken from Israel's encounter with God in Exodus and Deuteronomy (Exodus 19-20; Deuteronomy 4-5).[412] Without ever mentioning God, the author describes his terrifying presence with blazing fire, darkness, gloom, and the tempest. All these appeals to the listener's senses and speak to the unapproachable nature of God. The children of Israel were permitted from approaching God on the mountain. Only Moses was allowed to enter the presence of God on behalf of the people. God also spoke from the mountain, and his words instilled fear in the people which "made the hearers beg that no further message be spoken to them." This references the peoples' desire that Moses speak to God on their behalf (Exodus 20:18-19). The Old Testament account describes an unholy peoples' inability to approach a holy God. The author uses the description to show the futility of rejecting Christ. If fear and judgment were the experiences of those under the Old Covenant, then fear and judgment still remains for those who attempt to approach God apart from Christ.

As inmates, we all know what it is like to stand judgment. We violated the law and found ourselves caught in the web of the criminal justice system. We stood fearfully before our judges expecting the worst punishment for our crimes. The range of sentencing (2-20, 5-99) left us caught between hope and despair. And after the gavel sealed our fates, some walked away with relief but others with more years than any person could possibly serve. We received judgment with very little mercy. Thankfully, the judgments of the Lord are true and just (Rev. 16:7). In Christ, when we stand before the Lord, it will be a "festal gathering"

---

[412] Guthrie, "Hebrews" CNTUOT, 988.

because we will all know our sentences: eternal life in the presence of our savior.

Two further descriptions emphasize God's wrath toward unholy people and the terrifying experience of his presence. Not even an animal was allowed to wander into the holy presence of God without suffering a sentence of death. This highlights the sure death of a sinful person who touched the holy mountain. Verse 21 emphasizes the terrifying presence of God. God's faithful servant Moses trembled with fear in his presence. This statement alludes to Moses' intercession on behalf of the people after they worshipped the golden calf (Deuteronomy 9:19).[413] Under the law, even those who were faithful servants feared the presence of the holy God. This picture of judgment, fear, and uncertainty helps to distinguish the contrast of grace, peace, and certainty found in Jesus and the New Covenant.

The author now transitions from the judgment and lack of access on Mt. Sinai to the grace and access available on Mt. Zion. The author's statement, "but you have come," emphasizes the completion of the faithful traveler's journey. Those who are in Christ have already arrived into the heavenly Jerusalem. This statement shows the author's belief in the success of his listeners. "Innumerable angels" helps to signify the presence of God. "In festal gathering" emphasizes the welcoming atmosphere in contrast with the stormy gloom and darkness of Sinai. Zion is pictured as a place where the believer is welcomed. The heavenly Jerusalem is also home to "the assembly of the firstborn." This is a description of the faithful people of God encompassing both Testaments. This assembly includes both "the church militant and

---

[413] Cockerill, *Hebrews*, 650.

triumphant."[414] A description of the great cloud of witnesses and those who are still running the race. Mount Zion is also home "to God the judge of all." The author describes God as judge in order to emphasize the mediating role of Jesus. God still stands as judge of the universe but unlike at Sinai, the believer has Christ as their advocate. The fear of entering the courtroom of God has been removed because the penalty has previously been paid by the "sprinkled blood of Jesus."

Most all inmates are all too familiar with the fear and uncertainty of entering the presence of a judge. At the bare minimum our freedom was at stake, at the maximum, our very lives hinged on the decision of a judge and jury (Texas is a death penalty state). So naturally, we trembled with fear, our lives were in the hands of people who did not know us. We hoped that the circumstances of our crimes had not been misrepresented by overzealous prosecutors more concerned about their conviction rate than justice. We hoped that the jury was impartial, we hoped that the judge slept well; nevertheless, we all feared the outcome. Thankfully, when we stand before God in Christ, we do not have to fear. The sprinkled blood of Jesus has removed all uncertainty of the outcome. At the end of the age when we stand in the courtroom of God, it will be for enrollment into the heavenly city, it will be a festal gathering.

The author adds a further description of believers with "the spirits of the righteous." The previous description highlighted all the faithful of God, both living now, and those in glory. This description focuses on those in glory. They are those who have died in faith. This phrase also highlights the role of Jesus as mediator. They are described as "made perfect." The inability of

---

[414] Ibid., 655-56.

the Old Testament worshipper to approach God at Sinai is removed because the sprinkled blood of Jesus has made the believer perfect. Once again, the idea of perfection implies complete. What was lacking in the believer's ability to access God has now been made complete. They are now righteous and are not the wilderness generation (Hebrews 3) or those who crucify again the Son of God (Hebrews 6) and profane the blood of the Covenant (Hebrews 10). The author's listeners have not sold their birthright, but through faith in Christ, "have come to mount Zion, and to the city of the living God" (Heb. 12:22). The author once again demonstrates the two aspects of faith in Jesus: the "already" and the "not yet." In Christ, the believer is sealed with the promised Holy Spirit, the guarantee of one's inheritance. Yet, this guarantee awaits the day in which the believer will take full possession of the inheritance they have in Christ (Ephesians 1:14). As a result, the believer proves the validity of faith by persevering to the end. The true believer is a wanderer and exile in this world on a journey to a world where he/she is a citizen.

The author provides numerous points of contrast between Mt. Sinai and Mt. Zion. The listeners "have not come" to Sinai which implies judgment and lack of access but they "have come" to Mt. Zion, a place described by access and fellowship. The author provides three names for the listeners to consider, each adding a different aspect to the contrast with Sinai. Mount Zion was associated with the temple mount and where the people went to access God. "The city of the living God" highlights both the presence of God and people's ability to dwell in his presence (implied by the word city). Finally, "the heavenly Jerusalem" contrasts with the earthly Jerusalem, which was but a temporal shadow of its eternal reality.[415] The author's description of Sinai emphasized obstacles to worship, his description of Zion shows the blessings of worship provided by Jesus. Furthermore, the author describes Zion as a place of festive fellowship.[416] Zion is home to innumerable saints in right-standing before the judge of the universe. The final contrast between Sinai and Zion is the presence of Jesus, the mediator of a New Covenant, and to "the sprinkled blood." The author now focuses on the most important distinction between the two mountains: Jesus. This is important for his listeners to grasp. Jesus and the blood of the New Covenant provide what is lacking from the Old Testament religious practices. To turn away from Jesus is to turn away from the presence of God. The author has already made clear what the blood of Jesus has accomplished. To resort once again to the blood of animals is to reject the welcoming presence of God at Zion for wrathful judgment on Sinai. The distinction is also evident in the blood of Abel versus Jesus. Abel's blood cried out from the ground judgment upon his murderer, Cain. This judgment included exile form God and his people. The blood of Jesus cries out a "better word." The blood of Jesus speaks forgiveness of sins, access to God, and release from ultimate judgment.[417] This stands in stark contrast to the picture of Mt. Sinai or even the wilderness temple. The blood of Jesus accomplished what the whole of Old Testament rituals could not. As a result, the believer is to strive for that rest which is theirs in Christ. The person who turns back from Christ shows that they have not come to the heavenly Jerusalem, but like Esau, have forfeited any claim to a future inheritance in the heavenly kingdom.

---

[415] Cockerill, *Hebrews*, 651-52.
[416] Ibid., 653.
[417] Cockerill, *Hebrews*, 658-59.

Application

THE JUDGMENT OF GRACE

The author of Hebrews is clear, “It is appointed for man to die once, and after that comes judgment” (Heb. 9:27). In many Christian denominations, the idea of God’s judgment is misunderstood. They argue that believers will be judged according to their works. Here the believer, like the ancient Israelite, is left standing at the foot of Mt. Sinai uncertain of the outcome. Salvation by works nullifies the grace of God through faith in Jesus. Others, believe judgment from a loving God is unbiblical. They present God as the loving grandfather who forgives regardless of one’s behavior. God will ultimately save everyone, sin and all. Read Romans 4:1-5 and James 2:14-26 and meditate on these two texts. Do they contradict one another or teach the same truth from different perspectives? Write out your answer.

5. A Final Reminder to Persevere (12:25-29)

Prisoner's Insight for the Journey

The world is full of warning signs which scream caution from every direction: don't drink and drive, just say no to drugs, and most importantly, don't mess with Texas. Yet most of society navigates life paying little attention to all the warnings. They are often viewed as inconveniences meant for other people. However, warnings are supposed to be for the betterment of society.

For those of us in prison, we have thrown caution to the wind, and "refused" to heed any warning. As a result of our recklessness, we were judged and found guilty. Our disregard for the many warnings resulted in a temporal judgment. We must serve a certain amount of time to atone for our recklessness. However, there exists one warning sign that no person can afford to ignore: the word of God. The Bible tells the world that God will once more not only shake the earth but also the heavens (Hag. 2:6; Heb. 12:26). On that day, only those who have placed faith in Jesus will not be judged. If you have learned to fear the wrath of the judge from behind the bench, then fear even more the wrath of the judge from heaven. He is a consuming fire (Heb. 12:29).

The author of Hebrews warns his listeners one final time. The God from heaven will not be ignored. For those who "refuse him who is speaking" only judgment remains. However, those who have placed faith in his Son Jesus have received a "kingdom that cannot be shaken." Their penalty has been paid and their judgment waved. For this reason, the believer must be grateful while offering to God acceptable worship.

Commentary

12:25-29

The author addresses his audience with a final warning which also continues his theme of divine speech. Since the believer has come to mount Zion through "the sprinkled blood that speaks a better word" (Heb. 12:24), they must "not refuse the one who is speaking" (Heb. 12:25). In these last days, God has spoken in his Son (Heb. 1:2) and all those who hear his message "must pay close attention" to what is said (Heb. 2:1). God's voice from Sinai represented judgment because they hardened their hearts in rebellion (Heb. 3:8), however, he now speaks a welcoming word of grace through his Son.[418]

The author is concerned for his audience and appeals to them one last time to hear the voice of God and respond with obedience and perseverance. He introduces his warning with his signature lesser to greater argument. He contrasts the judgments (implied by the word escape) of Sinai and Zion. The lesser is the fearful judgment that fell on the disobedient generation in the wilderness. They hardened their hearts and did not enter into God's rest. As a result, their bodies fell in the wilderness (Heb. 3:17). The greater judgment will fall upon the one who rejects the word from heaven. Once again, the author contrasts Sinai with Zion. If God's people did not escape a temporal judgment, they shall surely not escape an eternal one.[419] The author emphasizes his listener's responsibility to persevere by warning them of turning away from God who speaks from heaven.

---

[418] Cockerill, *Hebrews*, 660.
[419] Ibid., 661.

God's voice from Sinai shook the earth in the past. This statement recalls the awesome presence of God from Hebrews 12:18-21. Yet God will once more shake the earth. The author once again uses a lesser to greater argument. God's voice shook the earth at Sinai. However, when he speaks judgment for a final time, he will shake both earth and heaven.

To highlight the totality of God's final judgment the author cites Haggai 2:6 and offers a brief interpretation. First, when quoting Haggai, the author provides his listeners with a paraphrased version. He shortens earth, sea, and dry land to simply earth and places it before heaven. Next, the original context of Haggai addresses God's judgment of the nations and subsequent glorification of Jerusalem. The author understands the nations to be the current opposition to God's people and Jerusalem to be the heavenly city mentioned in Hebrews 12:22. As a result, this verse becomes a prophecy concerning the "last days." By mentioning both the shaking of the earth and heaven, the author emphasizes that God will judge all of creation, nothing will escape the judgment of God. However, verse 27 helps clarify the author's intended meaning.[420]

The author begins his interpretation of Haggai by expounding on the phrase "once more." This reminds his listeners that God once judged the wilderness generation and he will "once more" judge all of creation. This means that God will remove what is man-made. "The phrase signals the removal of the present world and pictures all its idols crushed, broken, and cast down. God will destroy all that man has made. All that remains will be that which

---

[420] Cockerill, *Hebrews*, 665.

belongs to the Lord."[421] "The things that cannot be shaken" represent God's holy city and his faithful people.

The opposition which his listeners currently face will not withstand the judgment of God. Those who do not "refuse him who is speaking" and "have come" to God's heavenly city reside in a place that cannot be shaken. All those who depend on the earthly temporal institution will one day find themselves without a foundation on which to stand.[422] Haggai's prophecy, however, ended on a positive note for the people of God. Those who have heeded the message and placed faith in its messenger inherit a "kingdom that cannot be shaken." The author's listeners can be "grateful" that the coming judgment for them will be one of vindication.

Even believers construct idols that compete with the supremacy of the Lord in our lives. This is especially true for the incarcerated Christian. So much has been restricted and removed from our lives that we often cling to what we have left with all our strength. We focus so much attention on our relationship with family and friends because we feel that any minor neglect might result in further loss. Sometimes we become so obsessed with the future that we neglect the present. While family, friends, and the future are important, we cannot lose sight of what is most important, our relationship with Jesus. This is why Christ reminds his followers that they should not be anxious about what is outside of our control. Our main concern should be seeking God's kingdom; a kingdom that cannot be shaken (Luke 12:22-31; Heb. 12:28).

---

[421] Mohler, *Hebrews*, 216.
[422] Cockerill, *Hebrews*, 670.

The Lord will proclaim to his people "come, you who are blessed by my Father, inherit the kingdom prepared for you from the foundation of the world" (Matthew 25:34). The very thought of escaping a judgment which all people deserve should move God's people to "offer to God acceptable worship, with reverence and awe." In this sense, the church militant should join the "festal gathering" in praising the awesome nature of their Creator and Savior. The fear of Sinai is now replaced with a reverence and awe of God's graceful plan of redemption. The believer stands confounded by the majesty of God. All that does not belong to him will, one day, fall in judgment to his very presence. Christ will one day return to judge the world. Therefore, the church must live as if that day could arrive at any moment. The author concludes his warning with a final reminder of God's complete and final judgment. Nothing will escape his awesome presence because he "is a consuming fire."[423]

Application

ACCEPTABLE WORSHIP

The Bible often speaks of the believers' acceptable worship (Rom. 12:1; Heb. 12:28). The Lord has given the Christian so much to be thankful for. Take the time today and list some of the things you are thankful for that the Lord has given you. Now in the form of acceptable worship praise him for his glorious gifts.

[423] Cockerill, *Hebrews*, 670-71.

IV. God's Final Instructions for the Weary Traveler (13:1-25)

Section Summary

Any careful reader of Hebrews will notice the sudden shift in style at the beginning of Chapter 13. The author has moved through some of the most profound teachings of the Christian faith with the most beautiful language in all the New Testament. Now, he begins a series of brief exhortations which at first glance appear to have nothing to do with the rest of the sermon.[424] This has led many to assume that Chapter 13 was added at a later date. Some have argued that the style and vocabulary are too difficult to have come from the author of the first 12 chapters. Others have cited a shift in themes which they argue were added to make the sermon relevant for a later audience. Most scholars today reject these arguments and find a great deal of unity between Chapter 13 and the rest of the sermon. It is likely that the author's shift in style is a result of an ancient literary practice called peroration. This practice summarized selected themes and moved listeners to action.[425] This section is closely tied to the author's idea of "acceptable worship' from Hebrews 12:28. Here, the author

---

[424] Cockerill, *Hebrews*, 673; Moo, *Hebrews*, 502.
[425] Moo, *Hebrews*, 502.

provides concrete examples of what acceptable worship must look like.[426]

Introduction to the Section

In this section, the author begins with his concrete examples of acceptable worship. Most commentators see a natural break between verses 6 and 7. After verse 7, there is very little agreement on the structure of the final verses. Thus, this commentary follows Cockerill's divisions. In verses 1-6, the author provides his listeners with four pairs of exhortations which aim to address unity within the body of believers. Verses 7-17 address the need to imitate past leaders while submitting to present leadership.[427] Finally, 18-25 end in epistolary fashion with a prayer, benediction, and final greetings.

A. Showing Love to One Another (13:1-6)

Prisoner's Insight for the Journey

I am currently housed at the H. H. Coffield unit, the largest prison in Texas. At Coffield, there are literally four thousand inmates seemingly stacked upon one another four stories high. There are no places of solitude or privacy. Yet prison can feel like the loneliest place on earth. In Texas alone, there are over one hundred thousand men and women who have been removed from their families and communities. They are thrown into a foreign environment governed by archaic policies and procedures and expected to be miraculously reformed. The very make up of prison fights against the ideas of brotherly love and hospitality.

---

[426] Cockerill, *Hebrews*, 675-76.
[427] Cockerill, *Hebrews*, 676-677.

As I write this, we are currently on our bi-annual lockdown. This means weeks of sack lunches delivered to our cells: one PB&J and one meat sandwich per sack. Many men will go to bed hungry; I am not one of them. I am blessed to have family who send me money to purchase food from commissary. They heed the call "to remember those who are in prison." However, the archaic rules say that I cannot share my food with others. The rules tell me to disregard brotherly love and hospitality. Well, in this regard, I am a rule breaker. I would rather obey God than man (Acts 4:19). If I got it, then you can have it!

The author of Hebrews desires for his listeners to live out, in a practical way, their faith in God. This means emphasizing brotherly love, hospitality, remembrance of the less fortunate, and the sanctity of marriage. The author knows that a strong community is better equipped to weather the trials and tribulations. The congregation is called to support one another in their time need. Like Jesus, they must never leave or forsake their brothers and sisters in Christ.

Commentary

13:1-6

The author introduces this section with four pairs of exhortations.[428] These exhortations illustrate what the author means by "acceptable worship" (Heb. 12:28). He encourages his listeners to "Let brotherly love continue." The idea that faith in Christ unites believers into a spiritual family is prevalent in the New Testament. The author has previously introduced brother/sisterhood in Christ in the context of Jesus' suffering (Heb. 2:11). Therefore, letting brotherly love continue likely

---

[428] Moo, *Hebrews*, 506.

includes facing trials together as a unified family. In the ancient world, the bond between siblings was considered the closest of all familial relationships.[429] The New Testament authors draw on this imagery repeatedly in order to emphasize the need of family and community during uncertain times (Rom. 12:10; 2 Pet. 1:7).

In prison, it is often the case that people lose contact with their families. This can be the result of many factors: death, disagreement, or simply, out of sight, out of mind. As a result, inmates often develop new families within prison. I have spent more time with many of my incarcerated brothers than I ever did with my blood brothers on the outside. Many of the guys who are now released stay in contact with those still incarcerated. They develop bonds forged through trials that are virtually unbreakable. They heed the command to "Let brotherly love continue."

The author also encourages his listeners to "show hospitality to strangers." In the ancient world hotels or inns were not common. Those that did exist were often ill repute. Therefore, many attempted to avoid these establishments altogether. Traveling Christians often found shelter in the homes of other Christians. This allowed Christianity to flourish in the first century. Many of the earliest churches were located in the homes of Christians.[430] Therefore, these house churches became one-stop-shops of food, shelter, and worship. This bond of hospitality linked many of these groups together as seen through the various greetings at the conclusion of the New Testament letters. The author includes a rationale for hospitality that has often left believers seeing angels in every kind deed. Most likely, the author is recalling the Old Testament accounts of angelic messengers like

---

[429] Whitherington, *Letters and Homilies for Jewish Christians,* 354.
[430] Whitherington, *Letters and Homilies for Jewish Christians, 354.*

in Genesis 18 when angels appeared to Abraham and Sarah. He reminds his listeners that a message from God can even come from strangers; therefore, remember to be hospitable to all those they encounter.

Verse 3 reminds the listeners to "remember those who are in prison." In light of the persecution and imprisonment that the church faced in the first century, this statement was probably the most relevant to the author's current advice. The listeners are called to treat the incarcerated "as though" they are in prison with them. This is a high calling which requires more than "thinking" of those incarcerated. Douglas Moo states the situation well: "This 'remembering' is not simply a mental exercise or even only a matter of praying for them." It would often take the form of practical acts, such as bringing food for prisoners.[431] The author also calls the church to remember "those who are mistreated." The abuses the Christian church suffered during the first century are well known. Christians were often seen as outcasts and persecuted for their "strange" religious beliefs. The call to remember the mistreated is both a call to empathize with their suffering and a call to prepare for one's own possible persecution. No one was exempt from possible imprisonment and mistreatment. By showing brotherly love and hospitality, one identifies with the community. By identifying with the Christian community, one subjects themselves to possible persecution. However, to identify with one another in suffering became one of the greatest catalysts for the growth of early Christianity. To love one's brother/sister in the faith was to show it through actions. Lane states:

> Those who respond in love, providing shelter to persecuted brothers and sisters, visiting them in

[431] Moo, *Hebrews*, 509.

> prison, and caring for them when they are ill-treated, will through these acts, acknowledge themselves to be Christian. Their actions will complement and validate their public confession of Christian faith. In the absence of demonstration of love to other confessors of Christ, public confession is an empty gesture. Confession in the form of action is indispensable for exhibiting the quality of life within the confessing community.[432]

Verse 4 introduces exhortations for a healthy marriage. In light of the loose morals of the Greco-Roman society, it is not strange that the idea of marriage appears here in the context of brotherly love and hospitality.[433] Koester notes that allowing strangers into one's home and the possibility of the imprisonment of a spouse strengthens the need "to observe rigorous standards of propriety."[434] The rationale for the sanctity of the marriage relationship is found in the judgment of God. He will judge "the sexually immoral and adulterous." The blood of the New Covenant has cleansed the believers from all sin. To practice "sexual immorality is a breach of the New Covenant."[435]

The final pair of exhortations addresses the love of money and contentment, two common teachings of the New Testament. The rejection of the love of money will naturally flow from a call to show brotherly love and hospitality. It would be unimaginable for one to be greedy while also showing hospitality. The author

---

[432] Lane, *Hebrews*, 515.
[433] Moo, *Hebrews*, 510.
[434] Koester, *Hebrews*, 565.
[435] Cockerill, *Hebrews*, 684.

highlights the close connection between brotherly love, hospitality, and the love of money with a play on words. In the original language, these three phrases are constructed from the Greek word "phil" (love): the love of brothers "Philadelphia," the love of strangers (hospitality) "philoxenia," and the love of money "aphilargyros." However, the author negates the word love of money with the alpha privative [-a].[436] This helps to emphasize that the love of money is the opposite of brotherly love and hospitality.[437] The final exhortation is one to contentment. This phrase could be translated "be satisfied with what you have." This phrase likely goes beyond a call to material contentment. Lane states: "In Hebrews the injunction of contentment is a call to quietness in the situation, in confident reliance on the presence and provision of a faithful God."[438]

I believe that if many of us would reflect on the past actions which led us to our incarceration, we would see the love of money and a lack of contentment. I personally defined my early life by these two principles. I desired money, I was always discontented, so I was willing to do whatever it took to alleviate my seeming problems. Brotherly love and hospitality were not concepts which I was familiar with. I wanted more no matter the cost and I cared little for the needs of others. Today, as a minister, I am called to always put the needs of others first. This is not easy to achieve, especially when dealing with people who are often ungrateful. Nevertheless, believers are called to imitate Christ who gave his life in the perfect example of brotherly love.

---

[436] Moo, *Hebrews*, 511.
[437] Cockerill, *Hebrews*, 685.
[438] Lane, *Hebrews*, 519.

The author grounds his exhortations in the word of God. He employs two powerful texts which speak of God's providence over the lives of his people. First, the author cites a biblical truth that is found in numerous places throughout Scripture: "I will never leave you nor forsake you." This is likely taken from Deuteronomy 31:6 and Joshua 1:5. This is God's promise to his people as they are about to enter into the Promised Land. God's message of faithfulness is meant to reassure the audience of God's continual care even in the face of the unknown. The author follows this verse with Psalm 118:6: "The Lord is my helper. I will not fear; what can man do to me?" These two verses aim to comfort a struggling church. God is with them every step of their journey. If God is with them who can stand against them? They must simply show to one another the love and gratitude that God has bestowed on them.

Application

REMEMBERING THE INCARCERATED

As previously mentioned, prison can be a lonely place. Many men and women feel isolated even in the midst of a crowd. Some simply do not know how to develop healthy relationships, and many put up barriers to protect themselves from future pain and disappointment. They have never experienced true brotherly love and hospitality. Take the time today to fellowship with someone who may be in need of a kind word. Remember to show kindness to all, you never know who you may be entertaining!

B. Imitate and Obey Leaders (13:7-17)

Prisoner's Insight for the Journey

It is always hard to say goodbye. In prison we often spend years or even decades surrounded by the same people. We come to know their habits, their likes, and dislikes; they become our family inside the walls. In my 21 yrs. of incarceration, I have made some good friends: (1) Old men who were like father figures, who taught me to do time as a young man. (2) Guys my age who were like brothers. (3) Men I grew old with in prison. (4) Young men who I became a father figure to; the ones I taught to do time. I have seen countless men come and go. But goodbyes never get easier. There are never enough time or words to share with someone before you part ways. You do your best to give them a little piece of wisdom.

The author of Hebrews is ending his masterpiece. He knows his audience well and is concerned about their wellbeing. So, before he signs off, he leaves them with some truths, and a few warnings. A little something to help them persevere.

Commentary

13:7-17

In this section, the author introduces a brief summary of his sermon.[439] It is introduced by a call to imitate the former leadership (v.7) and concludes with a call to obey the current leaders (v.17).[440]

---

[439] Cockerill, *Hebrews*, 689.
[440] Moo, *Hebrews*, 512.

The author is still concerned with the overall perseverance of his listeners; therefore, he encourages them to "remember" those who spoke the Word of God. As Moo has noted, "Remember in Scripture means not just to 'recall' something in an intellectual sense, but to 'take to heart' with a view of affording one's thinking and conduct."[441] Correct thought should lead to correct actions. This statement looks back to the author's first warning at Hebrews 2:1-4.

The audience will avoid drifting away if they continue to consider and imitate their faithful leaders' way of life. This is a call to discipleship.[442] The listeners are being encouraged to follow the example of those who preceded them. This is a heavy calling, especially in light of their possible persecution. To drive home this point, the author reminds them of their ultimate example, their traveling companion who has walked with them thus far: "Jesus Christ is the same yesterday and today and forever." This statement is the believer's comfort; circumstances may change, but the Lord remains. Once again, the author recalls the eternal nature of the Son from Hebrews 1:10-12. The world will ultimately perish and the believer's only security is in the nature of Jesus.

For the incarcerated believer, this statement should provide a measure of peace in a chaotic world. Prison is constantly in a state of confusion fueled by the unknown. We are on lockdown at the Coffield unit and after four days we were finally allowed to shower; no warning, just go. Hundreds of men in a mad scramble at 5:00 am headed to the community shower. As I stood in the overcrowded shower waiting on an open showerhead, I

---

[441] Moo, *Hebrews, 512.*
[442] Lane, *Hebrews*, 527-28.

began to pray. I could do nothing else. The situation was totally out of my control. I was suddenly overcome by a sense of peace. Strangely in the midst of total chaos, I knew the Lord was in control.

In verse nine, the author warns against false teachings. Commentators have noted the difficulty of interpreting verses 9-14. This difficulty is related to many of the obscure phrases the author employs: "diverse and strange teachings … foods … altar." However, it is likely that these teachings oppose the word that was formerly spoken to them.[443] Other scholars question why the author waited so long to address contemporary false teachings.

It is possible that the author withheld addressing contemporary false teachings because it was rhetorically effective to do so. After a lengthy discourse on the superiority and sufficiency of Jesus, the author simply drives the nail into the coffin. No more on the issue needs to be said. It is also possible that false teaching is not the main point. The author aims to encourage his listeners to persevere.[444]

Strange things can hinder perseverance; therefore, the heart must be strengthened by grace. The strange teachings are closely tied to "food" which is a likely reference to sacrificial meals. The listeners were to find their comfort in Christ not some outward religious practice. The author, while not explicitly mentioning the works of the Law, alludes to them in the phrases: food, altar, sacrifice, and tent. Therefore, the common contrast between works of the Law and grace which is often emphasized in Paul's letters is also found here. The ritual practices "have not

---

[443] Lane, *Hebrews*, 530.
[444] Moo, *Hebrews*, 514-15.

benefited those devoted to them." There is also an implied contrast between being "led away" and drawing near to God. It is likely that the listeners were being influenced through attending meals tied to religious practices at the synagogue. As religious ceremonies, meals were thought to strengthen the heart.[445] Those who frequented these types of gatherings would likely be exposed to other types of diverse teachings which would draw listeners away from the sufficiency of Christ. However, the author has already made clear that gifts and offerings cannot perfect the conscience (Heb. 9:9-10). The seeming strength provided by "food" had no lasting effects on the worshipper. The author here appears to be advocating a more defined break between the religious practices of Judaism and what was becoming Orthodox Christianity. The listeners were doing themselves no favors attempting to live in both worlds.

The prison church is full of individuals who practice syncretism. Their religious beliefs are a mixture of numerous different faith groups and denominations. On Sundays, they're in protestant service worshipping Jesus, on Thursdays, they attend Eastern Religious meditation, and on Saturdays, they top it all off with a little Messianic Judaism! I am often amazed at how someone who has read their Bible could possibly attend so many different worship services which obviously contradict the teachings and the beliefs of the others. As a Field Minister, I spend a lot of time addressing the struggles of those individuals. Much like their theologies, their lives are also a mess. I believe this is also a direct result of their understanding of the Gospel. All the prosperity teachings, Jewish festivals, or chi-centering prayer cannot replace the grace which flows from knowing that Jesus is

[445] Lane, *Hebrews*, 532-37.

totally sufficient for all one's needs. The people do themselves no favors by looking for grace in all the wrong places.

In verse 10, the author further drives a wedge between Judaism and Christianity. Christians have "an alter" from which no one else has a right to eat. This altar is likely the sacrifice which Jesus has provided and the blessing which flows from it. Therefore, those who do not recognize the sufficiency of Jesus have no right to receive any blessings. Those "who serve the tent" is a clear allusion to Judaism. So once again, the author is reminding his listeners that a mixture of religious practices is no longer an option. They must choose by which altar they will approach God; the one which has become obsolete and without benefit (Heb. 9:10; 13:9), or the living altar that provides believers with boldness and confidence (Heb. 10:19-22).

In verses 11-13, the author directs his listeners' attention to Jesus. He accomplishes this through a comparison between the Old Testament sacrificial system and Jesus' offering of himself. The similarities in the author's example are often difficult to see. For example, verse 11 makes it clear that the blood of the sacrifice was offered in the temple, then the bodies of the animals were burned outside the camp. Jesus on the other hand, was crucified outside of the city (John 19:17-18). The author here is not attempting to compare or contrast the process of the sacrificial offerings. His point is to highlight where the sacrifice took place. Jewish religious practices were centered around the temple. Jews from all over the known world came to Jerusalem and the Temple in order to gain access to God's forgiveness. As a result, the Temple was the most holy of places. Anything deemed unclean, like an animal corpse, was disposed of outside the city in order not to defile the Temple. So, in verse 12, when the author states,

"Jesus also suffered outside the gate in order to sanctify the people." He is directing his listeners' attention away from the Temple and toward Jesus. The author drives home a powerful point; true sanctification is now found in an unsanctified place.[446] The author now calls his audience to "go to" Jesus "outside the camp." This obvious call to abandon all Jewish practices requires his listeners to hear the reproach Jesus endured; following Jesus comes with great sacrifices. Moo states:

> The Jewish imagery that pervades this passage, along with the notion of sacred space that is basic to the "outside the camp" idea, suggests rather that the author is calling his readers to leave the security of the Jewish system of sanctification. This is where Jesus is, as it were, 'located': to come to him demands renouncing the apparent security provides, then, some basis for thinking that at least one of the problems the author addresses in his sermon in the temptation facing, probably particularly, Jewish Christians to abandon their distinctive Christian identity and profile and find their spiritual security in Jewish ritual.[447]

In verse 14, the author reveals to his listeners the temporary nature of this world. The audience is to go to Jesus outside the camp in expectation of a greater city. They are much like Abraham because the city they are leaving is not their home. God has prepared for the faithful in a heavenly city. This city is

---

[446] Moo, *Hebrews*, 516-17.
[447] Moo, *Hebrews*, 518.

the final destination of all those who persevere in the faith. This is God's ultimate rest.

In verses 15-16, the author once again compares the Old Testament sacrifices with the New Testament offerings. In the Old Testament, the offerings were meant to achieve something for the offeror. The sinner brought his/her offering in the hopes of receiving forgiveness. However, as was the case the offeror left empty handed. The blood of animals could not achieve forgiveness. New Testament offerings on the other hand flow from the knowledge of the forgiveness provided to the believer. The author's listeners are to offer praises to God, not because praise can earn the favor of God, but because the listeners are thankful for the favor God has bestowed upon them. This is the worshipper's sacrifice to God. The worshipper also has a responsibility to their fellow believer. The author reminds his listeners "to do good and to share" with others. The church must resist the urge to separate from the larger community (Heb. 10:28); but instead exhort one another (Heb. 3:13) and practice brotherly love (Heb. 13:1). This exhortation to praise God and support one another is reminiscent of Jesus' summary of the Ten Commandments. Believers are called to love God and their neighbors (Matthew 22:36-40). In doing these two things, they are offering pleasing sacrifices to God.

The final verse in this section revisits the call to obedience and submission to leaders. This call to obedience and submission is likely a result of the negative influence of false teachings and teachers.[448] The listeners' leaders are distinguished from others. They are responsible for watching over the souls of their congregation and will one day give an account of their duty. The

[448] Moo, *Hebrews*, 520.

idea of watching over denotes caring for the outcome of the people.[449] Watching over should never be confused with lording over. The author's audience is already struggling with oppression from outsiders; they should not have to also struggle with oppression within. The picture of leadership in the New Testament is always one of servant leadership.[450] Leaders have a greater responsibility to others. Where there is greater responsibility, there is also greater accountability. This means leaders will one day have to give an account before God on how they cared for God's people. This theme of greater accountability is echoed in James' epistle (James 3:1). Leaders should not take their calling lightly. As a result, the people should be willing to submit to godly leaders. Those who serve God in a leadership position should be able to serve with Joy. This benefits all people. Lane notes that the author here is likely addressing an existing tension between the listeners and their leaders. In order for the community to persevere in the face of outward persecution, this inward difference must be resolved.[451] A divided church will not likely persevere.

In prison, churches are largely divided. This results from the fact that the prison church is designed to be seeker-friendly and non-denominational. This means that the incarcerated church encourages all forms of faith expression (Pentecostal to Baptist) and discourages the dogmatic proclamation of any particular view. Therefore, as one can imagine, there is very little consensus surrounding the content of practice of faith. Churches also lack formal leadership roles. There are no pastors or deacons. The church is overseen by a chaplaincy department which is meant to be religiously neutral. Despite the restrictions, somehow

---

[449] Cockerill, *Hebrews*, 708.
[450] Ferguson, 55-58.
[451] Lane, *Hebrews*, 556.

leadership seems to manifest itself. Men and women rise to the occasion. They see a need and fill it. They are not appointed leaders but are leaders because they lead. Prison churches may be divided but they succeed because of a few faithful servant leaders.

Application

SERVANT LEADERS

Leaders in prison are everywhere, some good, some bad. Some people choose to lead men and women further into their misery. They promote drug use and violence, and they punish disobedience. Others are beacons of hope, lights in a dark place. They lead those who follow to better places and better days. They lead by example. Consider those who you follow and ask yourself, "Am I moving in the right direction?" If you are a leader, ask yourself, "Am I leading my followers into darkness or the light?"

C. A Final Word of Exhortation (13:18-25)

Prisoners' Insight for the Journey

As they say: "All good things must come to an end." Writing this book was a journey of emotions. Like all new adventures, I started out excited. I relished the challenge of writing a book while still incarcerated. I started out strong, knocking out hundreds, or even thousands, of words a day. Then uncertainty reared its ugly head. I began to question if I was really capable of such an enormous project. I quickly learned that writing a book was not easy. Following closely behind my uncertainty was despair. Numerous times I told myself; "You can't do this. No one will read a book written by an inmate." I wanted to quit and leave this book unfinished like so many other projects of my past. Today, I am once again excited. The finish line is eight verses away. Today I will finish this journey even if I have to write all day and into the night. If no one ever buys a copy of this book, I will still be satisfied. Once again, I have overcome my inner critic. This book is written for all those thousands upon thousands of incarcerated men and women who have ever doubted the power of the Lord's perseverance: "The Lord is my helper, I will not fear, what can man do to me?" (Hebrews 13:6).

Commentary

13:18-25

The author begins this section with a request for prayer. The very person who has penned this lengthy sermon full of exhortations, warnings, and encouragements, now requests that the recipients pray for him. This reveals that even the godliest of leaders need the prayer and support of their people. The author appeals to his good conduct toward God's people to show that he is worthy of their prayers. Cockerill notes: "His authority [to request prayer] rests on his integrity as one who faithfully interprets and lives by the word of God. Spoken first in the prophets and now in his Son (1:1-4). He offers himself as example of one who has embraced Christ as the fully sufficient Savior and lived faithfully with the assured hope of God's promise for the future. What he claims for himself he would have his hearers emulate."[452]

In verse 19, the author gives his purpose for his request of prayer. He desires to return quickly to the recipients. This statement has led some commentators to believe that the author possibly had been imprisoned for his faith and was now desiring to quickly return to his congregation.[453] Other commentators caution against making the text say more than it does.[454] Regardless of the author's circumstances, he was obviously familiar with his listeners and desired to be reunited with them.

As a Field Minister, once a month we have a zoom call where every Field Minister in the state attends. We are able to see classmates and friends we haven't seen in years. During these calls, we reminisce about the past, marvel about how old we look, and inquire about one another's wellbeing. Through years of college and ministry, we have forged a strong bond. We always look forward to seeing one another and long for the day we will once again be reunited in ministry on the outside.

Verse 20 begins the author's benediction; however, this is not a generic closing but reveals the author's various themes

---

[452] Cockerill, *Hebrews*, 712.
[453] Ibid., 713-14.
[454] Moo, *Hebrews*, 527.

previously outlined in his sermon.[455] God is the God of peace. The listeners are struggling with trials and tribulations. They must understand that the God who journeys with them is the God who will provide peace. The peace which the Lord provides is grounded in the resurrection of Jesus. If God has raised Christ as a first fruit of one's future resurrection, then believers also have this hope. Through the power of the resurrection, Jesus has overcome death. This is why the author can confidently state: "The Lord is my helper, I will not fear, what can men do to me?" (Hebrews 13:6). Jesus is also proclaimed as "the Great Shepherd." Once again, Jesus is superior. He is the believers' "great High Priest" (Heb. 4:14), their "pioneer" (Heb. 2:10), and their "forerunner" (Heb. 6:20). Naturally then, he is also the great shepherd of Psalm 23.[456] Jesus has inaugurated with his blood an eternal covenant.[457] The Old Covenant may have become obsolete, but the New Covenant is established on the death, burial, and resurrection of the Son of God. This covenant will never grow obsolete.

The author prays that God will equip his listeners with every good that they may do his will. "The 'good' is the inner endowment required so that the will of God can be done." Lane further adds: "It is God who strengthens the heart with grace (13:9), who fills and supports the heart with charismatic gifts (2:4; 6:5; 13:9), so that it neither wavers nor suffers a deficiency but possesses the capacity to do the will of God."[458] The will of God in the narrowest sense is the perseverance of the saints. In a

---

[455] Lane, *Hebrews*, 560.
[456] Cockerill, *Hebrews*, 716.
[457] Moo, *Hebrews*, 528.
[458] Lane, *Hebrews*, 564.

broader sense, the will entails all that is pleasing to God. Doing the will of God brings glory to both the Father and the Son.

Verses 22-25 begin the author's final greetings. He appeals to his listeners to bear with his exhortation. The phrase a "word of exhortation," likely denotes that this letter is actually a sermon.[459] This means that the author likely adapted this ending because he would not be the one delivering the sermon. With reference to Timothy, the author places himself within the Pauline circle. He appears to be planning a return to his listeners accompanied by Timothy. Many scholars have debated exactly where this letter was destined for. The phrase "those who come from Italy" could possibly mean those who are presently located in Italy send greetings or those who were once in Italy send greetings.[460] Whichever translation one adopts will also likely affect one's view of the letter's destination. The letter was either written to Jewish believers in Rome or written to Jewish believers somewhere else who were from Rome. As with the case of many New Testament letters, both peace (v.20) and grace (v.25) season the author's final greetings. It is the peace and grace of God that will bring the author's weary travelers to their final destination.

Application

THE JOURNEY CONTINUES

Now that you have concluded your study, take the time to write your thoughts about what you have learned. I would love to hear your comments.

---

[459] Moo, *Hebrews*, 529.
[460] Moo, *Hebrews*, 530.

You may mail them to: Michael Nobles "Hebrews" 9470 C.R. 2188 Whitehouse, TX 75791. I hope this study has encouraged you to dig deeper into God's word. Semper Reformanda.

Bibliography

Allen, David. *Hebrews: New American Commentary.* Edited by Ray Clendenen. Vol. 35. 39 vols. Nashville, TN: B&H Academic, 2010.

Andrews, Stephen. "Melchizedek." In *Dictionary of the Old Testament: Pentateuch*, edited by Desmond Alexander, & David Baker, 562-564. Downers Grove: InterVarsity Press, 2003.

Bauckham, Richard. "The Divinity of Jesus Christ in the Epistle to the Hebrews." In *The Epistle to the Hebrews and Christian Theology*, edited by Richard Bauckham, Daniel Driver, Trevor Hart, & Nathan MacDonald, 15-36. Grand Rapids, MI: Eerdmans, 2009.

Bauer, W., F.E. Danker, W.F. Arndt, F.W. Gingrich, ed. *A Greek-English Lexicon of the New Testament and Other Early Christian Literature.* 3rd. Chicago: University of Chicago Press, 2000.

Beale, G.K. *A New Testament Biblical Theology: The Unfolding of the Old Testament in the New.* Grand Rapids: Baker, 2011.

Carson, D.A., and Douglas Moo. *An Introduction to the New Testament.* Grand Rapids: Zondervan, 1992.

Chilton, Bruce. "Purity and Impurity." In *Dictionary of the Later New Testament and Its Developments*, edited by Ralph Martin, & Peter Davids, 988-996. Downers Grove: IVP, 1997.

Cockerill, Gareth. *Hebrew: The New International Commentary on the New Testament.* Grand Rapids, MI: Eerdmans, 2012.

Duke, Rodney. "Priests, Priesthood." In *Dictionary of the Old Testament: Pentateuch*, edited by Desmond Alexnder, & David Baker, 646-655. Downers Grove: InterVarsity Press, 2003.

Ferguson, Everett. *Backgrounds of Early Christianity.* 2nd. Grand Rapids: Eerdmans, 1993.

Guthrie, Donald. *New Testament Introduction.* 4th. Dowbers Grove: IVP, 1990.

Guthrie, George. "Hebrews." In *Commentary on the New Testament use of the Old Testament*, edited by G.K. Beale, & D.A. Carson, 919-995. Grand Rapids, MI: Baker Academic, 2007.

Harris, Dana. *Hebrews: Exegetical Guide to the Greek New Testament.* Edited by Andreas J. Kostenberger and Robert Yarbrough. Nashville, TN: B&H, 2019.

Hauck, Friedrich. *Theological Dictionary of the New Testament.* Edited by and G. Friedrich G. Kittel. Translated by G.W. Bromiley. Vol. 3. 10 vols. Grand Rapids, MI: Eerdmans, 1964-1976.

Horton, Michael. *The Christian Faith: A Systematic Theology for Pilgrims on the Way.* Grand Rapids, MI: Zondervan, 2011.

Koester, Craig. *Hebrews: A New Testament Translation with Introduction and Commentary.* Vol. AB 36. New York: Doubleday, 2001.

Lane, William L. *Hebrews.* 2 Vols. WBC 47a-47b vols. Dallas, TX: Word Books, 1991.

McCabe, D.R. "Oaths and Swearing." In *Dictionary of Jesus and the Gospels*, edited by Joel Green, 629-631. Downers Grove: InterVaristy Press, 2013.

Moberly, R. Walker. "Exemplars of Faith in Hebrews 11: Abel." In *The Epistle to the Hebrews and Christian Theology*, edited by Richard Bauckham, Daniel R. Driver, Trevor A. Hart, & Nathan MacDonald, 353-363. Grand Rapids: Eerdmans, 2009.

Mohler, Albert R. Jr. *Christ-Centered Exposition: Exalting Jesus in Hebrews.* Edited by Daniel Akin, and Tony Merida David Platt. Nashville, TN: Holman Reference, 2017.

Moo, Douglas. *Hebrews. Exegetical Commentary on the New Testament.* Grand Rapids: Zondervan, 2024.

Oepke. "διώκω." In *Theological Dictionary of the New Testament*, edited by Gerhard Kittel. Grand Rapids: Eerdmans, 1964.

Schreiner, Thomas and Ardel Caneday. *The Race Set before Us: A Biblical Theology of Perseverance and Assurance.* Downers Grove: InterVarsity Press, 2001.

Tasker, R.V.G. "Hope." In *New Bible Dictionary*, edited by A.R. Millard, J.I. Packer, & D.J. Wiseman, 479-480. Grand Rapids: IVP, 1996.

Wallace, Daniel. *Greek Grammar Beyond the Basics: An Exegetical Syntax of the New Testament.* Grand Rapids, MI: Zondervan, 1996.

Witherington, Ben III. *Letters and Homilies for Jewish Christians: A Socio-Rhetorical Commentary on Hebrews, James, and Jude.* Downers Grove, IL: IVP Academic, 2007.

www.ingramcontent.com/pod-product-compliance
Lightning Source LLC
LaVergne TN
LVHW010638110826
845149LV00014B/2877
9798994588604